ECOLOGY, POLICY AND POLITICS

Human and non-human well-being is central to environmental concern. In this book John O'Neill develops an Aristotelian account of welfare that reveals the relationship between the good of non-humans and future generations and our own well-being. He shows that welfare and liberal justifications of market-based approaches to environmental policy fail, and examines the implications this has for debates about market, civil society and politics in modern society.

Accessible in approach, this book is ideal for student use in courses on applied ethics, environmental economics and environmental policy and politics. It will also appeal to the general reader.

John O'Neill is Lecturer in Philosophy at Lancaster University. His publications include *Worlds Without Content: Against Formalism* (Routledge, 1991).

ENVIRONMENTAL PHILOSOPHIES

Philosophy, in its broadest sense, is an effort to clarify the problems which puzzle us. Our responsibility for and attitude to the environment is one such problem which is now the subject of intense debate. Theorists and policy analysts often discuss environmental issues in the context of a more general understanding of what human beings are and how they are related to each other and to the rest of the world. So economists may argue that humans are basically consumers sending signals to each other by means of the market, while deep ecologists maintain that humans and other animals are knots in a larger web of biospheric relations.

This series examines the theories that lie behind different accounts of our environmental problems and their solution. It includes accounts of holism, feminism, green political themes and the other structures of ideas in terms of which people have tried to make sense of our environmental predicaments. The emphasis is on clarity, combined with a critical approach to the material under study.

Most of the authors are professional philosophers, and each has written a jargon-free, non-technical account of their topic. The books will interest readers from a variety of backgrounds, including philosophers, geographers, policy-makers and all who care for our planet.

ECOLOGY, POLICY AND POLITICS

Human well-being and the natural world

John O'Neill

London and New York

First published 1993
by Routledge
11 New Fetter Lane, London EC4P 4EE

Simultaneously published in the USA and Canada
by Routledge
29 West 35th Street, New York, NY 10001

Typeset in 10 on 12 point Palatino by
Ponting–Green Publishing Services,
Chesham, Buckinghamshire
Printed in Great Britain by
Clays, St Ives plc

British Library Cataloguing in Publication Data
O'Neill, John Francis
Ecology, Policy and Politics: Human well-being
and the natural world.
(Environmental Philosophies Series)
I. Title   II. Series
333.7

Library of Congress Cataloging in Publication Data
O'Neill, John
Ecology, Policy, and Politics: Human well-being and the
natural world / John O'Neill.
p.   cm.
Includes bibliographical references and index.
1. Environmental policy.   2. Human ecology.
3. Animal welfare.   4. Conservation of natural
resources.   5. Ecology.
I. Title.
HC79.E50513   1993
363.7–dc20   93–16367

ISBN 0–415–07299–9   ISBN 0–415–07300–6 (pbk)

To
Bill and Mary O'Neill
and
Bridie and Rosa O'Neill

CONTENTS

vii

CONTENTS

ACKNOWLEDGEMENTS

I am indebted to many people for helping me in a variety of different ways to produce this book. I would like to thank Andrew Brennan for inviting me to write it and for his assistance in producing the final text. I am also especially grateful to Andrew Collier, Roger Crisp, Russell Keat and Yvette Solomon to whom my thinking on the matters discussed in this book owes a great deal and who read and commented extensively upon an entire draft of the book. They pointed out many weaknesses of argument and made many suggested improvements. The flaws that still exist are there despite their best efforts. The arguments in the book owe much to discussions with colleagues at Sussex University. Rob Eastwood, Mary Farmer and Mark Peacock read earlier drafts of the chapters that deal with economic matters and saved me from a number of errors. Peter Dickens, Richard Gaskin, Ben Gibb, Luke Martell, Trevor Pateman and Neil Stammers all read and commented upon earlier versions of the book and made many helpful suggestions. I am also grateful to the friends and colleagues I have had in Bangor, Lancaster and Bolton: I would especially like to thank John Benson, Alan Holland, Geoffrey Hunter, Jeremy Roxbee-Cox, Frank Sibley and Suzanne Stern-Gillet for their conversations on issues discussed here. Earlier drafts of some of the chapters of this book were read to university seminars at Bangor, Brighton, Bristol, Kent, Lancaster, Liverpool, Southampton, and Sussex: my thanks to those who made numerous helpful comments on those occasions. There are many others whose thoughts, advice and critical comment have been important in writing this book: Robin Attfield, J. Baird Callicott, Alan Carter, Stephen Clark, Harro Hopfl, Paul Lancaster, Keekok Lee, David Miller, Carrie Rimes, Sean Sayers and Richard Sylvan all deserve special mention. Finally I would like to thank all those students with whom I have discussed issues in social philosophy and ethics: their acute comments on earlier versions of arguments developed here have taught me that research and teaching are not distinct activities.

Versions of chapter 2 and 3 appeared as 'The varieties of intrinsic value', *The Monist* 75 (1992), and 'Future generations: present harms', *Philosophy* (1993). Parts of chapter 9 are based on 'Marcuse, Husserl and the crisis of the sciences', *Philosophy of Social Science* 18 (1988) and 'Science, wonder and the lust of the eyes', *Journal of Applied Philosophy*. I would like to thank the editors and publishers for permission to use that material here.

1

HUMAN WELL-BEING AND THE NATURAL WORLD

What is it for us to live well? How should 'human well-being' be understood and characterized? Which social institutions best enable human beings to live a good life? How should we formulate policies to foster human well-being? What role do the sciences and arts have in its development? These are some of the central questions addressed in this book. Why? Should a book on *environmental* philosophy begin with questions about *human* well-being?

The place that considerations about human well-being should have in environmental concerns has been at the centre of recent debates. The literature on the environment is dominated by two broad approaches, each of which might be expected to respond very differently to my opening questions. This book argues that both are mistaken. The first position is that which holds that environmental problems can be accommodated within existing procedures of public decision-making and by the standard economic positions that found them. Thinkers who defend this view are likely to be quite happy to start from my initial set of questions about human well-being. Thus, for environmental economists who approach ecological problems from within the standard neo-classical paradigm that underpins the main tool of policy-making – cost-benefit analysis – the questions with which I begin are just those with which a book on environmental issues should begin. On this particular point the Austrian paradigm of Menger, von Mises and Hayek *et al.* would concur. Economics, for these thinkers, *is* concerned with human well-being, and that stance is not substantially changed when environmental issues are raised. Well-being is characterized in terms of the satisfaction of wants or preferences – the stronger the preference satisfied, the greater the well-being. The strength of a preference is captured in terms of the

1

price a person would pay at the margin for its satisfaction. For both neo-classical and Austrian schools, the best institutional framework for the realization of well-being is the market. Thus a basic theorem of *neo-classical* economics is that 'ideal' markets are an efficient mechanism for satisfying preferences.[1] 'Ideal' markets are not, however, found in reality – and cost-benefit analysis is introduced as a way of rectifying the 'failures' that result from the departures of real markets from 'ideal' conditions. Cost-benefit analysis still, however, begins with human well-being understood in terms of the satisfaction of preferences, the strength of which are expressed in terms of willingness to pay: it aims to maximize well-being thus understood. So these thinkers would apparently have no problems with my initial questions, with the possible exception of that about the sciences and arts.

Opposed to this position in the recent literature is a second 'deep green' or 'deep ecological' approach popular with both environmental philosophers and green activists. This argues that dominant economic, political and ethical approaches to the environment cannot accommodate proper environmental concern: standard approaches are 'anthropocentric' or 'shallow', in that they treat the non-human world as having only instrumental value for human satisfaction. The argument goes that we need to develop an 'environmental ethic' which recognizes the intrinsic value of non-human entities. The range of entities to which intrinsic value should be ascribed standardly includes some or all of the following: non-human animals, plants and other non-sentient living things, the collectives to which they belong, such as species and ecosystems and, occasionally, inanimate entities such as rivers and mountains. Those who hold a deep position often extend the target of their criticisms to include modern science itself which is also taken to entail an ecologically malignant anthropocentrism. For many green theorists science is part of the ideology of industrial society and presupposes an instrumental picture of nature as a separate object which is of value only as a resource for humans. Others, while they allow that science, like art, need not presuppose a narrow view of nature as a resource to satisfy basic material needs, still suggest that it involves a view of the world as a means for the development of specifically *human* practices.

From this deep perspective, to begin with questions about human beings and their well-being is to begin at precisely the wrong place. It betrays just that anthropocentric approach to the

2

non-human world which the deep perspective aims to reject. A book that opens with my questions is likely to be 'shallow': it will treat the non-human world as having only instrumental value as a means to human well-being. Indicative of that shallowness is the question about science and the arts: it privileges the value that the world has for specifically human practices. In addition to this shallowness, the sins of the first paragraph are made still worse by the first question 'what is it for *us* to live well?': a view that begins with 'us', whoever 'we' may be, is unlikely to take on the temporally neutral perspective that proper environmental concern requires.[2] It will not give proper due to the interests of future generations. So even if one mistakenly begins with human well-being, 'our' well-being is not the proper starting point. This would be the likely 'deep' response to my initial set of questions.

This book rejects both the 'standard' and the 'deep' approaches to the environment just outlined. In opposition to both, it develops an Aristotelian conception of well-being according to which well-being should be characterized not in terms of having the right subjective states, as the hedonist claims, nor in terms of the satisfaction of preferences as modern welfare economics assumes, but rather in terms of a set of objective goods a person might possess, for example friends, the contemplation of what is beautiful and wonderful, the development of one's capacities, the ability to shape one's own life, and so on. On the basis of this conception I show the relationship between concerns for the goods of both non-humans and future generations and components of our own well-being, and I highlight the role the sciences and arts play in the development of such concerns. The hedonistic and preference-based accounts of well-being presupposed by market-based approaches to environmental policy are not, however, simply arbitrary mistakes. Those conceptions of well-being are institutionally fostered by the market itself: the environmental problems engendered by the market stem in part from the forms of self-understanding it develops. As Aristotle himself was aware, an Aristotelian conception of well-being contains a critique of the market.

This position entails a rejection of both sets of responses to my opening set of questions. Against the second, 'deep', response, it argues that there is no incompatibility between a concern for human well-being and the recognition of and care for the intrinsic value of the non-human world, or between concern for the well-being of present generations and that of past and future generations. The term 'intrinsic value' itself is an ambiguous one. In chapter 2 I clarify its different senses and argue that, even if non-human entities have intrinsic value in its strongest sense, i.e., value independent of human valuations, the defender of such intrinsic value still needs to show how concern for it increases human well-being. I then sketch an account of how the two are related which is filled out in chapters 5 and 9. Chapter 9 focuses in particular on the special place that science and the arts have in the development of human excellence and the appreciation of the intrinsic value of the non-human world. In doing so it rejects the anti-scientific views prominent in recent green writing. In chapter 3 I argue that concern for our own well-being, properly understood, ties our well-being to that of future generations, and I examine the reasons why this tie is not recognized in modern market societies.

The case against the mainstream economic response is developed in chapters 4, 5, 6, 7 and 9. The focus of most of my arguments against market-based approaches to environmental policy will be on cost-benefit analysis. In developing my criticism I point to more general problems in the neo-classical foundations of cost-benefit analysis, and also in the very different approach of Austrian economics. In chapter 4 I examine the difficulties in incorporating into cost-benefit analysis the interests of those unable to articulate preferences – non-humans and future generations. While sophisticated versions of environmental economics show that the value and interests of non-humans and future generations can be incorporated into cost-benefit analysis, they cannot give them proper weight. This failure is particularly evident in the role of social discounting in cost-benefit analysis in which future goods and harms are valued at less than those of the present. I show that the standard arguments for social discounting fail. Radically revised versions of cost-benefit analysis attempt to respond to these problems by including the 'preferences' of non-humans and future generations directly. In arguing that these also fail, I highlight the problems of starting with preferences in the first place. The problems with purely 'want-regarding' principles of policy, i.e., principles that confine policy-making to the satisfaction of wants individuals happen to have, are examined in chapters 5 and 6.

Chapter 5 outlines and rejects the want-regarding accounts of well-being that provide one of the main theoretical under-pinnings of neo-classical economics and cost-benefit analysis. I argue that well-being consists not in the satisfaction of preferences as such, but in the possession and realization of a set of objective goods. It is shown that sophisticated want-regarding views of well-being, which identify it with satisfaction of *informed* preferences of competent agents, are unstable and in the end collapse into an objective account. An objectivist account of well-being entails that the gap between well-being and ideals is narrower than is usually assumed, and, more specifically, it reveals that the capacity to appreciate environmental goods is a component of human well-being. The relationship between them is spelt out in more detail in chapter 9 on science and value.

Welfare arguments form, however, only one part of the case for the want-regarding principles that underlie market-based approaches to environmental policy. A second and quite independent case for such principles is one that appeals to liberal values. A departure from want-regarding principles of policy, the argument goes, is illiberal and at worst totalitarian. It presupposes a classical account of politics according to which politics aims at the promotion of a particular 'correct' conception of the good. Modern liberalism is often defined in opposition to that view: the liberal political order is one that is procedurally neutral between that plurality of different conceptions of the good which is characteristic of modern society. Chapter 6 shows this position to be mistaken: the classical account of politics is compatible with 'liberal' values, notably that of autonomy, and the existence of a plurality of goods and ways of life. Indeed, J. S. Mill's liberalism quite rightly starts from just such a classical account.

Environmental policy does, however, raise in a stark form a related problem for both liberal and socialist theory concerning the role of authority within democracy and its compatibility with the value of autonomy. Rational environmental policy requires citizens to accept as authoritative the judgements of others, in particular scientists, without being able to appraise the grounds for those judgements. How can it be rational to hold beliefs on the authority of others? Is it compatible with individual autonomy and political democracy? Chapter 8 examines the grounds and conditions for the acceptance of authoritative judgements and suggests that, despite its arid appearance, the argument for rational acceptance to authority provides fertile soil for a defence of democracy and social equality, and is compatible with the value of autonomy.

Another major problem for cost-benefit analysis as an approach to environmental policy is that of value-pluralism and value-incommensurability. Cost-benefit analysis depends on a particular algorithmic conception of practical rationality, according to which the lack of a common measure by which to compare different options signals irrationality. This assumption is built into the neo-classical foundations of cost-benefit analysis, and is shared by those in the Austrian tradition where it played a central part in their case against planning in the socialist calculation debate. In chapter 7 I argue that this assumption is false. Environmental policy calls on a plurality of incommensurable values. The existence of that plurality does not entail irrationality, but rather points to the inadequacy of algorithmic conceptions of practical rationality. It reveals the role that judgement plays in practical choice. Why is there an assumption of value-commensurability in market-based approaches to policy? The answer lies in an inference at the heart of the marginal revolution in economics – that the commensurability of objects in market exchange entails value-commensurability. This inference is invalid. It fails to appreciate the social meaning of acts of exchange and betrays a misconception about what ethical commitment involves. I show that a proper understanding of these explains and justifies the widespread refusal of the economist's request to put a price on environmental goods.

The problems in market-based approaches to environmental policy raise more general issues in political theory concerning the place and justifiability of market institutions which are often missed in standard accounts of the relation between markets and environmental damage. Discussion has focused on the market's direct effects on environmental goods, for example on the damage that results where environmental goods are 'public goods'. While these are important, the discussion ignores the patterns of understanding about the self, self-interest and well-being that the market fosters. Indeed, those understandings themselves inform the hedonistic and preference-based views of welfare assumed in mainstream economic theory. The market as an institution systematically undermines an objectivist conception of well-being that ties our own well-being to the realization of the goods of future generations and non-humans. I show in chapter 4 that through its mobilization of land and labour the market has undermined those institutions which developed a sense of the way harms to the future are harms to the present and the past. In other chapters I show similarly that market-based understandings of welfare undermine an appreciation of the way that the good of non-humans is tied to our own.

This theme is treated more systematically in the final chapter of the book. That different institutions carry with them different definitions of well-being and self-interest is an insight developed by Aristotle in his influential account of the relation of household and market in the *Politics*. His analysis still has relevance in the context of modern environmental problems. It highlights the way in which the market encourages a view of well-being defined in terms of the unlimited acquisition of material goods. Other institutional contexts encourage quite different conceptions which allow limits to the material goods required for well-being and are more compatible with an appreciation of environmental goods and sustainable economics. In chapter 10 I examine the relationship between the market and other institutions, particularly political institutions and non-market associations. I argue that it is primarily within the latter that an understanding of the relation between our own well-being and that of future generations and non-humans is fostered.

This critique of the market and the case against market-based approaches to policy developed in the rest of the book are compatible with two conflicting views of the relationship of market and other institutions: the first allows the market a central place in economic life, but attempts to place boundaries around it; the second is critical of the market within the economic sphere itself. I finish by arguing that the first position has many more problems, and the second many more virtues, than recent discussion has allowed. The case against market economies remains a strong one that is still owed a reply.

2

NATURE, INTRINSIC VALUE AND HUMAN WELL-BEING

To hold an environmental ethic is to hold that non-human beings and states of affairs in the natural world have intrinsic value. This seemingly straightforward claim has been the focus of much recent philosophical discussion of environmental issues. Its clarity is, however, illusory. The term 'intrinsic value' has a variety of senses and many arguments on environmental ethics suffer from a conflation of these different senses: specimen hunters for the fallacy of equivocation will find rich pickings in the area. This chapter is partly the work of the underlabourer. I distinguish different senses of the concept of intrinsic value and, relatedly, of the claim that non-human beings in the natural world have intrinsic value; I exhibit the logical relations between these claims and examine the distinct motivations for holding them. It is not however merely an exercise in conceptual underlabouring. It defends the thesis that while it is the case that natural entities have intrinsic value in the strongest sense of the term, i.e. in the sense of value that exists independently of human valuations, such value does not as such entail any obligations on the part of human beings. The defender of nature's intrinsic value still needs to show that such value contributes to the well-being of human agents. At the end of the chapter I sketch an account of how care for the goods of non-humans might be a constitutive of our well-being.

2.1 THE VARIETIES OF INTRINSIC VALUE

The term 'intrinsic value' is used in at least three different basic senses:

(1) Intrinsic value$_1$. Intrinsic value is used as a synonym for non-instrumental value. An object has instrumental value in so far as it

8

is a means to some other end. An object has intrinsic value if it is an end in itself. Intrinsic goods are goods that other goods are good for the sake of. It is a well-rehearsed point that, under pain of an infinite regress, not everything can have only instrumental value. There must be some objects that have intrinsic value. The defender of an environmental ethic argues that among the entities that have such non-instrumental value are non-human beings and states. It is this claim that Naess takes to be a central component of deep ecology:

> The well-being of non-human life on Earth has value in itself. This value is independent of any instrumental useful-ness for limited human purposes[1]

(2) Intrinsic value$_2$. Intrinsic value is used to refer to the value an object has solely in virtue of its 'intrinsic properties'. The concept is thus employed by G. E. Moore:

> To say a kind of value is 'intrinsic' means merely that the question whether a thing possesses it, and in what degree it possesses it, depends solely on the intrinsic nature of the thing in question.[2]

This account is in need of some further clarification concerning what is meant by the 'intrinsic nature' of an object or its 'intrinsic properties'. I discuss this further below. However, as a first approximation, I will assume the intrinsic properties of an object to be its non-relational properties, and leave that concept for the moment unanalysed. To hold that non-human beings have in-trinsic value given this use is to hold that the value they have depends solely on their non-relational properties.

(3) Intrinsic value$_3$. Intrinsic value is used as a synonym for 'objective value', i.e. value that an object possesses independently of the valuations of valuers. As I show below, this sense itself has sub-varieties, depending on the interpretation that is put on the term 'independently'. Here I simply note that if intrinsic value is used in this sense, to claim that non-human beings have intrinsic value is not to make an ethical but a meta-ethical claim. It is to deny the subjectivist view that the source of all value lies in valuers – in their attitudes, preferences and so on.

Which sense of 'intrinsic value' is the proponent of an environ-mental ethic employing? To hold an environmental ethic is to hold that non-human beings have intrinsic value in the first sense:

it is to hold that non-human beings are not simply of value as a means to human ends. However, it might be that to hold a defensible ethical position about the environment, one needs to be committed to the view that they also have intrinsic value in the second or third senses. Whether this is the case I examine later in this chapter.

2.2 SOURCES AND OBJECTS OF VALUE

In much of the literature on environmental ethics the different senses of 'intrinsic value' are used interchangeably. In particular senses (1) and (3) are often conflated. Typical is the following passage from Worster's *Nature's Economy*:

> One of the most important ethical issues raised anywhere in the past few decades has been whether nature has an order, a pattern, that we humans are bound to understand and respect and preserve. It is the essential question prompting the environmentalist movement in many countries. Generally, those who have answered 'yes' to the question have also believed that such an order has an intrinsic value, which is to say that not all value comes from humans, that value can exist independently of us: it is not something we bestow. On the other hand, those who have answered 'no' have tended to be in an instrumentalist camp. They look on nature as a storehouse of 'resources' to be organized and used by people, as having no other value than the value some human gives it.[3]

In describing the 'yes' camp Worster characterizes the term in sense (3). However, in characterizing the 'no's he presupposes an understanding of the term in both senses (1) and (3). The passage assumes that to deny that natural patterns have value independently of the evaluations of humans is to grant them only instrumental value: a subjectivist meta-ethics entails that non-humans can have only instrumental value. This assumption is widespread.[4] It also underlies the claims of some critics of an environmental ethic who reject it on meta-ethical grounds thus: to claim that items in the non-human world have intrinsic value commits one to an objectivist view of values; an objectivist view of values is indefensible; hence the non-human world contains nothing of intrinsic value.[5]

The assumption that a subjectivist meta-ethics commits one to the view that non-humans have only instrumental value is false. Its apparent plausibility is founded on a confusion of claims about the source of values with claims about their object.[6] The subjectivist claims that the only source of value is the evaluative attitudes of humans. But this does not entail that the only ultimate objects of value are the states of human beings. Likewise, to be an objectivist about the source of value, i.e. to claim that whether or not something has value does not depend on the attitudes of valuers, is compatible with a thoroughly anthropocentric view of the objects of value – that the only things which do in fact have value are humans and their states, such that a world without humans would have no value whatsoever.

To enlarge, consider the emotivist as a standard example of a subjectivist. Evaluative utterances merely evince the speaker's attitudes with the purpose of changing the attitudes of the hearer. They state no facts. Within the emotivist tradition Stevenson provides an admirably clear account of intrinsic value. Intrinsic value is defined as non-instrumental value: '"intrinsically good" is roughly synonymous with "good for its own sake, as an end, as distinct from good as a means to something else"'.[7] Stevenson then offers the following account of what it is to say something has intrinsic value:

> 'X is intrinsically *good*' asserts that the speaker approves of X intrinsically, and acts emotively to make the hearer or hearers likewise approve of X intrinsically.[8]

There are no reasons why the emotivist should not fill the X place by entities and states of the non-human world. There is nothing in the emotivist's meta-ethical position that precludes her holding basic attitudes that are bio-centric. Thus let H! operator express hurrah attitudes and B! express boo attitudes.[9] Her ultimate values might for example include the following:

H! (The existence of natural ecosystems).

B! (The destruction of natural ecosystems by humans).

There is no reason why the emotivist must assume that either egoism or humanism is true, that is that she must assign non-instrumental value only to her own or other humans' states.[10]

It might be objected, however, that there are other difficulties in holding an emotivist meta-ethics and an environmental ethic. In making humans the source of all value, the emotivist is committed to the view that a world without humans contains nothing of value. Hence, while nothing logically precludes the emotivists' assigning non-instrumental value to objects in a world which contains humans, it undermines some of the considerations that have led to the belief in the need to assign such value. For example, it is not compatible with the standard last man argument[11] in defence of an environmental ethic. The argument runs thus: if non-humans have only instrumental value, then the last man whose last act was to destroy a forest or magnificent oak would have done no wrong; the last man does do wrong; hence it is false that non-humans only have instrumental value. However, given a subjectivist account of value, the last man does no wrong, since a world without humans is without value.

This objection falls for just the same reason as did the original assumption that subjectivism entails that non-humans have only instrumental value. It confuses the source and object of value. There is nothing in emotivism that forces the emotivist to confine the objects of her attitudes to those that exist at the time at which she expresses them. Her moral utterances might evince attitudes towards events and states of affairs that might happen after her death, for example,

H! (My great grandchildren live in a world without poverty).

Likewise her basic moral attitudes can range over periods in which humans no longer exist, for example:

H! (Rain forests exist after the extinction of the human species).

Like the rest of us she can deplore the vandalism of the last man. Her moral utterances might evince attitudes not only to other times but also to other possible worlds. Nothing in her meta-ethics stops her asserting with Leibniz that this world is the best of all possible worlds, or, in her despair at the destructiveness of humans, expressing the attitude that it would have been better had humans never existed:

H!(the possible world in which humans never came into existence).

That humans are the source of value is not incompatible with their assigning value to a world in which they do not exist. To conclude, nothing in the emotivist's meta-ethics dictates the content of her attitudes.

Finally it needs to be stressed that while subjectivism does not rule out non-humans having non-instrumental value, objectivism does not rule it in. To claim that moral utterances have a truth value is not to specify which utterances are true. The objectivist can hold that the moral facts are such that only the states of humans possess value in themselves: everything else has only instrumental value. Ross, for example, held that only states of conscious beings have intrinsic value:

> Contemplate any imaginary universe from which you suppose mind entirely absent, and you will fail to find anything in it you can call good in itself.[12]

Moore allowed that without humans the world might have some, but only very insignificant, value.[13] It does not follow from the claim that values do not have their source in humans that they do not have humans as their sole ultimate object.

The upshot of this discussion is a very traditional one, that meta-ethical commitments are logically independent of ethical ones. However, in the realm of environmental ethics it is one that needs to be re-affirmed. No meta-ethical position is required by an environmental ethic in its basic sense, i.e. an ethic which holds that non-human entities should not be treated merely as a means to the satisfaction of human wants. In particular, one can hold such an ethic and deny objectivism. However, this is not to say that there might not be other reasons for holding an objectivist account of ethics and that some of these reasons might appear particularly pertinent when considering evaluative statements about non-humans. It has not been my purpose in this section of the chapter to defend ethical subjectivism and in 2.4 I defend a version of objectivism about environmental values. First, however, I discuss briefly intrinsic value in its Moorean sense, intrinsic value$_2$ – for this sense of the term is again often confused with intrinsic value$_1$.

2.3 VALUES AND NON-RELATIONAL PROPERTIES

In its second sense intrinsic value refers to the value an object has solely in virtue of its 'intrinsic properties': it is value that 'depends solely on the intrinsic nature of the thing in question'.[14] I suggested earlier that the intrinsic properties of an object are its non-relational properties. What is meant by 'non-relational properties'? There are two interpretations that might be placed on the phrase:

(1) The non-relational properties of an object are those that

persist regardless of the existence or non-existence of other objects (weak interpretation).

(2) The non-relational properties of an object are those that can be characterized without reference to other objects (strong interpretation).[15]

The distinction between the two senses will not concern me further here, although a similar distinction will take on greater significance in the following section.

If any property is irreducibly relational then rarity is. The rarity of an object depends on the non-existence of other objects, and the property cannot be characterized without reference to other objects. In practical concern about the environment a special status is ascribed to rare entities. The preservation of endangered species of flora and fauna and of unusual habitats and ecological systems is a major practical environmental problem. Rarity *appears* to confer a special value to an object. This value is related to that of another irreducibly relational property of environmental significance, i.e. diversity. However, it has been argued that such value can have no place in an environmental ethic which holds non-humans have intrinsic value. The argument runs something as follows:

(1) To hold an environmental ethic is to hold that natural objects have intrinsic value.

(2) The values objects have in virtue of their relational properties, e.g. their rarity, cannot be intrinsic values.

Hence (3) the value objects have in virtue of their relational properties have no place in an environmental ethic.[16]

This argument commits a fallacy of equivocation. The term 'intrinsic value' is being used in its Moorean sense, intrinsic value$_2$ in the second premise, but as synonym for non-instrumental value, intrinsic value$_1$, in the first. The senses are distinct. Thus, while it may be true that if an object has only instrumental value it cannot have intrinsic value in the Moorean sense, it is false that an object of non-instrumental value is necessarily also of intrinsic value in the Moorean sense. We might value an object in virtue of its relational properties, for example its rarity, without thereby seeing it as having only instrumental value for human satisfactions.

This point can be stated with greater generality. We need to distinguish:

(1) values objects can have in virtue of their relations to other objects; and

14

(2) values objects can have in virtue of their relations to human beings.[17]

The second set of values is a proper subset of the first. Moreover, the second set of values is still not co-extensive with:

(3) values objects can have in virtue of being instrumental for human satisfaction.

An object might have value in virtue of its relation with human beings without thereby being of only instrumental value for humans. Thus, for example, one might value wilderness in virtue of its not bearing the imprint of human activity, as when John Muir opposed the construction of the dam in the Hetch Hetchy valley on the grounds that wild mountain parks should lack 'all . . . marks of man's work'.[18] To say 'x has value because it is untouched by humans' is to say that it has value in virtue of a relation it has to humans and their activities. Wilderness has such value in virtue of our absence. However, the value is not possessed by wilderness in virtue of its instrumental usefulness for the satisfaction of human desires. The third set of values is a proper subset of both the second and the first. Intrinsic value in the sense of non-instrumental value need not then be intrinsic in the Moorean sense.

What of the relation between Moorean intrinsic value and objective value? Is it the case that if there is value that 'depends solely on the intrinsic nature of the thing in question' then subjectivism about values must be rejected? If an object has value only in virtue of its intrinsic nature, does it follow that it has value independently of human valuations? The answer depends on the interpretation given to the phrases 'depends solely on' and 'only in virtue of'. If these are interpreted to exclude the activity of human evaluation, as I take it Moore intended, then the answer to both questions is immediately 'yes'. However, there is a natural subjectivist reading to the phrases. The subjectivist can talk of the valuing agent *assigning* value to objects solely in virtue of their intrinsic natures. Given a liberal interpretation of the phrases, a subjectivist can hold that some objects have intrinsic value in the Moorean sense.

2.4 OBJECTIVE VALUE AND THE NATURAL WORLD

In 2.2 I argued that the claim that nature has non-instrumental value does not commit one to an objectivist meta-ethics. However,

I left open the question as to whether there might be other reasons particularly pertinent in the field of environmental ethics that would lead us to hold an objectivist account of value. I show in this section that there are.

The ethical objectivist holds that the evaluative properties of objects are real properties of objects, that is, that they are properties that objects possess independently of the valuations of valuers. What is meant by 'independently of the valuations of valuers'? There are two readings of the phrase which parallel the two senses of 'non-relational property' outlined in the last section:

(1) The evaluative properties of objects are properties that exist in the absence of evaluating agents (weak interpretation).

(2) The evaluative properties of objects can be characterized without reference to evaluating agents (strong interpretation).

The distinction is a particular instance of a more general distinction between two senses in which we can talk of a property being a real property of an object:

(1) A real property is one that exists in the absence of any being experiencing that object (weak interpretation).

(2) A real property is one that can be characterized without reference to the experiences of a being who might experience the object (strong interpretation).

Is there anything about evaluations of the environment that make the case for objectivism especially compelling? I begin by considering the case for the weak version of objectivism. For the purpose of the rest of the discussion I will assume that only human persons are evaluating agents.

2.4.1 Weak objectivity

A popular move in recent work on environmental ethics has been to establish the objectivity of values by invoking an analogy between secondary qualities and evaluative properties in the following manner:

(1) The evaluative properties of objects are analogous to secondary qualities. Both sets of properties are observer-dependent.

(2) The Copenhagen interpretation of quantum mechanics has shown the distinction between primary qualities and secondary qualities to be untenable. All the properties of objects are observer-dependent.

Hence, (3) the evaluative properties of objects are as real as their primary qualities.[19]

The argument fails at every stage. In the first place the conclusion itself is too weak to support objectivism about values: it is no argument for an objectivist theory of values to show that all properties of objects are observer-dependent. The second premise should in any case be rejected. Not only is it the case that the Copenhagen interpretation of quantum theory is but one amongst many,[20] it is far from clear that the Copenhagen interpretation is committed to the ontological extravagance that all properties are observer-dependent. Rather it can be understood as a straightforward instrumentalist interpretation of quantum theory. As such it involves no ontological commitments about the quantum domain.[21]

More pertinent to the present discussion, there are also good grounds for rejecting the first premise. The analogy between secondary qualities and values has often been used to show that values are not real properties of objects. Thus Hume remarks:

> Vice and virtue ... may be compared to sounds, heat and cold, which, according to modern philosophy, are not qualities in objects, but perceptions in the mind.[22]

For the Humean, both secondary qualities and evaluative properties are not real properties of objects, but, rather, illustrate the mind's 'propensity to spread itself on external objects': as Mackie puts it, moral qualities are the 'projection or objectivication of moral attitudes'.[23] The first premise of the argument assumes this Humean view of the analogy between secondary qualities and values. However, there are good grounds for inverting the analogy and that inversion promises to provide a more satisfactory argument for objectivism than that outlined above.

On the weak interpretation of the concept of a real property, secondary qualities are real properties of objects. They persist in the absence of observers. Objects do not lose their colours when we no longer perceive them. In the kingdom of the blind the grass is still green. Secondary qualities are dispositional properties of objects to appear in a certain way to ideal observers in ideal conditions. So, for example, an object is green if and only if it would appear green to a perceptually ideal observer in perceptually ideal conditions.[24] It is consistent with this characterization of secondary qualities that an object possesses that quality even though it may never actually be perceived by an observer. Thus, while in the strong sense of the term secondary qualities are not real properties of objects – one cannot characterize the properties without referring to the experiences of possible observers – in the weak sense of the term they are.[25]

This point opens up the possibility of an inversion of the Humean analogy between secondary and evaluative qualities which has been recently exploited by McDowell and others.[26] Like the secondary qualities, evaluative qualities are real properties of objects. An object's evaluative properties are similarly dispositional properties that it has to produce certain attitudes and reactions in ideal observers in ideal conditions. Thus, we might tentatively characterize goodness thus: x is good if and only if x would produce feelings of moral approval in an ideal observer in ideal conditions. Likewise, beauty might be characterized thus: x is beautiful if and only if x would produce feelings of aesthetic delight in ideal observers in ideal conditions. Given this characterization, an object is beautiful or good even if it never actually appears as such to an observer. The evaluative properties of objects are real in just the same sense that secondary qualities are. Both sets of properties are independent of observers in the sense that they persist in the absence of observers. The first premise of the argument outlined above should therefore be rejected. Furthermore, in rejecting this premise, one arrives at a far more convincing case for the reality of evaluative properties than that provided by excursions into quantum mechanics.

However, the promise of this line of argument for environmental ethics is, I believe, limited. There are a variety of particular arguments that might be raised against it. For example, the Humean might respond by suggesting that the analogy between secondary and evaluative properties is imperfect. The arguments for and against the analogy I will not rehearse here.[27] For even if the analogy is a good one, it is not clear to me that any point of substance specifically about the nature of values divides the Humean and his opponent. The debate is one about preferred modes of speech, specifically about how the term 'real property' is to be read. For the Humean such as Mackie, the term 'real property' is understood in its strong sense. It is a property that can be characterized without reference to the experiences of an observer. Hence neither secondary qualities nor values are real properties of objects. The opponent of the Humean in employing the analogy to establish the reality of evaluative properties substitutes a weak interpretation of 'real property' for the strong interpretation. There may be good reasons for doing this, but disagreement lies there and not on the nature of values as such.[28] Moreover, there seems to be nothing about evaluative utterances concerning the natural environment which adds anything to this debate. Nothing about specifically environmental values tells for or against this argument for objectivism.

2.4.2 Strong objectivity

A more interesting question is whether there are good reasons for believing that there are objective values in the strong sense: are there evaluative properties that can be characterized without reference to the experiences of human observers? I will now argue that there are and that use of evaluative utterances about the natural world provide the clearest examples of such values.

Consider the gardener's use of the phrase 'x is good for greenfly'. The term 'good for' can be understood in two distinct ways. It might refer to what is conducive to the destruction of greenfly, as in 'detergent sprays are good for greenfly', or it can be used to describe what causes greenfly to flourish, as in 'mild winters are good for greenfly'. The term 'good for' in the first use describes what is instrumentally good for the gardener: given the ordinary gardener's interest in the flourishing of her rose-bushes, detergent sprays satisfy that interest. The second use describes what is instrumentally good for the greenfly, quite independently of the gardener's interests. This instrumental goodness is possible in virtue of the fact that greenflies are the sorts of things that can flourish or be injured. In consequence they have their own goods that are independent of both human interests and any tendency they might have to produce in human observers feelings of approval or disapproval.[29] Such goods I will follow Von Wright in terming the 'goods of X'.[30]

What is the class of entities that can be said to possess such goods? Von Wright in an influential passage offers the following account:

> A being, of whose good it is meaningful to talk, is one who can meaningfully be said to be well or ill, to thrive, to flourish, be happy or miserable . . . The attributes, which go

19

along with the meaningful use of the phrase 'the good of X', may be called *biological* in a broad sense. By this I do not mean that they were terms, of which biologists make frequent use. 'Happiness' and 'welfare' cannot be said to belong to the professional vocabulary of biologists. What I mean by calling the terms 'biological' is that they are used as attributes of beings, of whom it is meaningful to say they have a *life*. The question 'What kinds or species of being have a good?' is therefore broadly identical with the question 'What kinds or species of being have a life'.[31]

This biological use of the terms 'good for' and 'good of' is at the centre of Aristotelian ethics. The distinction between 'good for' and 'good of' itself corresponds to the Aristotelian distinction between goods externally instrumental to a being's flourishing and those that are constitutive of a being's flourishing.[32] And the central strategy of Aristotle's ethics is to found ethical argument on the basis of this broadly biological use of the term 'good'. I discuss this further in 2.5.

The terms 'good' and 'goods' in this biological context characterize items which are real in the strong interpretation of the term. In order to characterize the conditions which are constitutive of the flourishing of a living thing one need make no reference to the experiences of human observers. The goods of an entity are given rather by the characteristic features of the kind or species of being it is. A living thing can be said to flourish if it develops those characteristics which are normal to the species to which it belongs in the normal conditions for that species. If it fails to realize such characteristics then it will be described by terms such as 'defective', 'stunted', 'abnormal' and the like. Correspondingly, the truth of statements about what is good for a living thing, what is conducive to its flourishing, depend on no essential reference to human observers. The use of the evaluative terms in the biological context does then provide good reasons for holding that some evaluative properties are real properties on the strong interpretation of the phrase. Hence, evaluative utterances about living things do have a particular relevance to the debate about the objectivity of values. The use of evaluative terms in biological contexts does tell for objectivism.

However, while the use of value terms in the specifically biological context provides the clearest examples of the existence of objective goods, the class of entities that can be meaningfully said to have such goods is not confined to the biological context. Von Wright's claim that the question 'What kinds or species of being have a good?' is identical with the question 'What kinds or species of being have a life?' should be rejected. The problem case for this identity claim is that of collective entities. Wright is willing to entertain the possibility that such entities have their own good but only if they can also be said to have their own life in a non-metaphorical sense.

> But what shall we say of social units such as the family, the nation, the state. Have they got a life 'literally' or 'meta-phorically' only? I shall not attempt to answer these ques-tions. I doubt whether there is any other way of answering them except by pointing out existing analogies of language. It is a fact that we speak about the life and also the good (welfare) of the family, the nation and the state. This fact about the use of language we must accept and with it the idea that the social units in question *have* a life and a good. What is arguable, however, is whether the life and *a fortiori* also the good (welfare) of a social unit is not somehow 'logically reducible' to the life and therefore the good of the beings – men or animals – who are its members.[33]

This passage conflates two distinct issues: whether collective entities have a life and whether they have their own goods. It does not appear to me that we can talk of collective entities having a life in anything but a metaphorical sense. They lack those properties typical of living things – reproduction, growth and suchlike. However, it does make sense to talk about the conditions in which collective entities flourish and hence of their goods in a non-metaphorical sense. Correspondingly, we can meaningfully talk of what is damaging to them. Furthermore, the goods of collective entities are not reducible to the goods of their members. Thus, for example, we can refer to the conditions in which bureaucracy flourishes while believing this to be bad for its constituent members. Or to take another example, what is good for members of a workers' co-operative can be quite at odds with what is good for the co-operative itself: the latter is constituted by its relative competitive position in the market place, and members of co-operatives might find themselves forced to forego the satisfaction of their own interests to realize this.[34] The question 'What class of being can have a good?' is identical with the question 'What class of being can be said to flourish in a non-metaphorical sense?'. The class of living things is a proper subset of this class.

This point is central to environmental questions. It makes sense to talk of the goods of collective biological entities – colonies, ecosystems and so on – in a way that is irreducible to that of its members. The realization of the good of a colony of ants might in certain circumstances involve the death of most of its members. It is not a condition for the flourishing of an individual animal that it be eaten: it often is a condition for the flourishing of the ecosystem of which it is a part. Relatedly, a point central to Darwin's development of the theory of evolution was that living beings have a capacity to reproduce that outstrips the capacity of the environment to support them. Most members of a species die in early life. This is clearly bad for the individuals involved. But it is again essential to the flourishing of the ecosystems of which they are a part. Collective entities have their own goods. In defending this claim one need not show that they have their own life.[35]

2.5 INTRINSIC VALUE AND HUMAN WELL-BEING

Both individual living things and the collective entities of which they are members can be said, then, to have their own goods. These goods are quite independent of human interests and can be characterized without reference to the experiences of human observers. It is a standard at this juncture of the argument to assume that possession of goods entails moral considerability: 'moral standing or considerability belongs to whatever has a good of its own'.[36] This is mistaken. It is possible to talk in an objective sense of what constitutes the goods of entities, without making any claims that these ought to be realized. We can know what is 'good for X' and relatedly what constitutes 'flourishing for X' and yet believe that X is the sort of thing that ought not to exist and hence that the flourishing of X is just the sort of thing we ought to inhibit. The case of the gardener noted earlier is typical in this regard. The gardener knows what it is for greenfly to flourish, recognizes they have their own goods, and has a practical knowledge of what is good for them. No moral injunction follows. She can quite consistently believe they ought to be done harm. Likewise one can state the conditions for the flourishing of dictatorship and bureaucracy. The anarchist can claim that 'war is the health of the state'. One can discover what is good both for rain forests and the HIV virus. One can recognize that something has its own goods, and quite consistently be morally indifferent to these goods or believe one has a moral duty to inhibit their development. That Y is a good of X does not entail that Y should be realized unless we have a prior reason for believing that X is the sort of thing whose good ought to be promoted. While there is not a logical gap between facts and values, in that some value statements are factual, there is a logical gap between facts and oughts. 'Y is a good' does not entail 'Y ought to be realized'.

This gap clearly raises problems for environmental ethics. The existence of objective goods was promising precisely because it appeared to show that items in the non-human world were objects of proper moral concern. The gap outlined threatens to undermine such concern. Can the gap be bridged? There are two ways one might attempt to construct such a bridge. The first is to invoke some general moral claim that linked objective goods and moral duties. One might for example invoke an objectivist version of utilitarianism: we have a moral duty to maximize the total amount of objective good in the world.[37] There are a number of problems of detail with such an approach. What are the units for comparing objective goods? How are different goods to be weighed? However, it also has a more general problem that it shares with hedonistic utilitarianism. Thus, the hedonistic utilitarian must include within his calculus pleasures that ought not to count at all, e.g. those of a sadist who gets pleasure from needless suffering. The hedonistic utilitarian fails to allow that pleasures themselves are the direct objects of ethical appraisal. Similarly, there are some entities whose flourishing simply should not enter into any calculations – the flourishing of dictatorships and viruses for example. It is not the case of that goods of viruses should count, even just a very small amount. There is no reason why these goods should count at all as ends in themselves (although there are of course good *instrumental* reasons why some viruses should flourish, in that many are indispensable to the ecosystems of which they are a part). The flourishing of such entities is itself a direct object of ethical appraisal. The quasi-utilitarian approach is unpromising.

A second possible bridge between objective goods and oughts is an Aristotelian one. Human beings like other entities have goods constitutive of their flourishing, and correspondingly other goods instrumental to that flourishing. The flourishing of many other living things ought to be promoted because they are constitutive of our own flourishing. This approach might seem a depressingly familiar one. It looks as if we have taken a long journey into objective value only to arrive back at a narrowly anthropocentric ethic. This however would be mistaken. It is compatible with an Aristotelian ethic that we value items in the natural world for their own sake, not simply as an external means to our own satisfaction. Consider Aristotle's account of the relationship of friendship to human flourishing.[38] It is constitutive of friendship of the best kind that we care for friends for their own sake and not merely for the pleasures or profits they might bring. To do good for friends purely because one thought they might later return the compliment not for their own sake is to have an ill-formed friendships. Friendship in turn is a constitutive component of a flourishing life. Given the kind of beings we are, to lack friends is to lack part of what makes for a flourishing human existence. Thus the egoist who asks 'Why have friends?' or 'Why should I do good for my friends?' has assumed a narrow range of goods – 'the biggest share of money, honours and bodily pleasures'[39] – and asked how friends can bring such goods. The appropriate response is to point out that he has simply misidentified what the goods of a human life are.

The best case for an environmental ethic should proceed on similar lines. For a large number, although not all, of individual living things and biological collectives, we should recognize and promote their flourishing as an end itself.[40] Such care for the natural world is constitutive of a flourishing human life. The best human life is one that includes an awareness of and practical concern with the goods of entities in the non-human world. On this view, the last man's act of vandalism reveals the man to be leading an existence below that which is best for a human being, for it exhibits a failure to recognize the goods of non-humans.[41] To outline such an approach is, however, only to provide a promissory note. The claim that care for the natural world for its own sake is a part of the best life for humans requires detailed defence. The most promising general strategy would be to appeal to the claim that a good human life requires a breadth of goods. Part of the problem with egoism is the very narrowness of the goods it involves. The ethical life is one that incorporates a far richer set of goods and relationships than egoism would allow. This form of argument can be made for a connection of care for the natural world with human flourishing: the recognition and promotion of natural goods as ends in themselves involves just such an enrichment.[42] But this position is still incomplete. Why should a concern for non-human goods *enrich* human life? I answer that question in chapters 5 and 9.

3

FUTURE GENERATIONS AND THE HARMS WE DO OURSELVES

The philosophical literature on future generations centres on a debate between two types of ethical theory: those theories which hold that we have ethical obligations only to those with whom we have reciprocal relations of a specified kind; and those that start from a purely impersonal perspective. Two forms of ethical theory are typical of the first approach:

(1) Ethical theories according to which the point of moral rules is to serve as a means by which individuals of limited altruism can realize their long-term interests in conditions where they are roughly equal in power and vulnerability – Humean and contractarian theories of justice and obligation provide standard examples;[1]

(2) Ethical theories according to which we have moral obligations only to those who belong to our moral community or to whom we have special ties – Golding is the theorist most often cited in discussion of this view.[2]

These theories are taken to entail that obligations to future generations are either absent – since there is an inequality of power and vulnerability (we can harm them, they cannot harm us) the circumstances of justice or obligation do not exist – or restricted – we have obligations only to those in the immediate future with whom we share ties of community or affection.

On the other side of the debate stand moral theories which begin from a purely impersonal perspective and which entail stronger obligations to future generations. There are two favourites:

(1) Classical Utilitarianism. Classical utilitarianism holds that the best action is that which maximizes total happiness, characterized hedonistically in terms of pleasure and the absence of pain. This view involves no temporal indexing of the pleasures,

and entails that pleasure should be maximized across generations, be this by increasing pleasure or by increasing future populations.[3]

(2) Modified versions of Rawls's theory of justice. Rawls ensures impersonality and impartiality in justice by specifying that the principles of justice are those that would be chosen by self-interested individuals in conditions of ignorance of their position in society, their dispositions to take risks, and their beliefs about the good. Rawls assumes in his own account that those in this original position belong to the same generation, and introduces obligations across generations by the *ad hoc* proviso that each cares about someone in the next generation.[4] Later theorists, however, have assumed that some or all generations are represented, where representatives do not know to which generation they belong.[5]

Both of these impersonal perspectives have generated a voluminous literature which addresses either paradoxes they are taken to involve[6] or the variety of the forms that these doctrines can take.[7]

In this chapter I will not address the intricacies of the debates around these positions. Rather I will focus on an assumption that is presupposed by all sides: that there is a special problem with respect to our obligations to future generations which is that we can benefit or harm them but that they cannot benefit or harm us. Goodin summarizes the point well:

> No analysis of intergenerational justice that is cast even vaguely in terms of reciprocity can hope to succeed. The reason is the one which Addison . . . puts into the mouth of an old Fellow of College, who when he was pressed by the Society to come into something that might redound to the good of their Successors, grew very peevish. 'We are always doing', says he, 'something for Posterity, but I would fain see Posterity do something for us'.[8]

This assumption, shared by the various protagonists in the philosophical debate about our obligations to future generations, is one which this chapter will reject. I reject it not because I believe that we only have obligations to those who can benefit or harm us. I would defend no such position. I reject it rather because the assumption that future generations cannot benefit or harm us highlights a peculiarly modern attitude to our relation with the past and the future which is at the centre of our environmental problems. The assumption that future generations cannot benefit or harm us entails that we can do no harm or good to the generations of the past. It is tied to the modern loss of any sense of a community with generations outside of our own times – of any sense of reciprocal action or dialogue with them: the good of any generation is a purely local affair; it reaches only as far as those with whom we might have direct sympathies. If we have obligations to future generations they are obligations to strangers which are generated from a purely impersonal perspective.

This temporally local perspective on our goods is founded in part on a pervasive but mistaken view of what goods and harms can befall us – that only that of which we are aware can harm us: what you don't know can't hurt you. Hedonism provides the clearest example of this view: harm is what produces pain, a good is what produces pleasure. Since on our death we lose consciousness, nothing can harm us. The greatest apparent harm or good that future generations can do to us is to our reputations. But a good reputation that cannot be enjoyed is of no value, and a bad reputation of which we are unaware is of no disvalue. Even amongst those who do not presuppose a hedonistic view of goods and harms and allow that posthumous damage to one's reputation is a harm, such damage is considered the only harm possible, and a minor one at that.[9] While it is not true that future generations cannot harm us at all, there is little that they can do. These accounts of the goods and harms that can befall us are mistaken.

In 3.1 I provide *prima facie* examples that show that what happens after death can harm us – and not just via our reputations – and I highlight the relevance this has for the more general arguments about obligations to future generations. In 3.2 I criticize the subjectivist account of well-being that underlies the temporally local perspective on the goods and harms that can befall us. In 3.3 I explore the social conditions responsible for the prevalence of that perspective.

3.1 FUTURE GENERATIONS, PRESENT HARMS

William Rowan Hamilton is remembered in science for his early work on optics, which a century later was to prove central to the wave mechanics of quantum theory. (His achievement is recorded in the form of eponymy: 'Hamiltonian' is the term given to the mathematical function he developed.) This work was an early achievement in Hamilton's career – it was published in 1828 when he was 23 – and his later work, while of significance, does not have the reputation of his early work. This is not, however, what Hamilton thought of it at the time. He believed that his later mathematical discovery, quaternions, first published in 1840, was to be a contribution to mathematics and the physical sciences of a status equivalent to that of Newton and Leibniz's development of calculus. It was to be his major contribution to the sciences. He wrote narratives about their discovery that befitted this projected status:[10] thus, for example, while in his initial accounts of the discovery, the basic equations of the system were simply jotted into a notebook, in later accounts they were literally carved in stone, on Broughm Bridge in Dublin where in fact a future generation was to lay a commemorative stone. He spent the last twenty-two years of his life on the elaboration of his theory.

E. T. Bell's *Men of Mathematics* includes a chapter on Hamilton entitled 'An Irish tragedy', the tragedy being the waste of Hamilton's talents on quaternions:

> Hamilton's deepest tragedy was . . . his obstinate belief that quaternions held the key to the mathematics of the physical universe. History has shown that Hamilton tragically deceived himself when he insisted '. . . I still must assert that this discovery appears to me to be as important for the middle of the nineteenth century as the discovery of fluxions . . . was for the close of the seventeenth'. Never was a great mathematician so hopelessly wrong.[11]

The description of Hamilton's life as a tragedy may be overstated. Quaternion theory was not worthless. It played a significant role in the development of vector analysis.[12] However, it is true that quaternions were not the achievement Hamilton thought they would be, and the development of vector analysis from the theory meant that certain features of it that Hamilton believed to be particularly important were put aside – a fact that led to a controversy between supporters of Hamilton's theory, notably Tait, and its 'opponents' Heaviside and Gibbs[13] who developed vector analysis. Measured against the projected status that Hamilton had hoped for, his later work was a comparative failure. There is indeed something approaching tragedy about Hamilton's work on quaternions.

Or so it seemed until 1992. A Chinese physicist, Li He, in a paper entitled 'Quaternions and the paradoxes of quantum dynamics', resurrected quaternion theory and showed that the replacement of quaternions by vectors had disguised important assumptions in quantum theory. He demonstrated the usefulness of a development of quaternion theory along the lines that Hamilton had originally projected, and in particular showed the way in which quaternions allowed one to dispense with representations of vectors in terms of Cartesian co-ordinates. A sophisticated re-working of quaternion theory solves some of the basic paradoxes in quantum theory, and suggests quite new avenues of research. The importance of Li He's work has only recently been understood in the English-speaking world, and there is now talk of his being a potential winner of the Nobel Prize. More important from our point of view, it has meant a total reassessment of Hamilton's work. Far from constituting a tragedy, his later work on quaternions will be remembered in the terms Hamilton believed it would be, as one of the greatest achievements in the history of mathematics.

The last paragraph is total fiction. However, were it the case that it was true, then the reassessment of Hamilton's later life and work expressed in its last sentence would be a proper one: Li He's work would have transformed it from comparative failure to success. He would have done for Hamilton that which, from Hamilton's own perspective, would have been the greatest good he could have done for him. This is true despite the fact that Hamilton has been dead for over 125 years. This point can be made in terms of the different narratives that can be written about a life. In my discussion of Hamilton, three narratives have been outlined: the projected narrative that Hamilton assumed, the tragic narrative recounted by Bell, and my fictional narrative. Each tells a different story: Hamilton's own is a simple success story, Bell's one of tragic failure, and my own one of vindication of the individual after neglect and misunderstanding. Which story is true will also affect the way in which one tells of the lives of others involved. Thus a vindication of Hamilton might also be a vindication of Tait but a re-casting of Gibbs and Heaviside as individuals who *failed* to appreciate the import of Hamilton's work. Narratives do more than describe lives; they contain an evaluative component about how well those lives went, an evaluation which is visible only from the viewpoint of the end of the story. Only at the end can we determine the genre to which a life-story belongs – tragic, comic, heroic and so on. The point of my story about Hamilton is that a person's death may not be the end of their life-story. The proper end from which an evaluation is to be made may occur a century or more after the person died.

It is important to note that what is at stake in terms of which narrative is true is not just Hamilton's reputation. It is whether his later life was itself a success or a failure. Consider another possible story: an historian, Felix Taylor, has shown that Hamilton's early work on dynamics was not the work of Hamilton at all. It was the work of another mathematician, Robert Young, who died early in life unknown, and whose work was plagiarized by Hamilton. Felix Taylor's findings would do terrible damage to Hamilton's reputation as a mathematician and would do much good for that of Robert Young. If the findings were true, the changes in reputation would be quite proper. If they themselves were falsifications, they would constitute a slur on a dead man's name and character of a kind which is often, quite rightly, seen as worse than a slur on the name and character of the living: the dead cannot reply. Be that as it may, Taylor's work would be concerned *only* with reputation. It would not as such affect whether the person's life itself was a success or a failure. If 'Hamiltonians' had been the work of Robert Young, then Robert Young's short life would have been one of great achievement. The question of reputation is one of whether or not that achievement is recognized, and not whether or not a work *is* an achievement.

The work of Li He would have had quite a different import for Hamilton's work. It would affect the degree to which the discovery of quaternions was an achievement at all. Thus, while Li He's paper would have an impact on Hamilton's reputation, it would do so indirectly, by rendering Hamilton's work itself a success, and hence something for which recognition is called. Reputation as a good is parasitic on other goods, the achievement of which is such that they deserve recognition. Where Taylor's work would affect who deserves recognition, Li He's work affects the existence of the good for which recognition is deserved.

Consider now another possible story concerning the fate of Hamilton's work – one which we know to be false. Shortly after Hamilton's death, a fundamentalist religious movement swept the globe, according to which all science and mathematics was a sin of human pride against God, and the cause of Man's fall. A second inquisition against scientists was instigated and scientists were forced to recant their work. All scientific works were burnt, the word of God being the only word allowed to be taught. The movement was a total success with the result that science and mathematics were lost to humankind for all time. What would be the consequences of this subsequent history for Hamilton's work? One possible answer is that it would have no consequences; the work of the nineteenth-century mathematicians was an achievement, whether or not it was subsequently recognized as such. While this answer is attractive, it is not completely satisfactory. For, as just noted in contrasting the impact of our fictional characters Taylor and Li He, it is not just *recognition* that depends on the actions of future generations, but also the question as to whether or not a work actually *is* an achievement.

The status of scientific works depends on their relation to both a particular past and a particular future. In relation to the past, a piece of scientific work makes sense only within a particular history of problems and theories to which it makes a contribution. Its success or failure depends on its capacity to solve existing problems where others fail. However, it also depends on a projected relation to the future in terms of its capacity to solve not just existing problems, but also problems unenvisaged by its author, and in its fruitfulness in creating new problems to be solved and new avenues of research. A scientific result exists in relation to a possible future in terms of which it is rendered a success or failure. My fictional religious movement robs all scientific work of that future by making the potential success or failure of theories unavailable. The consequence is not that all scientific work is a failure, but rather, that the possibility of both future failure and success disappears. That possibility depends on the existence of generations competent to judge and develop a theory.

The claims which I have defended here concerning the role that future generations can have in determining the success or failure of the work of previous generations are not true only of scientific work. They are also true of other activities and apply to other intellectual disciplines. Thus it has been said of Aristotle that his greatness lies in his interpreters. The continual discussion of his work, the discovery of new arguments and the development of new interpretations in the context of new problems and intellectual climates is the source of Aristotle's success. For example, without Aquinas, Aristotle would be a lesser figure than he is. The same points apply in the arts; the greatness of many works of art lies in their continuing to illuminate human problems and predicaments in contexts quite foreign to that in which they were originally constructed. Likewise, many of the aesthetic qualities of a work of art may only become apparent in virtue of its relation to other works. In that minimal sense, Eliot's comment is right that 'the past should be altered by the present as much as the present is directed by the past'.[14] For this reason, if the arts were robbed of a future by the production of generations unable to appreciate them and contribute to them, they would to that extent be robbed of the conditions for success or failure.

Similar points apply to more 'prosaic' activities. They apply, for example, to politics. The success or failure of major political projects normally becomes apparent only well after the political actors have ceased to be active. Witness that of the Bolsheviks in contemporary Eastern Europe. They apply also to everyday working activities, where these involve skilled performance. It is true, for example, of crafts. Consider the hedgerows of Britain: these are the product of the skilled work of labourers that stretches back for centuries. If a succeeding generation with no sense of the skill embodied in the hedgerows and no appreciation of their value destroys them as mere impediments to more profitable agriculture, then that generation harms not only itself but also the past. The disappearance of the hedgerows is more than 'just' an act of environmental vandalism. This is not to say that respect for past generations and a desire to do well by them entails that we leave all embodiments of their activities untouched. It does mean, however, that such concerns should form an important component of our practical deliberations.

I finish my story-telling by giving a twist to my last tale about the fate of Hamilton's work. Imagine that the religious movement so destructive to science was largely an outcome of the Romantic movement of which Hamilton was a part. After his death, many in Hamilton's Romantic circle were among the first to denounce the sins of science, and his Romantically inclined scientific acquaintances among the first to recant their own work. Hamilton's own Romantic views were a source of attacks on liberal enlightenment thought, and his name often referred to in such cases. Let us also suppose that Hamilton was aware of the possible anti-scientific import of his Romantic views. If this story were true, then there would be a sense in which Hamilton had failed himself. In so far as he was responsible, through his influence on this religious movement, for the appearance of future generations incapable of understanding the worth of his work and pursuing mathematical work consequent on it, then he also undermined the possibility of success for his own work.

The same point can be made in a less artificial manner by a consideration of the value of education. Education is a good not just for the pupil but also for the educators – it is through the education of succeeding generations that one establishes not only an audience for one's work, but also participants in the same enterprise who are able to render it a possible success. Hence, to fail to educate succeeding generations is not only to damage them, it is also to damage oneself.

These final points have particular relevance to our relations to future generations. Future generations can benefit or harm us: the success or failure of our lives depends on them for it is they that are able to bring to fruition our projects. Our failures with respect to them can be of two kinds.

(1) We can fail to produce works or perform actions which are achievements. Future generations may not be able to bring our deeds to a successful fruition.

(2) We can fail to produce generations capable of appreciating what is an achievement or contributing to its success. This tends to be ignored by those discussing future generations.[15] Thus Golding asks 'what obligations do we have to future generations since they may not belong to our moral community?',[16] and answers that we have none. Others have responded that we do have duties to strangers, whatever their nature, appealing either to utilitarian considerations,[17] to impersonal principles of justice,[18] or to intuition.[19] Both sides fail to acknowledge that our primary responsibility is to attempt, as far as it is possible, to ensure that future generations do belong to a community with ourselves – that they are capable, for example, of appreciating works of science and art, the goods of the non-human environment, and the worth of the embodiments of human skills, and are capable of contributing to these goods. This is an obligation not only to future generations, but also to those of the past, so that their achievements continue to be both appreciated and extended; and to the present – ourselves – so that we do not, like my final mythical Hamilton, undermine our own achievements by rendering impossible our own success.

Thus it might be that the products of modern society will be mindless consumers, with no interest in knowledge of the natural world, little concern for the quality of the lives of those contemporaneous with them, no sense of what it is for public life to thrive, no concern with the natural environment in which they live, no taste for the arts or understanding of the fundamental sciences beyond a pragmatic concern for successful techniques. The nightmares of science fiction might come to pass. If that were to be the case, then, to the extent that the current generation was responsible for it, that generation would have failed not only the future but also itself and the past. Our obligations to future generations are obligations both to those of the past and to those of the present.

A number of qualifications and points of clarification need to be made to the position I have thus far developed. Consider the phrase 'a community with ourselves' which I used earlier. This notion disguises differences within any generation of value and interest; such differences entail that what counts as an achievement or a success in the lives and work of those in the past is often contested – consider, for example, the differing status one might accord to the theoretical works of Locke, Hegel, Mill or Marx, or to the political actions of Cromwell, Jefferson, Luxemburg, Lenin and Mao. Examples drawn from the history of science, like that of Hamilton, can be misleading in this regard, for there is a high degree of consensus concerning the achievements of the past within the scientific sphere which is absent in others, particularly the political and social. Differences in values and interests among the present generation affect not only the past, but also more clearly the future. Such conflicts are associated with conflicting aspirations for the future and hence, indirectly, with the kinds of people that will inhabit the future. It is not, then, a question of passing on a 'shared set of values' to future generations, but rather an ongoing argument concerning what those values are to be and, within the political domain, what kind of society those generations will inhabit. This is not, of course, to say that historical outcomes decide correctness in such conflicts – barbarism is always a possible outcome.

It is not only within generations that values conflict, but also across generations. The works and actions of one generation are subject to the critical scrutiny of the later, and also the values that inform such works. Again, examples from science can be misleading; claims concerning paradigm shifts notwithstanding, there has been a remarkable continuity in scientific values over the past three centuries, a point Kuhn himself concedes.[20] In other spheres, value discontinuity over time is more pronounced, and the reassessment of earlier works is often consequent on such changes. Within the political context, consider the changing views of Bolshevik revolution within this century; within the ethical context, the resuscitation of the Stoics in the new paganism of the Enlightenment;[21] within a literary context, the reassessment of the Metaphysical poets in this century by T. S. Eliot and others.[22] Present, future and past are linked, then, not by some single set of values which the present passes from past to future, but by arguments both within generations and between them. The conservative image of a quiet and contented continuity of past, present and future needs to be rejected.[23]

3.2 HEDONISM AND THE TEMPORALLY LOCAL PERSPECTIVE

The view defended in the last section – that future generations can harm us, and that we can harm ourselves in virtue of the kind of future we bring into being – presupposes the rejection of a subjectivist account of human well-being. For the subjectivist, well-being or happiness consists in having particular psychological states such as pleasure or feelings of satisfaction.[24] Hence, since our deaths end our mental states, nothing can harm us after our deaths.[25] The hedonistic account of happiness provides the clearest example of this perspective.

The subjectivist allows of no distinction between a life that feels good and a life that is good. However, the failure to make such a distinction leads to incoherence. Consider again my example of Hamilton's life, and assume that it had become apparent during his lifetime that quaternions were not likely to be the achievement that he had thought, and that this was evident to other mathematicians. Hamilton's beliefs were, we may suppose with E. T. Bell, delusions. As long as he maintained his self-deception, Hamilton might have felt good, but whether his life was good is a different matter. Let us assume that at the end of his life he realized that quaternions were not likely to be the success he had believed them to be. He would have experienced great disappointment. For the subjectivist, this is bad because for Hamilton it *feels* bad. But this gets everything the wrong way around, for Hamilton feels bad

36

because he recognizes that his life itself is not a success.[26] The disappointment is parasitic on the objective failure of his project. The subjectivist can make no sense of this emotion since, in the absence of the emotion, there is nothing wrong.

A similar point can be made with regard to reputation. What is good for an individual about a good reputation? For the subjectivist, it can only consist in its feeling good. However, this fails to appreciate the way in which concepts such as reputation and honour are parasitic on objective goods. Reputation and honour are goods only in so far as they involve recognition by others who are believed competent to judge the goods which an individual has achieved. Individuals seek then to confirm the worth of their own achievements. Hence, it does not make sense to seek reputation and honour as an end in itself. To receive honour and recognition from those one does not believe able to judge competently the worth of an achievement is self-defeating.[27] Thus, one feels good in achieving recognition by others competent to judge the worth of one's work because it confirms the independent worth of the work. Subjectivism, since it has no place for objective goods, fails to make sense of the good of reputation. It can make no sense of the distinction between reputation and fame, honour and status.

If reputation is a good simply because it feels good, then posthumous reputation makes no sense at all. If, on the other hand, honour is a good in virtue of its reflecting an objective good, then it does. It was this perception of honour that informed the classical concern with the future. In the classical world, each generation looked to the future for its continuity. Thus when Herodotus begins his history by stating that his aim is 'to preserve the memory of the past by putting on record the astonishing achievements both of our own and of Asiatic peoples',[28] those whom he primarily means to benefit are those whose memory he perpetuates. Their success depends on such memories since through them they are immortalized. As Augustine puts the classical view he himself in part rejected:

> what else was there for them to love, but glory? For, through glory, they desired to have a kind of life after death on the lips of those who praised them.[29]

Significantly, that desire for posthumous honour was rejected by the Epicureans on the grounds that it was unnecessary since it led to no pain when it remained ungratified.[30] Given a subjectivist theory of well-being, such desires no longer makes sense and ought to be eliminated.

A subjectivist theory of well-being undermines our ties to the future, for it fails to allow that the success of our own lives is tied to those of the future, just as the good of those of the past is in our own hands. If the only thing that is good for us is particular mental states, then there is no perspective from which to defend obligations to future generations, except an impersonal perspective. One is forced to treat the problem of future generations as a concern for strangers whose own goods are not bound up with our own. Each generation is isolated into itself.

3.3 THE MARKET AND THE TEMPORALLY LOCAL PERSPECTIVE

Recent philosophical arguments about future generations are symptomatic of a temporal myopia that infects modern society. The question of obligations to future generations is posed in terms of abstract obligation to possible future people who are strangers to us. The argument is premised on the lack of a sense of continuity of the present with both past and future. Our projects, and interests in the success of such projects, are not understood as tied to the future. What is the source of that myopia?

One way to begin to answer that question is by noting that the problem of our obligations to future generations can be stated as a version of Hardin's mis-characterized 'tragedy of the commons'.[31] Hardin's tragedy is mis-characterized in that it highlights a problem not of common ownership of a resource, but of no ownership at all. The problem of the commons is one of open access in a context of private ownership of particular assets. In its original form the tragedy is as follows.

A pasture is open to a number of herdsmen, each one of whom acts in isolation from the others and attempts to maximize his own utility. Each considers the utility to himself of adding another animal to his herd. For any individual, the positive benefit of adding another animal to the herd will be greater than the loss from overgrazing, since the benefit accrues entirely to the individual, while the loss is shared among all the herders. Hence, a set of rational, self-maximizing herdsmen will increase their herds even though collectively it is to the detriment of all.

With respect to the earth, successive generations occupy a temporal 'commons'. This is true even given complete private ownership of resources. To re-use Hardin's example, consider a plot of land owned by successive generations of herders. The herders of each generation, if they are rational self-maximizers, will add to their herd and graze the land to its limits within that generation; the benefit accrues to themselves, while the loss is shared by all successive generations. Hence, given Hardin's logic, we should expect each generation to deplete the resources it passes on to following generations.

What is the solution to this temporal tragedy? One possibility that is not open is the standard solution that is offered to the original spatial tragedy of the commons, which is to place the 'commons' under private ownership. As I have just noted, the result occurs even given private ownership within each gener-ation. However, an answer to the problem can be achieved if we re-cast the question: why is it the case that successive generations did not knowingly deplete resources until recently? Indeed, why did they improve the land, even given that they knew they would not reap the benefits?

The answer is that, until recently, for successive generations, their identity and the projects through which they expressed their identity spread over time. They did so, ironically, because land *across* generations was seen as the *common* property of particular families or communities. Thus land was owned by a family over many generations, or held in common by a community with a stable set of families over generations. Each generation had a sense of identity over time with future owners. They understood themselves to be members of a collective with continuity over time, and saw their own interests as bound up with those of future members of that collective. They engaged in projects the success of which relied on successive generations. Consider tree planting, for example. As a project it is tied to the future in two ways: it will benefit individuals living in a future generation, but to do so successfully it requires the co-operation of another, intermediate, generation. One's concern with the future entails projects whose success depends on the future. Individuals of different generations did not see each other as temporally local actors; rather, their interests and projects were seen as inextricably tied to those of other generations. In medieval Europe, the family and village community were sources of a sense of identity that spread across time.

In modern society such continuity is missing. In contrast with the past, the present generation acts on the land in terms of a temporally local horizon without a sense of identity or projects spread over time. It engages knowingly in resource depletion. This is most evident in the fate of topsoil, one-third of which has now been removed from the world's agricultural areas. The present generation does indeed appear to act like Hardin's rational self-maximizing herder, concerned for immediate high returns from the land. Why is this? The answer lies partly in the immediate economic pressures that the market places on use of the land. Even given a sense of identity over time, it is difficult to express that identity when in order to survive in the market place each must maximize her current returns from the land even at the cost of its long-term deterioration.[32]

More significantly, the market also undermines the existence of an identity across generations. On the land, two developments have relevance to the decline in continuity across time. One is the replacement of family ownership of the land by corporate ownership. Modern corporations have no concerns with identity across time. Second is the advent of mobility in ownership of land, which entails that on non-corporately owned land the family as an intergenerational owner of the land often no longer exists. Hence there is no sense of a tie to future owners of the land. Indeed, this point was at the heart of the debates about land and commerce in Britain in the seventeenth and eighteenth centuries. Thus, for example, the eighteenth-century civic humanist criticism of commercial society was founded on the belief that the civic virtues had their basis in stable ownership of landed property.[33] The material foundation of a good society lay in 'real property recognizable as stable enough to link successive generations in social relationships belonging to, or founded in, the order of nature'.[34] Commercial society, by mobilizing land, undermined that link between generations.

The relation between the market and the mobilization of land points to another feature of market economies that is at the basis of the modern shrinking of identity across time. It is not just the mobilization of landed property by the market that undermines intergenerational identity, but also the mobilization of labour. Specific ties to a particular locality and place, to a stable extended family within a locality, and commitments to a particular craft and profession are inimical to and undermined by the workings of a market society. On the one hand, workers in a market society must be prepared to shift location and occupation if they are to achieve the market price for their labour – hence the element of truth in von Mises's claim that low wages and unemployment are the consequence of the acts of those who refuse to change their profession and place of work.[35] On the other hand, the 'efficiency' of the market requires individuals to be thus mobile. Mobility of labour is built into the concept of 'the perfectly competitive market' central to arguments for the efficiency of the market in modern welfare economics. The advocacy of the mobility of labour has been central to the defence of the market economy, from Smith's strictures against guilds and corporations to recent objections to professions and trade unions.[36] This mobilization conflicts with a self whose identity is constituted by relations to place, kin and occupation. A consequence is the lack of a sense of identity that extends across generations in modern society.

Consider ties of place. A humanized environment contains within it the presence of those generations who created the land.[37] To have a tie to a place is to have a tie with an environment which reveals a particular past history. It is to recognize the skills embodied in dry stone walls, hedgerows and buildings and to have a sense of continuity with those whose skills are thus made public. Hence, to disrupt ties to place is not merely to remove persons from a particular spatial location, but also to divorce them from relations to previous generations. Similar points apply to relationships of kinship. The contraction of the family in the modern world has a temporal dimension: a relationship like that of being a second cousin, or even a cousin, means less in part because generational continuity and the common sources that constitute such relations are themselves of less significance. Ties to the past and future tend to be limited to two or at best three generations in either direction. Finally, with respect to occupation, ties across generations have been weakened also by the disappearance of continuity in craft and work. If a craft does persist today, it often does so outside of any history and in the context of the production of tourist bric-a-brac. The relation of craftsman and apprentice has been undermined, and with it the sense in which success in craft work was tied to past and future. As Weil notes:

> A corporation, or guild, was a link between the dead, the living and those yet unborn, within the framework of a certain specified occupation. There is nothing today which can be said to exist, however remotely, for the carrying out of such a function.[38]

The mobilization of labour by the market, like the mobilization of land, has undermined a sense of community across generations. Both lie at the basis of the temporal myopia of modern society.

To make these points is not to advocate a return to stable ownership of the land and limited mobility in labour. The particular ties of pre-modern societies were often oppressive, and the dissolution of old identities a liberation from personal servitude and narrow horizons.[39] Moreover, even if it were desirable to limit mobility, in modern conditions it would not be practicable without excessive coercion. However, to highlight the sources of the temporal myopia of modern society is to point to the need for forms of community that allow an extension of our sense of identity over time, something like that which the older family and community ties provided. This parallel between the possibility of general community across time and that previously provided by the family is exploited by Marx:

> a whole society, a nation, or even all simultaneously existing societies taken together, are not the owners of the globe. They are only its possessors, its usufructuaries, and, like *bone patres familias*, they must hand it down to succeeding generations in an improved condition.[40]

Such a sense of identity both requires and would encourage participation in those projects the success of which requires cooperation across generations. Success in our own lives needs to be clearly bound up with those of future generations. The problem of obligations to future generations is a social and political problem concerning the economic, social and cultural conditions for the existence and expression of identity that extends across generations. At the heart of that issue is the problem which has been the focus of much social and political theory for the last two centuries – that of developing forms of community which no longer leave the individual stripped of particular ties to others, but which are compatible with the sense of individual autonomy and the richness of needs that the disintegration of older identities also produced. One part of a solution to that problem lies in those surviving practices and related associations in which individuals become part of a tradition. These persist despite the market. They form a necessary component of an ecologically rational social order, a point to which I return in chapter 10.

The current environmental crisis has made this problem more pressing. Paradoxically, however, it might also reinforce the narrow time-horizon of moderns. The doomsday predictions of environmentalists can encourage a sense that we are already within the final generations. Ecological fear without a sense of the possibility of change can induce an image of our approach to an end after which there is no future. The confidence in long-term projects across generations which informed pre-modern societies was based on a feeling of certainty that such generations would exist, a feeling only punctuated by outbreaks of millenarianism. The ecological crisis may induce a secular millenarianism which threatens to undermine the very sense of a relation to the future which is needed if that future is to exist.

4

THE CONSTITUENCY OF ENVIRONMENTAL POLICY

A feature of successful computer chess programs is that they combine powerful methods for calculation with weak procedures for evaluating their outcomes. The same might be said of standard cost-benefit analysis: a sophisticated mathematical analysis is combined with crude measures of value. The unit of value is human preference satisfaction, measured by monetary units in actual or hypothetical markets. The object is to refine the monetary instruments of measurement so that all preferences are included, and to apply a principle for the aggregation of preferences thus measured. Public policy is to be based on the aggregation of preferences. In the next four chapters I argue that this approach to public policy fails to provide the basis for rational and ethically defensible environmental policies. The present chapter examines problems concerning the constituency of environmental policy – who counts in policy decisions. I argue that while cost-benefit analysis is able to incorporate the intrinsic value of nature and the preferences of future generations and non-human beings – criticism to the contrary being unfounded – it fails to give them proper weight. In the following chapters I argue that treatment of policy decisions purely as a process of preference aggregation is misconceived.

4.1 COST-BENEFIT ANALYSIS: AN OUTLINE

Cost benefit analysis arrives at public policy through the aggregation of individual preferences. The strength of an individual's preference for an object is expressed in terms of the amount she is willing to pay for that object at the margin, or alternatively, the amount she is willing to accept as compensation for its loss.[1]

Weighted preferences, as measured by willingness to pay or accept compensation, provides the starting point of analysis. The analyst must identify the parties affected by a proposal, and consider the benefits and costs for each party where benefits are understood as the satisfaction of preferences and costs their non-satisfaction.

As a tool of social policy-making the analyst requires a principle for deciding which projects are worthwhile and how different proposals are to be ranked. *Economic* cost-benefit analysis employs only 'efficiency' principles of aggregation. The basic criterion of efficiency employed in neo-classical economic analysis is the Pareto improvement criterion – a proposed situation A represents a social improvement over a prior situation B if some individual prefers the new situation A to the old situation B and no one prefers B to A. However, where policy decisions involve both winners and losers, this Pareto criterion has little practical force. In actual policy decisions the analyst employs the *potential* Pareto improvement criterion on the Kaldor–Hicks compensation test. According to this criterion a proposal is 'efficient' if the gains are greater than the losses so that the gainers would be in a position to compensate the losers and still be better off.[2] On the Kaldor–Hicks criterion a proposal is efficient if aggregate benefits are greater than average costs whoever the gainers and losers happen to be. Where there are a number of proposals, projects can be ranked in terms of their total aggregate benefit. Neither the Pareto criterion nor the Kaldor–Hicks test for policy touches on questions of the distribution of losses or gains. *Social* cost-benefit analysis does attempt to do so either by placing some further distributional constraint on projects that pass the efficiency test[3] or by directly attaching different weights to the benefits and costs of different social groups, so that the benefit that accrues to an under-privileged group is weighted more heavily than that of a privileged group.[4]

Cost-benefit analysis – both 'economic' and 'social' – also standardly weights benefits and costs differently depending on the time at which they occur. Future benefits and costs are valued less the further into the future they occur. The future is discounted. Thus, by applying a social-discount rate, the analyst converts future benefits and cost to current values when aggregating costs and benefits, the further in the future the lower the value. Where the discount rate is r, the benefit B_t in any year t will convert to a current value at year 1 of $B_t/(1+r)^t$. The arguments typically offered for discounting will be outlined and discussed in 4.3.

Having identified parties affected by a set of proposals, calculated the weighted benefits and costs to different parties, and applied the relevant efficiency rules, the analyst has to rank the proposals. There are two modes of ranking proposals. The first I have mentioned already in discussing the Kaldor–Hicks criterion of efficiency. Costs at present value are subtracted from benefits at present value: the proposal which maximizes benefits over costs is the preferred proposal. Where there are limitations on the amount of capital that can be used in various projects, this ranking rule is often replaced by another: the best proposal is that which gives the best returns per unit of resource. Proposals are ranked in terms of the ratio of total benefits to total costs, and that with the highest benefit to cost ratio is preferred.

Two further problems which have led to further refinements will be of particular importance in what follows. They are:

(1) Should one begin with 'actual' preferences in cost-benefit analysis or fully informed preference?

(2) How is one to measure the value of goods that are not exchanged on the market?

The way in which cost-benefit analysis might deal with such problems will be examined in chapter 5.

4.2 THE CONSTITUENCY OF POLICY

A standard objection to cost-benefit analysis in environmental decision-making is that, by taking preference satisfaction as basic, it necessarily fails to consider those who cannot articulate their preferences by the willingness to pay criterion, in particular (1) non-humans and (2) future generations.

4.2.1 Non-humans

It might be objected that if only the preferences of currently articulate adults count in policy decisions, then there is no place in cost-benefit analysis for consideration of the intrinsic value of non-humans. The strength of this objection depends on what is meant by 'intrinsic value'. As noted in chapter 2, the term intrinsic value has a number of distinct senses. I argued there that if by 'intrinsic value' is meant 'non-instrumental value', then the claim that non-humans have intrinsic value is quite compatible with a subjectivist theory of value. That point has relevance here. The preferences of articulate humans might express non-instrumental concern for non-humans. Thus, if we let Pxy be the predicate 'x prefers y', while the x variable may only range over articulate persons, there is no reason why the y variable should not range over the states of the inarticulate. Among an individual's basic preferences might be the preservation of some threatened habitat or of some endangered species, independently of any benefit that might accrue to that individual. Intrinsic value in the sense of non-instrumental value can therefore be incorporated into cost-benefit analysis via the preferences of articulate humans. Within the economic literature, values founded in such preferences are termed 'existence values'. There is nothing conceptually in-coherent about introducing the intrinsic value of non-humans into cost-benefit analysis via 'existence values'. What cost-benefit analysis does have difficulty in incorporating is the intrinsic value of non-humans where by intrinsic value is meant the value an object has independently of the evaluations of valuers.

4.2.2 Future generations

Just as the non-instrumental value of non-humans can be included through the preferences of humans, so also the interests of future generations can be represented by the preferences of present generations. The present generation includes individuals who have preferences concerning the well-being of their children, grandchildren and generations beyond. Such values are some-times incorporated into economic analysis as a part of the 'option-value' of an object, where this refers to the value an object has in virtue of its potential beneficial uses by humans. Individuals, it is argued, can assign 'option value' to an object, not only in virtue of its potential use by themselves, but also in virtue of its potential use by others – both contemporaries and future generations.[5] Again, there appears to be nothing conceptually improper about this employment of 'option values'. Individuals can have among their preferences a preference that something be used by others, and such preferences can appear in cost-benefit analysis. Cost-benefit analysis can, then, incorporate the interests of future generations and non-instrumental value of non-humans via the preferences of current generations.

4.2.3 Problems of incorporation

The value of an object is taken then to be a representation of three kinds of preferences – a preference for the actual use of the object, a preference for the optional use of an object by self and others, and a preference for the object's existence and well-being independent of its actual or potential use by others.[6] The problem with cost-benefit analysis is not the *possibility* of incorporating non-humans and future generations, but the *way* in which they are incorporated. There are two problems here. First, the representation of non-humans and future generations is precarious. Second, the weights given to their interests are inadequate.

(1) The representation of non-humans and future generations by the preferences of current generations is precarious. What analysis thus far has shown is that they can be indirectly represented. It does not follow that they *will* be represented. They are represented only in so far as the current generation are not egoists, that is in so far as they do not prefer only to satisfy that set of interests that can be satisfied exclusively of others. I have argued in chapters 2 and 3 that our well-being incorporates the interests of future generations and non-humans. However, our preferences need not. For representation of future generations and non-humans to be possible, enough of the current generation must possess non-egoistic preferences. The vicarious representation on which cost-benefit analysis relies to defend itself against the charge of failing to incorporate future generations and non-humans exists only if one assumes that the preferences current generations have are those they *ought* to have. However, to begin to refer to preferences individuals *ought* to have rather than those they in fact have is to move away from a view that takes preference satisfaction as the basis of decision-making. I will discuss this point in more detail in the next chapter.

(2) The weight that is ascribed to the interests of future generations and non-humans given indirect representation of their interests by current preferences is less than it ought to be. Two points are of relevance here. The first is a continuation of that just made: the vicarious representatives of the interests of future generations and non-humans are less numerous than those they represent. Thus, given a society like ours, in which the majority in their purchasing behaviour do not exhibit great concern for the interests of future generations and non-humans, those interests

may not receive the weight they ought to. The interests of one of the affected parties of a policy – the *articulate* current generations – are likely to receive greater weight than the *inarticulate*. The second is a problem peculiar to the representation of future generations, namely that social discounting necessarily entails that their interests receive less consideration. This I consider in detail in the next section.

4.3 Discounting the future

To discount the future is to value the costs and benefits that accrue to future generations less than those of the present. Since benefits and costs are in cost-benefit analysis measures of preference satisfaction and dissatisfaction, the preferences of future generations weigh less than those of the present. Thus the assumed preferences they might be supposed to have for an absence of toxic waste, expressed in their willingness to pay for that absence or their willingness to accept compensation for its presence, is valued at less than that of current generations. If their preference expressed by willingness to pay for the absence of toxic waste is £n, and the discount rate is r, then preference in t years' time is £$n/(1 + r)^t$. Thus if we assume a constant preference for the avoidance of toxic poisoning at some arbitrary figure, say £1,000, then, using the standard discount-rate employed in the UK of 5 per cent, the same preference in fifty years is now to be valued at only £$1,000/(1.05)^{50}$ = £87.2. The further into the future, the lower the weight. Likewise with benefits. Consider tree growing. A tree that took fifty years to grow, worth £100 at current prices, would in a cost-benefit analysis be given a value of just £8.72. Likewise with non-renewable resources. £100 worth of oil at present rates would be discounted at £8.72. Social discounting appears then to provide a rationale for displacing environmental damage into the future, and valuing current consumption of benefits over future consumption. Our current preferences count for more than both our future preferences and those of future generations. Given the way in which discounting appears to provide an ethically indefensible bias against future generations, how is it justified?

Four justifications of discounting are to be found in the literature.

(1) Uncertainty. Individuals value present benefits over those of the future since they are uncertain about their future preferences,

the existence of a future benefit or cost, and finally of their own existence to receive expected benefits. Similarly, in social policy, uncertainty about future preferences and the existence of future benefits and costs justifies discounting the future.

(2) Increasing wealth. On the assumption that wealth increases over time, the marginal utility of any future benefits will be less than those of the current period. Hence future benefits are to be weighted less than current benefits, in just the same way that benefits to the current wealthy are to be weighted less than those to the current poor.

(3) Pure-time preferences. Individuals have pure-time preferences – they prefer benefits now to benefits tomorrow simply in virtue of the time at which they occur. They are impatient. Any aggregation of preferences in cost-benefit analysis must reflect these pure-time preferences.

(4) Social opportunity costs. Any future benefits of a proposal have to be compared to the future benefits that might have accrued had the resources been invested at the going rates of interest. Future benefits and costs have to be discounted by the projected interest rates.

I now show that none of these arguments provides sound grounds for discounting.

4.3.1 Uncertainty

Uncertainty about the future provides no justification for discounting. Uncertainty about personal existence does not entail uncertainty about species existence. One can assume that, given care on our part, future generations will exist. While uncertainty about specific preferences of future generations does exist, uncertainty about their *needs* does not. One can assume that toxic materials will be harmful and that they will need sources of energy, food and basic raw materials. It is of course possible that scientific progress will mean that measures counteracting or neutralizing the toxins in question will have been developed, or that the tree planted will die of disease before it reaches maturity or will have been destroyed by fire, or that substitutes for wood will have been developed and so on. However, there is no reason to suppose that the uncertainty of future benefits and costs, even if it may have a loose relation to distance in time, obeys a discount factor of $B_t/(1 + r)^t$. Indeed, there is no reason to suppose that any probability function at all can be ascribed to the uncertainty of future benefits and costs. In particular, the future progress of science is in principle unpredictable, for reasons Popper has outlined. If we could predict the future progress of scientific knowledge we would already possess it.[7] Hence, there is no rational foundation to the assignment of any probability function to the discovery of a solution to a particular scientific problem. Hence, since such technical solutions depend on scientific theories, there is no rationally founded probability function that can be assigned to the discovery of technical solutions to any particular pollution problems or to the existence of new materials that can be substituted for the old.

We need to distinguish *uncertainty* from *risk*, where risk describes contexts in which probability functions can be assigned to possible outcomes (as in card games) and uncertainty contexts in which they cannot. Given contexts where there are unresolvable uncertainties other rules need to be applied. One such rule is the 'maxi–min' rule – given a choice of proposals or a choice between acting on a specific proposal or not so acting, assume the worst outcome will result from each course and choose that option which has the least bad worst outcome, i.e., play safe. A related rule is the 'mini–max regret' rule – follow that proposal which minimizes the maximum regret we will have. Where potential environmental disasters are possible consequences of a proposal, such risk aversion strategies are rational. Likewise, so also is the strategy of not making irreversible decisions for which the same rationale applies. Where the worst consequences of a reversible decision are avoidable, those of an irreversible decision are not. Whatever rules are applied in the context of uncertainty, given that no meaningful probability function can be applied to such outcomes, it makes no sense to appeal to uncertainty to provide a foundation for discount rates.

4.3.2 Increasing wealth

If wealth is increasing at a certain rate then it makes sense within the theoretical presuppositions of social cost-benefit analysis to weight a unit of value in the future as less than it is now. To do so is simply to apply social cost-benefit analysis across generations. A unit of wealth has a lower marginal utility with increased wealth. However, the assumption that future generations will be wealthier is not one that has a rational foundation. Given the depletion of non-renewable resources, changes in global climate, the limits of substitutibility of materials, there are good grounds for believing that the average wealth of future generations might be a great deal less than that of current generations. Indeed, there is something paradoxical about discounting when applied to non-renewable resources, in that it undermines its own justification. Given discounting, current consumption is to be preferred to future consumption, but given a finite non-renewable resource this entails that at some point t_n that generation will be likely to be less well off than current generations. The application of discounting entails the disappearance of the wealth that justifies, in terms of diminishing marginal utility, its very application.

4.3.3 Pure-time preferences

The claim that individuals have a time preference for present over future goods and that the value assigned to a good diminishes in direct proportion to its distance into the future is commonly cited as a justification for social discounting. Since it is the task of social policy to aggregate the preferences of affected parties, time preferences must be incorporated into public policy. This defence of discounting is open to two sets of objections: (1) those concerning the move from intrapersonal preferences to interpersonal preferences, and (2) those concerning the rationality of such preferences for any individual in the first place.

(1) For any individual who has a pure-time preference for the present over the future consumption of goods, that preference concerns her own future preference satisfaction. When one moves to consideration of a social-discount rate this is no longer the case. One is concerned not with the satisfaction of one's own preferences, but with those of others. Now it is one thing to say that I would be willing to pay only £8.72 for a tree I received in fifty years for which I would currently be willing to pay £100. It is another to value that tree for another person who lives in fifty years' time at £8.72. Social discount rates do just this. Even given unanimity in time preferences in the current generation, the goods and harms about which preferences are expressed satisfy or dissatisfy the preferences of a different population. Cost-benefit analysis does not aggregate the preferences of all affected by the

decision. There is no defensible way of moving from intrapersonal preferences to interpersonal preferences.

(2) Are pure-time preferences rational for an individual? Two conflicting views are to be found within both neo-classical and Austrian economics. Both hold that individuals have pure-time preferences – that, other things being equal, individuals prefer the satisfaction of wants sooner rather than later. They differ, however, in their view of the way the satisfaction of time preferences bears on human well-being. The defender of pure-time preferences argues that human well-being demands their satisfaction.[8] The opponent of pure-time preferences holds that well-being demands that we ignore such time preferences since to include them will be to fail to maximize the satisfaction of desires over a person's lifetime. Time preferences show only that 'our telescopic faculty is defective';[9] one should take a temporally neutral view of the satisfaction of desires. I will argue here that both views are mistaken. Neither can make sense of the reference to narrative order in the evaluation of how well a person's life goes.

Consider the following stories.

(A) A newly married couple, couple A, go on a two-week honeymoon. The holiday begins disastrously: they each discover much in the other which they had not noticed before, and they dislike what they find. The first two days are spent in an almighty row. However, while they argue continuously over the next seven days, they begin to resolve their differences and come to a deeper appreciation of each other. Over the last five days of the holiday they are much happier and both feel that they have realized a relationship that is better than that which they had before their argument. The holiday ends happily. Sadly, on their return journey, the plane that carries them explodes and they die.

(B) A newly married couple, couple B, go on honeymoon. The first twelve days proceed wonderfully. On the thirteenth day their relationship deteriorates badly as each begins to notice and dislike in the other a character trait which they had not noticed before, at the same time realizing that the other had a quite mistaken view of themselves. On the last day of the holiday they have a terrible row, and sit on opposite ends of the plane on the return journey. They both die in an explosion on the plane.

Which lives go better? Or, to stay with the language of consumer choice, given a visitation on the day before the holiday begins by an angel who presents you with a choice between the two lives, which would you choose? (The visitation and the choice itself will be instantly forgotten, so can be ignored.) What would the consumer with a time preference choose? All other things being equal, nobody wants the stress that arguments bring. All other things being equal, everyone wants to have an enjoyable time. In holiday B, the preference satisfactions occur early, and the preference dissatisfactions occur late. The defender of time preferences suggests that we include time preferences for goods that occur sooner rather than later. With weight given to preference satisfaction sooner rather than later, the choice must be holiday B. The opponent of time preferences will ignore such relative weighting and advise a temporally neutral perspective. But, given identical dissatisfactions from arguments and satisfactions from enjoyable times together, holiday B still contains more satisfactions than dissatisfactions. Given that when these occur is of no matter, one should still choose holiday B.

However, most individuals, given a visitation from my angel, would, I suspect, choose holiday A; they would characterize the story of holiday A as a happier one than that of holiday B. They would do so neither because the temporal order of events is irrelevant nor because it is the case that it is always better to have goods sooner rather than later. What counts in favour of holiday A is the *narrative* order of events, and crucial to that order is the way in which that story ends. As I argued in the last chapter, people's lives have a narrative structure, and the ending of a narrative is crucial to the genre to which a person's life, or an episode of that life, belongs – tragic, comic, pathetic and so on. Our evaluation of how well a person's life goes depends on the narrative we can truly tell of it. Time is relevant, but not in the way that either of the protagonists in the debate about time preferences assumes.

Both the standard perspectives on time preferences make sense only if one pictures a person's life as consisting of a series of momentary acts of desire satisfaction. Given such a life a pure-time preference for consumption now over consumption in the future makes sense. However, it does so at the cost of coherence in a person's life. Just as such a picture of lives across generations isolates each generation into itself, such a picture of an individual's life isolates each act into itself. A strong sense of identity across time is lacking. At any moment t_0 Jones cares for $Jones_0$, who exists now, more than for $Jones_1$ – who is physically related to $Jones_0$ – at time t_1, and more than for $Jones_2$, who exists at time t_2, for $Jones_2$ is a distant relation of $Jones_0$, more distant than $Jones_1$. The critic of pure-time preferences is an economic maximizer who demands equal consideration for future preferences, but on the basis of an oddly impersonal perspective. A life is still a series of discrete acts of consumption, but the maximizer instructs us to plan to maximize satisfaction over a life-time. The old self at time t_{70} is a distant relative of the self of t_0 – someone about whom $self_0$ should care – and the value placed on that $self_{70}$'s consumer satisfaction ought to be identical to that we place on the young person who now consumes. However, there is no sense of continuity, save physical relatedness, between the person at t_{70} and that at t_0. The lives described lack internal coherence. The economists' pictures of lives as acts of discrete consumption can make no sense of the ways in which lives as a whole are to be evaluated.

What is absent from these accounts is a view of human lives as ones which have a narrative structure – as stories of physical and moral growth and decline, of the success and failure of projects, of their re-evaluation, and so on. There is a narrative continuity between the self of t_0 and that of t_{70}.[10] Our concern for the self of t_{70} is a concern about the way our intervening lives have gone. As I noted earlier, the genre to which a story belongs depends on the way it ends. Our concern with the future is, hence, a concern with now: how well our life at present is proceeding depends on its relation to a projected future. Thus, what from the present perspective appears to be the best part of one's life might, at a future date, turn out to be a prelude to failure. What at present appears to be a segment of one's life that has gone disastrously wrong may from a future perspective appear to be a turning point which leads to a happy conclusion.

Consider again my honeymoon stories. In holiday A, the argument at the start of the holiday is not simply a 'cost' – a moment of pain or desire dissatisfaction. Rather, taken in context, it might be that which clarifies the relationship and lays the foundation for the ensuing happiness. Within the context of the individuals' entire lives, it has another significance. Likewise, the moments of happiness in holiday B are not 'benefits' – feelings of satisfaction. Rather, within the context of the whole story, they are moments of illusion, when each person has a false view of the other, an illusion shattered by the final argument. Had their lives continued beyond that present, the argument also may have become something else, but the ill fortune of untimely deaths robs the participants of such a future. Whether moments of pain and pleasure are goods or evils depends on their context of a life as a whole. They do not come ready-tagged as such.

The failure to allow this significance of the narrative order stems, in part, from one standard view of well-being assumed in economic literature. If one assumes, with Pigou, that 'the elements of welfare are states of consciousness',[11] then *when* an event occurs is irrelevant to its contribution to a person's welfare. Whether an event at time t_0 is a 'satisfaction' or a 'dissatisfaction', a 'pleasure' or a 'pain', remains unchanged by any future event. It might be the case that at time t_1 its *recollection* causes pleasure, but its characterization at t_0 cannot be altered. Just as hedonism entails that our well-being cannot be affected by what happens after our deaths, so it entails that my current well-being is quite independent of what may happen later. As I noted in chapter 3, it is only if one moves towards an objectivist account of well-being which ties it to real achievements that narrative order can play a part in the evaluation of a person's life, and the characterization one gives to a particular event will be changed in terms of later events.[12]

4.3.4 Social opportunity costs

Unlike the justifications of social discounting thus far considered, that which appeals to social opportunity costs need not be understood as valuing the goods and harms of future generations at lower rates than those of the present. Rather, interest rates provide a bench-mark against which possible benefits for future generations need to be evaluated. For any project, the capital invested in it has an alternative investment within banks at the current rate of interest. If the return of a project at year t_n is less than that given at current interest rates at t_1, then the project fails to provide the best outcome for future generations. Thus, for example, if the project is one of planting trees, on the assumption that the trees have a market value £v at year t_n, whereas the return at t_n at current rates of interest is £v + w, it follows that an investment of money at current rates of interest more than compensates the future for the loss of potential trees. Similarly, for oil and other natural resources, we discount at the current rate of interest, since investment at such rates provides future generations with compensation for any losses.

There are two related problems. The first and less serious problem concerns the way in which interest rates are often misleadingly presented as simply given, with banks acting as a kind of money-generating institution independent of the rest of the economy. This instrument generates pound notes at a particular rate of interest to compensate future generations for their losses. Interest rates are of course no such thing. They rather are a measure of the cost of borrowing within an economy at a particular moment, and that cost of borrowing, in ideal market conditions, is determined by the demand for capital loans to invest in other private or public projects and the supply of savings. The expectations of each rational potential borrower is that the return on her project will be greater than that of the rate of interest. In other words, what is being compared when one uses the interest rate as a measure for discounting is the return from the project under consideration as against the return possible on other projects competing for capital investment. This point serves merely to clarify the argument from social opportunity costs and it might seem to provide a stronger case for discounting the future at the current rate of interest. The rate of interest represents a market measure of the expected returns on projects. Those that fail to meet that rate are shown to be less advantageous for future consumption than those that do.

However, as far as future generations are concerned, the argument fails. The returns on capital investment on alternative projects are likely, within a competitive market economy, to reflect expectations for immediate to medium-term gains. The capital invested in such projects might be – indeed in terms of energy and resource use is likely to be – costly to future generations. (Hence Pearce's defence of high discount rates, viz. that low discount rates 'will increase the demand for resources and environmental services',[13] has a grain of truth in it. The statement is true if one substitutes 'interest rate' for 'discount rate'.) In considering the effects of different projects on future generations what is relevant is not the gross rates of profit that can be expected from different projects, but rather the direct consequences of different projects for the well-being of those generations. It might be that clearing a forest and selling the wood will produce more immediate profit per unit of investment than employing the same capital to plant trees. Hence, in market terms, it might be rational to borrow capital at a certain rate of interest for the first project, while irrational to borrow capital at the same rate for the second. However, with respect to the possibility of sustainable development which will benefit future generations the second project is likely to prove preferable to the first. Interest rates do not provide a measure of return on projects that is relevant in consideration of the interests of future generations.

This points to the second problem with the compensation argument for using interest rates as a bench-mark for discount rates for projects. The argument assumes that all goods are commensurable – that for the loss of any good there is a level of compensation losers are willing to accept. This assumption is one that I will reject in chapter 7. A point to note here, however, is that the compensation argument depends on the existence of alternative goods one can buy and substitute for that loss. Money is never its own reward. However, given the loss of basic environmental resources such as top soil, clean air, clean water, an atmosphere that filters out harmful rays, and so on, it is not clear what the substituted goods are supposed to be. Even if goods *were* commensurable such that all are replaceable by others at particular rates, it is simply nonsense to point to a nominal compensation sum in the absence of arguments to show that goods to be substituted will exist. One needs *direct* comparison of different projects in terms of the real possibilities they leave open to future generations.

The argument for discounting by appeal to social opportunity costs reveals at a deep level an old confusion between wealth and money that was noted as far back as Aristotle and again by Adam Smith in his critique of mercantilism.[14] Wealth refers to goods which can, in a market economy, be purchased with money, not money itself:

> A guinea may be considered as a bill for a certain quantity of necessaries and conveniences upon all the tradesmen in the neighbourhood. The revenue of the person to whom it is paid, does not so properly consist in the piece of gold, as in what he can get for it, or in what he can exchange for it. If it could be exchanged for nothing, it would, like a bill upon a bankrupt, be of no more value than the most useless piece of paper.[15]

The last sentence is of quite direct relevance to the debate about the use of interest rates as a ground for discounting – although it takes on a quite different meaning. What matters is not a nominal sum of wealth, but the goods, in particular the environmental goods, it can be exchanged for. What does it profit a man who gains a fortune and yet loses the world?

The appeal to market-based discount rates in the discussion of planning for the future is a mistake. It is not that discount rates should be zero, negative or positive, but that they are on the whole *irrelevant* to the discussion of the policy one should adopt to the future. There are good principles that govern our dealings with the future – that we minimize resource depletion, that we avoid irreversible changes, that we engage in sustainable economic activity and so on. Moreover, with any specific resource, there are rates of use and of return on projects that need to be considered. However, the appeal to general discount rates governing all activities, projects and resources cannot form the basis of rational planning for the future. More specific comparisons need to be made. To a limited extent the rule is already followed, for example in the particularly low discount rates for forestry projects. These *ad hoc* adjustments are not irrational: they are a rational departure from an irrational procedure. It would be better if the use of market-based discount rates were avoided completely.

4.4 COST-BENEFIT ANALYSIS AND THE INARTICULATE

Given that standard cost-benefit analysis does fail to give sufficient weight to the interests of the inarticulate, can it be revised to do so? One possible simple refinement of cost-benefit analysis is to include the preferences of the inarticulate directly. Thus, it might be argued, while the inarticulate cannot express their preferences, we can with a fair degree of reliability impute certain preferences to them. Indeed, that is what in practice cost-benefit analysts actually do for its standard constituency. Thus while we cannot know the detailed preferences of future generations, we do know enough of their needs to impute some preferences to them. We can assume, for example, that they will have a preference for unpolluted air, clear water and freedom from physically harmful substances – say highly radioactive substances.

Likewise, it might be argued that we can feasibly impute certain preferences to higher animals. Thus to take an example of Stone's: there is no reason, he suggests, why biologists might not construct a 'preference profile' of the bowhead whale – its preferred route through the Beaufort Sea, its preferred foods and so on. Using such a preference profile one might then also compute a related compensation rate for a project that interfered with the whales' current paths.[16] A similar position is developed in the Ramsey Centre Report on environmental ethics. Where standard cost-benefit analysis represents the preferences of non-humans only indirectly, the Ramsey Centre Report suggests we include them directly. Like Stone, it holds that it makes sense to refer to the preferences of non-humans:

> we consider it is not improper to speak of animals' 'prefer-ences', nor impossible to identify them ... Desires and preferences may be readily located in the drives and other behaviour-patterns of non-human animals, as may, corres-pondingly, their interests.[17]

Those preferences imputed to sentient beings should enter directly into cost-benefit analysis: 'in environmental decisions all sentient beings should receive equal consideration, and non-sentient beings, none.'[18] Two measures for including the preferences and interests of non-humans are suggested. The first is for the decision maker to act as a trustee and directly weigh the interests of non-humans as they might those of children and future generations alongside those of existing adults. The second is to include interests by adding a moral side-constraint on decisions.

Direct representation of the inarticulate clearly solves a problem concerning the disproportionate weight that might otherwise be placed on the interests of current generations. What is peculiar, however, is the inclusion of their interests via their *preferences*. The detour through preference is irrelevant in the inclusion of the inarticulate. What we know of future generations is what their *needs* will be – for clean air, unpolluted waters and so on. Their preferences might be quite different. They might themselves be quite unconcerned about the quality of their environment. If that were the case, then, for reasons noted in in the last chapter, that might represent a failure of ourselves and intermediate genera-tions. However, in considering current projects that will affect future generations, we consider their needs. Their possible prefer-ences are irrelevant.

Similar considerations apply to non-humans. In considering the interests of whales, what counts is not some hypothetical preference profile that might be imputed to them, but rather what is known of their needs. Whales might show in their behaviour a preference for substances which are harmful to them – domestic animals often reveal preferences for sugary food that is harmful, while on the impeccable authority of my children's *I-Spy Book of Nature* I learn that the kinkajou has a keen taste for alcohol and literally hangs around in tropical bars, ready to drop down and steal customers' drinks.[19] There are no good reasons to respond to such preferences. Indeed where non-human animals are concerned there are good paternalistic reasons to deny them. Neither does it make sense in this context to employ 'informed preferences' in place of 'actual preferences' as the authors of the Ramsey Centre Report suggest.[20] While it makes sense to refer to possible 'informed preferences' of adult humans, i.e., to impute conditional claims of the form 'if they knew x, they would prefer y', it is unintelligible to impute such preferences to animals. They lack the cognitive capacities to possibly satisfy the antecedent of the conditional. Talk of 'informed preferences' in this context is simply a misleading way of referring to an animal's needs.

In the context of the inarticulate, then, what needs to be considered are not possible preferences, but needs. The concept of need in turn is based on non-subjective criteria of well-being. In saying 'A has a need for X', we are saying that X is required if A is to flourish. The detour into preference structure is irrelevant. In the following chapter, I will argue more generally against purely preference-regarding principles of policy. The view that environmental policy should proceed by way of an aggregation of preferences is misconceived.

5

JUSTIFYING COST-BENEFIT ANALYSIS: ARGUMENTS FROM WELFARE

5.1 JUSTIFYING COST-BENEFIT ANALYSIS

Why should cost-benefit analysis be thought an appropriate tool of policy? The standard story begins with neo-classical economics and the efficiency of 'ideal markets'. Cost-benefit analysis is introduced to resolve problems that arise from the departure of real markets from 'ideal' conditions. The story runs as follows.

A fundamental theorem of neo-classical economics is that ideal markets yield Pareto-optimal outcomes.[1] A state S_1, is Pareto-optimal if there is no other state S_2 such that one person prefers S_2 to S_1 and no one prefers S_1 to S_2. An ideal market is one which satisfies the following conditions: (1) Individuals have available to them at no cost full information about the quality of all goods and services and the costs of all alternative ways of producing them.[2] (2) Costs of enforcing contracts and property rights are zero. (3) Individuals are rational in the sense that their preference orderings are transitive (i.e., if an individual prefers A to B and B to C, she prefers A to C).[3] (4) Transaction costs – for example the costs of bringing goods to the market, and of formulating and agreeing contracts, are zero. (5) The market is perfectly competitive. There are no externalities, i.e. third-party effects on the satisfaction or dissatisfaction of individuals' preferences that are not taken into account in market exchanges e.g. the benefits to others of an unspoiled landscape (positive externality) or the cost to others of pollution from nitrates (negative externality) by a farmer. Relatedly, there are no 'public goods' – that is goods such that (a) the action of some or all of a group is a necessary and sufficient condition for the existence of a good, action by one or a few is insufficient, (b) such action is a cost to the contributing individual, (c) the good is available to all, including those who do not contribute, and (d) non-contributors cannot be excluded from the good.[4] The common described by Hardin is a 'public good' – its existence requires action by most individuals – the cost of not adding a cow is born entirely by each contributor, but the benefits of a flourishing common are shared by non-contributors.

Clearly, ideal markets are not met with in reality. Conditions in which the market fails to meet Pareto-optimality through departure from ideal markets are referred to as 'market failures'.[5] Cost-benefit analysis is standardly justified in terms of solving problems of market failure – in particular in contexts of externalities and public goods.[6] Environmental goods, preferences for which are not revealed in markets since they are unpriced[7] and which are often public goods, and environmental harms, which are negative externalities, are taken to be particularly open to treatment by cost-benefit analysis.[8] Pareto-optimality is restored by the methods of cost-benefit analysis. Cost-benefit analysis produces ideal market outcomes by other means. This justificatory story is open to further elaboration, for example in a social direction, but the restoration of ideal market outcomes provides the basic plot. But why should 'ideal markets' be thought to be ideal? What makes them the ideal framework for decision-making? Why should Pareto-optimal outcomes, potential Pareto-optimal outcomes and their social relatives be thought to be optimal *per se*?

A central feature of the optimality criterion employed in neo-classical economics and cost-benefit analysis is that they are couched in terms of preferences and preference satisfaction. Both the neo-classical account of the market and cost-benefit analysis in so far as they *justify* the market or the use of quasi-market procedures in public spheres, begin with the preferences individuals happen to have. In thus starting with people's preferences as they are, neo-classical economics and cost-benefit analysis provide examples *par excellence* of what Barry characterizes as 'want-regarding principles':

> want-regarding principles ... are principles which take as given the wants which people happen to have and concentrate attention entirely on the extent to which a certain policy will alter the overall amount of want satisfaction or on the way in which the policy will affect the distribution among people of opportunities for satisfying wants.[9]

Such principles are contrasted with 'ideal-regarding principles' which do not take existing wants as given, but rather conceive of procedures and policies cultivating certain wants. That principles of policy should be want-regarding is built into the neo-classical foundations of cost-benefit analysis. The purpose of procedures – markets or policy procedures – is to satisfy the wants people happen to have and the justification of policy must be thus purely want-regarding. The next two chapters reject that justification and defend an ideal-regarding position. The defence of environmental goods requires reference not to preferences as they are, but to preferences as they ought to be. Policy formation under ideal conditions should be understood as a process whereby, through rational dialogue, citizens arrive at those preferences.

Why should justification of procedures, institutions and policies be purely want-regarding? There are three forms of argument that might be offered for starting with existing preferences and wants: (1) meta-ethical arguments, (2) welfare arguments and (3) liberal arguments.

(1) Meta-ethical argument. It is sometimes assumed that a subjectivist theory of value commits one to want-regarding procedures and justifications. The argument goes something like this: since value-utterances are merely expressions of preferences, no one set of preferences should be given special privilege. Hence, public policy and institutions should be such that they merely meet preferences in the most 'efficient' way possible, where efficiency is defined in terms of 'Pareto-optimality' or 'Hicks–Kaldor optimality', welfare maximization and the like. The appeal to such 'efficiency' criteria is often justified in terms of 'value-freedom'. Since economics is value-free, it must be neutral between different ends individuals happen to have and address only questions of 'efficiency'.

Any move from a subjectivist meta-ethic to standard economic efficiency criteria is illegitimate. Whatever the truth or falsity of subjectivism, one cannot justify standard preference-aggregation principles by reference to it, for these principles themselves incorporate substantive first-order value commitments. Thus, nothing, for example, rules out the alternative principle which Mussolini took to form the basis of a link between relativism and fascism:

everybody has the right to create for himself his own

ideology and to attempt to enforce it with all the energy of which he is capable.[10]

It should be added, against Mussolini, that nothing forces the subjectivist to accept the fascist principle that the preferences of those with the strongest will should be enforced. Subjectivism in meta-ethics is logically neutral between *any* principles for arriving at public policy. Any principle of public policy including 'efficiency' principles must itself be treated as a preference by the subjectivist – and it is open for others to chose a different and less neutral principle for aggregating preferences. Subjectivism provides no foundation for standard preference-aggregation principles. They need foundation not in meta-ethics, but in first-order ethical principles.

The other two defences of cost-benefit analysis recognize this.

(2) The *welfare* justification is broadly utilitarian in origin, and defends preference aggregation principles in terms of their maximizing human well-being. This justification I consider in the rest of this chapter.

(3) The *liberal* justification appeals to the desirability of political neutrality between the values of citizens – I discuss this in the next chapter.

5.2 WELFARE JUSTIFICATIONS

A central argument for starting with preference satisfaction lies in an equivalence that is taken to exist between preference satisfaction and well-being. Pareto-optimality and potential Pareto-optimality start with preferences since these indicate the effects of different states of affairs on the well-being of affected parties. Thus the 'ideal market' is taken to be optimally efficient in the sense that there is no departure from it which could leave some person 'better off' and no one 'worse off'. Cost-benefit analysis which employs *potential* Pareto-optimality becomes equivalent to standard utilitarianism – it defines the best policy as that which maximizes the 'well-being' or 'utility' of affected parties.

One argument, then, for holding to purely want-regarding justification of procedures, institutions and policies lies in a connection that is taken to exist between the satisfaction of wants and preferences, and well-being. To satisfy a person's preferences is to increase their well-being, the stronger the preference the greater the increase in well-being. Why? There are two kinds of answer. The first is that there is a conceptual connection between well-being and the satisfaction of preferences. Well-being is defined in terms of preference satisfaction. The second is that a person's preferences may provide an *indicator* of what is likely to increase a person's well-being, although well-being itself needs to be characterized in other terms.

There are two standard versions of the 'indicator' position. The first is the subjective-state position – that well-being consists in having certain psychological states, for example states of pleasure, and a person's preferences provide a generally reliable indicator of what will produce such states. This position is defended by Pigou.[11] The second is the objectivist's position: well-being consists in the possession or realization of certain objective goods, e.g. the development of capacities, of friend-ships and so on. A person's preferences indicate a person's beliefs about these goods: thus Aristotle 'we desire the object because it seems good to us'.[12] Both 'indicator' views allow that persons' preferences and their well-being can come apart. The subjective-state account allows that individuals may make mis-takes about what will maximize their pleasure. Hence, some wants might be rejected – Pigou thus suggests that time prefer-ences should be overridden.[13] However, in general wants are taken to be reliable indicators of what objects will produce the valued subjective states. The journey in an ideal-regarding direc-tion is likely to be a short one.

The objectivist is likely to allow a larger departure of well-being from the satisfaction of the preferences individuals have. The objectivist allows that individuals might make mistakes about what the goods of good life are. Hence well-being is a question not of satisfying preferences *per se*, but of educating our capacities of judgement and our desires, such that we come to prefer what is good. Well-being consists not in the satisfaction of preferences people have, but in the satisfaction of some ideal set of prefer-ences. In this chapter I defend an objectivist position against want-regarding accounts of well-being.

Purely want-regarding accounts of well-being that define well-being in terms of preference satisfaction are open to immediate criticism on the basis of obvious discrepancies between the satis-faction of actual preferences and well-being, for example, the satisfaction of a preference for a certain food that unbeknownst to me causes chronic ill health or the satisfaction of desires I have when delirious. Proponents of want-regarding accounts recognize these and standardly refine the theory by discounting certain preferences, for example in cases where they are not fully informed or the agent not fully competent. One begins not from raw preferences that individuals actually have, but from the preferences of the agent when fully informed and/or fully competent. Clearly, I might prefer food X to Y, only to discover later that X is highly carcinogenic. If I had known that about X, I would have preferred Y to X. One starts then not from actual preferences, but the preferences an agent *would* have if fully informed and/or competent. Hence Griffin's initial definition of utility: '"utility" is the fulfilment of informed desires, the stronger the desires, the greater the utility'.[14]

In this chapter I will suggest that any such refinement to a want-regarding account of well-being is unstable. The problem with it is one that Griffin himself raises:

> What makes us desire the things we desire, when informed, is something about them – their features or properties. But why bother then with informed desire, when we can go directly to what it is about objects that shape informed desires in the first place? If what really matters are certain sorts of reasons for action, to be found outside desires in qualities of their object, why not explain well-being directly in terms of them?[15]

This objection I will argue in the following is a sound one – although the connection between the objects of value and an individual's well-being needs some spelling out. I develop this point by way of an excursion into what appears to me to be the most telling criticism of cost-benefit analysis – that it allows no role for reasoned argument in public policy: it treats all preferences as non-rational wants – political debate is replaced by a surrogate market mechanism which is supposed to mimic the workings of an ideal market. I show that any attempt to introduce a proper role for reason takes us away from a preference-satisfaction account to one that is concerned with the *objects* of our preferences. The result is an objectivist and ideal-regarding account of well-being and it is thus that well-being should be conceived.

5.3 COST-BENEFIT ANALYSIS, SCIENCE AND ARGUMENT

How might one arrive at a judgement as to how good this book is? How might you arrive at a comparative judgement of its merits against others that defend competing views? Or given two competing physical theories A and B how might one judge their worth? Or, again, to give these questions a policy-orientated feel, given a choice of research projects A' and B' within competing theoretical frameworks A and B, how might one decide which project to resource? Here are some possible methods.

(1) Consider the book sales for competing theories. A person's willingness to pay for a book will be a function of a number of variables – style, packaging, the author's personal qualities, the arguments and conclusions it contains. Identify all such variables and, by the use of statistical techniques, infer how much individuals are willing to pay for the arguments and conclusions the book contains.

(2) Carry out a survey of the audiences that attend papers given by proponents of competing theories to discover: (a) their travel costs, (b) the loss of income incurred by listening to the paper, and (c) where appropriate, the conference fee. From these one can infer the cost of attendance and hence how much a person is willing to pay to hear the different arguments and conclusions.

(3) Ask individuals how much they would be willing to pay for projects informed by their favoured theory to be resourced, or how much they would be willing to accept in compensation for forgoing the resourcing of their favoured project.

By employing such methods one will arrive at a shadow price for each theory which reflects the weighted preferences of individuals expressed in their willingness to pay for their satisfaction. One can then arrive at a measure of how good each theory is by applying the standard efficiency criteria for aggregating preferences: (1) Pareto-optimality criteria – theory A is an improvement on theory B, if someone prefers A to B and no one prefers B to A; or (2) the more applicable potential Pareto-improvement criteria – theory A is an improvement on B if gains measured by willingness to pay are greater than losses, so that gainers – those who prefer A to B – would be in a position to compensate losers and still be better off. Where there are a number of competing theories, the best is that which produces the greatest preference satisfaction, where preferences are weighted by willingness to pay.

How appropriate would such methods be for deciding how to allocate resources between different physical theories – or for deciding whether this book is a good or bad one? An initial point to note is that the introduction of such principles would have quite radical consequences for the distribution of scientific resources. For example, an examination of the public market place in ideas – in books, willingness to travel to and pay for lectures – show widespread and strong preferences for non-normal science. Research into astrology or personal auras would be a beneficiary. To make this point is, indeed, to note the extent to which the distribution of resources in the world of ideas is at odds with the liberal assumptions that underpin neo-classical economics.

The possible radical consequences of applying such decision procedures is however merely symptomatic of their problems. Even if the outcomes were to turn out to be identical to those at which existing methods arrive, the procedures would still be flawed. They fail to take into account the soundness of the arguments for the different theories involved. Questions concerning the evidence for different theories, their testability, their consistency with other well-supported theories, their internal consistency disappear. There is no reference in the procedures to those cognitive values which tell for or against different theories. Relatedly, argument between proponents of different theories which makes reference to such values likewise plays no part in the consideration of a choice between them. The choice of theories is reduced to a question of preference, whether or not those preferences are supported by good reasons. Preferences that are mere wish-fulfilments stand equal to those with a ground in argument – superficial anecdotal arguments for personal auras and the influence of stars on personal life take an equal place alongside those for theories of molecular biology.

Could a purely want-regarding procedure be saved from this criticism of cost-benefit analysis? It might be argued that a preference aggregation can deal with it by moving from actual preferences to *informed* preferences. What we need to consult is not the preferences individuals actually have, but those they would have if fully informed about the object of their preference. Such a move has immediate difficulties, however, for it begs the question. Part of what is at issue in a choice between two or more competing theories is precisely what does and what does not count as an item of information. One either gives an account of the difference between information and non-information in terms of preferences, in which case the appeal is circular, or one makes a direct appeal to cognitive norms – to norms of reliable evidence, consistency and so on – in which case preferences disappear from the picture. The appeal to 'informed' preferences is simply a disguised way of appealing to cognitive values.

The same conclusion can be reached from another direction. Why is it that one appeals to 'informed' preferences to choose between different theories, rather than preferences as such? The only plausible answer is that the informed preference is that which will more likely get the theory choice right – and it does so because the preference is one that answers to good evidence and argument. It is this that is doing the work. The only appropriate procedure for aggregating preferences for scientific theories is reasoned debate – since only this appeals to the relevant criteria for theory choice. Any purely want-regarding procedure misses the point.

It might be objected that this argument is too hasty. A non-circular appeal to preference can be made by appeal to the preferences of *competent* judges. The appeal here refers not to information about the *objects*, but to the capacities and skills of the *subject* who has the preference. The best theory is that preferred by those whose preferences have been educated by an apprenticeship in the practice of science. Thus, as Kuhn puts it, 'trained scientists are, in such matters, the highest court of appeal'.[16] The best theory is simply that on which competent scientific judges agree – 'what better criterion than the decision of the scientific group could there be?'[17]

This defence fails. One can still properly ask why it is that the preferences of the competent should count as against the incompetent. And why should competence be defined in terms of a particular training within the scientific community and not, say, a training in astrology? The answers, I take it, are these: that the preferences of the competent count because their judgements about the merits of different theories are more likely to be right; and competence is defined in terms of a scientific training, rather than a training in astrology, because the practice of science embodies certain norms of arguments and evidence, certain skills of observation and experimentation, and finally a background of knowledge, such that those trained within that practice will arrive at judgements which are more likely to be true of their objects than those who lack that training. Without such background assumptions, the distinction between competent and incompetent is either arbitrary or, as some sociologists of science would have it, an exercise in arbitrary power.[18] The 'best' theory cannot be simply defined as that which competent scientists prefer. Competence relies on the idea of getting something right.[19]

To attempt to remedy the problems of using preference-regarding principles for scientific choice by distinguishing between preferences – between informed and uninformed, those of competent and incompetent – fails because, in letting in reason elsewhere, preferences *per se* drop out of the picture. Once reason and argument enter, policy becomes a matter not of aggregating given preferences, but of arguing about what preference one ought to have. It is the desirability of the *object* of the preference – a true theory – that is basic. We prioritize certain preferences because they are preferences for what is likely to be true. Truth, not preference satisfaction, does the work. One necessarily moves to ideal-regarding principles of choice.

This argument is open to the following rejoinder. That we must thus move in an ideal-regarding direction might be accepted and a cost-benefit analysis approach to science policy on these grounds rejected. However, it might be objected that this has nothing to do with well-being – it is rather that human well-being must take its place amongst other goods – including truth. One might hold to a want-regarding account of well-being, but hold that other ideals determine our choices. Cost-benefit analysis, interpreted in purely want-regarding terms, on these grounds might still be accepted as a *welfare* measure, but one that must now take a place with other values.

Now, I think that such a manoeuvre fails to save a want-regarding account of well-being for reasons already developed. There is a relation between what we desire, want or prefer, and what we believe to be good. Desires answer to goods. If we prefer apples to pears it is because we value gustatory pleasure and apples happen to give us more pleasure than pears.[20] We prefer theory A to theory B because we value theories that are true and we believe that A is a better candidate for truth than B. Values are doing the work.

To make this point does not, however, dispose of the disquiet

71

behind the attempt to prise apart well-being and ideals. It shows only that want-regarding accounts of well-being won't do the job. The point behind the objection, I take it, is this – that some ideals appear to be external to a person's life such that a person can sacrifice their well-being for the sake of an ideal – an artist who lives a miserable life because of his commitment to art, or a person who sacrifices career and comforts to work amongst the poor. It might be that there is a bridge to be built between a proper understanding of what is good for a person and the realization of ideals, but it cannot be a simple definitional one – that we define a person's well-being in terms of ideals.[21] One needs to show why the realization of that ideal is not simply good *of* a person (as in 'it was good of you to do that'), but good *for* that person. The good needs to be one that makes *that* person's life go better.

However any general attempt to separate ideals from well-being would be mistaken. A commitment to particular goods and ideals is internally linked to the well-being of an agent. Consider again the case of Hamilton discussed in chapter 3. Mathematics and the excellences of the practice of mathematics – the proof of a significant result – cannot be treated as separate from the question of how well his life is said to go. His early life goes well in virtue of the mathematical skills he develops and what he achieves with those skills. Our accounts of how well his life goes cannot be considered separately from the excellences of mathematics. Similar points hold of other of the sciences. To the person who is a scientist, the development of fruitful theories and the elimination of those that are false are not merely external goods, but are partly constitutive of how well a person's life goes. More generally, the practices and projects in which persons engage are internal components of their lives, not something external to them. Hence, success or failure within them in part determines how well their lives can be said to go.[22]

Nor is it the case that *any* ideal or any project will do – that how well an individual's life goes can be identified with the realization of whatever he or she happens to value. Individuals make mistakes as to what is of value. Of a promising physics student who gives up the subject for the study of tarot cards, of a promising philosophy student who suddenly becomes enamoured of post-structuralism, or of a promising artist who gives up her life to the production of kitsch, we are apt to say that their lives have taken a turn for the worse. If a reader disagrees with any of my assessments – say of the philosopher who turns to post-structuralism – it is in virtue of their disagreeing with my estimate of its worth. Our estimation of the value of different activities determines whether or not we count them and the objects they realize to be achievements. Hence as I noted in chapter 3 the arguments within and across generations. The same points can be made of less lofty examples – literacy programmes increase well-being because they enlarge the capacity of individuals to achieve significant goods in their lives. This is true also of good health – which is both itself a good and a means to other goods – and those prerequisites for good health – decent food, sanitation, health services and so on.

There is a second answer one might make to the question 'Why should engaging in the rational activities of science, or discovering and contemplating what is true, be good *for* me and not just *of* me?'. This appeals to a specific Aristotelian account of the goods of human life. One part, if not all, of the goods of a person's life lies in the development of her characteristically human capacities. Now there is a necessary relation that exists between the development of that person's human capacities and attributes, and certain ideals. Consider again the value to a person of a scientific education. One might say that such an education is good *for* that person, because it develops certain capacities – powers of observation, of judgement, of reason. But specification of such desirable capacities presupposes some reference to the goods in which they issue. One says a person has good powers of observation, judgement and reason if she is disposed to see what is there, to judge correctly, to argue validly and so on. Excellences of character are parasitic on the goods in which they issue.[23] Hence my earlier point – that the distinction between the competent and incompetent in science presupposes the ideal of truth-finding. It makes no sense without it. Hence, some ideals at least are required to make the distinction between what it is for persons to develop their powers and what it is for them to fail to do so. Well-being is thus tied up with a commitment to their realization. A similar point can be made with respect to environmental goods for reasons I develop at the end of the next section.

Still economists may baulk at these moves on the grounds that it makes the notion of an individual's well-being *too* broad to be treated within the discipline. One of the most sophisticated of recent arguments to keep commitments out of any account of well-being is that of Sen. Sen's approach to well-being in his recent work has much in common with that defended in this book. However he still insists on a distinction 'between a person's overall achievements (whatever he wishes to achieve as an "agent") and his personal well-being'.[24] He writes:

> The distinction between agency achievement and personal well-being arises from the fact that a person may have objectives other than personal well-being. If, for example a person fights successfully for a cause, making a great personal sacrifice (even perhaps giving one's life for it), then this may be a great agency achievement without it being a corresponding achievement of personal well-being.[25]

He continues later:

> At the risk of over-simplification, it may be said that we move from agency-achievement to personal well-being by narrowing the focus of attention through ignoring 'commitments'.[26]

Sen offers two distinct arguments here which need to be kept apart. The first runs: since 'a person may have objectives other than personal well-being', those objectives are not constituents of well-being. This argument fails – that x is not the objective of a person's action does not entail that x is not constitutive of her well-being. This is true even of goods that are necessary for well-being in the narrowest conception. Assume a narrow medical sense of well-being as health: I eat a meal for the gustatory pleasure it brings – not because it increases my well-being in the sense of my health. But it does not follow that the meal does not contribute to my health. Or consider friendship. If friendship is well-constituted I act towards my friend for my *friend's* sake, not my own. It does not follow that having friendship is not an element of well-being.[27] (The point has a parallel in the paradoxes of hedonism and self-realization. If one wants a life of pleasure then do not make pleasure one's object; if one wants self-realization, then do not make self-realization one's object.)

Sen's second argument runs thus: 'an ideal x cannot be a part of a person's well-being, for a person can sacrifice their well-being for the sake of x'. This argument I raised at the outset of this discussion and I still owe it an answer. It is invalid. That one sacrifices one's well-being for the sake of x does not entail that x is not constitutive of one's well-being. The argument depends on a failure to note the plurality of goods that are constitutive of a person's well-being.[28] It certainly makes sense to say of an artist, say Van Gogh, that he sacrificed his own well-being for his art. What we normally mean by this is that there are certain goods which are necessary to lead a minimally good life – friends, health, sanity – and that the artist sacrificed these for his art. However, that does not mean that art and aesthetic achievement were external goods irrelevant to his well-being. If he had given up a promising artistic career for a comfortable but dull existence one might still want to say his life had gone ill. Nor need it be the case that only the goods necessary for a minimally good life are those for which one can sacrifice one's well-being. One can sacrifice the possibility of other achievements to realize one that is central to one's life. Thus for example E. R. Dodds properly asks of MacKenna's much admired translation of *The Enneads* of Plotinus, the central project of some nine years of his life, 'whether in fact MacKenna's Plotinus is worth the enormous price that was paid for it not only in effort and suffering, but in the sacrifice of other potentialities that lay in his rich natural endowment'.[29]

The problem with Sen's second argument can be revealed in another way. One can sacrifice one's well-being for the sake of goods which the narrowest conception of well-being would include. Persons might sacrifice their health in the pursuit of gustatory pleasure: it does not follow that gustatory pleasures are not a component of well-being. Persons might be so committed to their health that they live a spartan life devoid of pleasures and friends – they sacrifice their well-being for their health. It does not follow that health is not a component of well-being. That some commitments are constitutive of a person's well-being is consistent with the claim that he can sacrifice his well-being for the sake of these commitments.

Economists may still be unhappy with the broadening of the concept of well-being. Some who recognize sources of well-being other than those that can be exchanged in the market have still attempted to narrow down a conception of well-being. Pigou, for example, draws the distinction between 'economic welfare' and 'total welfare', where economic welfare is characterized as 'that part of social welfare that can be brought directly or indirectly into a relation with the measuring-rod of money'.[30] More recent economists have tended to accept that starting point, but have attempted to bring all possible sources of welfare into the 'economic' category by holding that, of any good, an agent can be asked 'how much would you be willing to pay for it?'. All goods can be brought under 'the measuring-rod of money'.[31] Pigou's position is in this regard, for all the weaknesses I discuss in chapter 7, at least better than that of his successors. For reasons I shall develop in 7.6, to apply the 'measuring-rod of money' to all goods – including for example friendships and kin-relations – is to fail to understand what it is to have such goods. A person who could say 'I'd be willing to pay £X as compensation for a loss of friendship' would reveal a failure to understand commitments of friendship and what it was to betray such commitments. Similar points apply to commitments to environmental goods. To the extent that Pigou's distinction is a proper one, it highlights the way in which the market as an institution presupposes a particular conception of a person's interests that conflicts with those presupposed in other institutional contexts.[32] What is problematic about Pigou's treatment is the way that it focuses the study of human well-being on that which the market as an institution presupposes. There is no theoretical justification for the move. It merely gives theoretical dignity to a widespread misconception about well-being that results from the dominant place of the market in modern life.

5.4 REASON, PREFERENCE AND ENVIRONMENTAL GOODS

Nobody, to my knowledge, has seriously advocated the applicability of cost-benefit analysis to questions of choices in the area of scientific research. In the case of environmental policy, however, it is the standard approach and has considerable influence. The kinds of surrogate pricing mechanism outlined with respect to scientific theories in the last section are all employed in environmental cost-benefit analysis. They stand, for example, at the heart of the influential Pearce Report.[33] They are required, the argument goes, because the market puts no proper price on environmental goods – as a source of 'utility' to individuals, as a supplier of primary resources, or as a sink for wastes. Such value functions of the environment are all characterizable as 'economic'

because they all have a positive economic value: if bought

and sold these functions in the market-place would all have positive prices. *The dangers arise from the mistreatment of natural environments because we do not recognise the positive prices for these economic functions.*[34]

The first function of the environment – as an object of 'utility' – can be brought into a proper economic account of the environment's value by placing a monetary value on preferences for environmental quality. The methods employed are variants of those outlined for scientific theories in the last section.

(1) Examine property prices. The prices will be a function of a number of variables – the quality of the property itself, of the neighbourhood, its accessibility to roads, entertainment etc., and finally the quality of environment. By comparing property values in different locations one can identify how far differences in prices reflect environmental differences and hence infer how much individuals are willing to pay for such environmental goods.

(2) One can study a sample of individuals who attend an environmental amenity – say for example a national park. Discover the time it takes individuals to travel to the park, the loss of income to an individual in terms of hours lost in possible work time. Add to this costs of travel and entry. One can then infer how much individuals are willing to pay for it.

(3) Ask individuals how much they are willing to pay for an environmental benefit, for example an unspoilt national park, or for its continued existence, even if they have no intention of travelling to it or alternatively how much they would be willing to receive by way of compensation for loss of that benefit – say to accept an industrial or commercial development within the park.

By employing such techniques, a monetary value can be attached to preferences such that they can be brought into standard cost-benefit analysis. The best policy is that which meets the standard criteria outlined earlier – the Pareto improvement criteria or potential Pareto improvement.

The introduction of such shadow prices is hailed by environmental economists as a way of making standard economic analysis environmentally friendly. However, it is so only given the 'right' prior preferences. An environmentally friendly outcome depends on the shadow price picking up a predominance of strong preferences for environmental goods.[35] If people prefer marinas to mud flats, Disneyland to wetlands, and roads to woodland, then no amount of shadow-pricing will deliver environmentally friendly results. Why should that matter? What grounds are there for complaint?

The grounds for complaint are not that the procedure might produce 'bad' results *per se*. Even if it produced 'good' results it would be wrong. The complaint is that as in the science case, the procedure itself is misconceived. It treats all preferences as identical save in the 'intensity' with which they are held. It is blind to the reasons and arguments that individuals have for or against different proposals. Standardly, environmentalists appeal to features of the site on which a development is to take place, to its aesthetic merits, its landscape qualities, to its value as a habitat, to the variety of species it holds, to its value as a place, its history and so on. Cost-benefit analysis is blind to such reasons. The strength or weakness of the *intensity* of a preference count, but the strength or weakness of the *reasons* for a preference do not. Preferences grounded in aesthetic, scientific or historical judgements about the site are treated as on a par with preferences for a particular flavour of ice-cream. They are priced and weighed with the others. Cost-benefit analysis provides policy without debate. Politics becomes not a forum for discussion and argument about policy, but a surrogate market which completes what an 'ideal' market is supposed to do – which aggregates most efficiently given preferences. That is indeed the justification offered for cost-benefit analysis.

The standard response from a want-regarding perspective to such objections is that which we have discussed in relation to science – to move from actual preference to the preferences of the informed or competent agent. Only certain preferences are taken as inputs into policy analysis. This response fails for reasons similar to those I have already considered with respect to scientific policy.

To focus discussion consider a real world example – the proposed siting of a theme park, film studios and commercial facilities by MCA in 1,600 acres of Rainham Marshes in the UK, 1,250 acres of which was declared a site of special scientific interest (SSSI) in 1986.[36] The the case is interesting in that it is a particularly difficult one for conservationists. To the uninformed observer the value of the marshes is difficult to discern. One sees a flat, muddy patch of ground infested by daddy-long-legs. It appears to have little aesthetic appeal as a landscape. Indeed to some it appears an industrial wasteland containing factories and warehouses and used as a dump. The informed observer sees something different. She sees a valuable habitat with a particular mix of flora and fauna. She sees not a daddy-long-legs but a lesser spotted crane-fly. She knows its particular history – that it is one of the few ancient grazing marshes still in existence. For these reasons she prefers the marsh to remain undeveloped and opposes the development, even though she is aware of its aesthetic faults. To oversimplify the real debate a little,[37] assume then that she is a fully informed and competent agent.[38] Why should those preferences count?

As I noted earlier, there are cases in which information and competence straightfowardly count within a purely want-regarding position. If I had known that tasty X caused cancer I would not have eaten it. Why? Because I have a settled preference for good health which generally overrides that of taste. My mental competence is disturbed during an illness, and I have no desire for liquids, even though I require them for my health. Had I been fully competent, I would have a preference for liquids. The case in question is not like these, however. To acquire through education in the subject of ecology new information about the site, and new powers of observation and judgement, is to develop new preferences. It is to begin to find value in and hence a preference for a lesser spotted crane-fly and a marsh where before all that was seen was a daddy-long-legs and an uninteresting mush of mud and grass.[39] Information and training develop new interests and preferences. What is it about those preferences that make them count? A person trains in ecology. Why should her new preferences have priority over those she had before? The education and experience have transformed the person's wants. Why should the preferences of the person P_0 at t_0 count over those P_1 at the later time t_1 given a purely preference-regarding theory of well-being? What is it about their *preferences* that give them priority, rather than the *reasons* that she would give for those preferences, those that concern the ecological value of the habitat?

The problems with the informed preference account of well-being parallel the well-known difficulties with J. S. Mill's account of why the preferences of an informed or competent agent be given priority. Mill appeals to a subjective-state account of well-being.[40] P_1 gets a higher quality of pleasure than P_0. One starts from the informed agent because only she is in a position to judge:

she knows 'both sides' of the question, the uninformed only one. That answer is unsatisfactory for standard reasons – it relies on the introduction of some criterion of excellence independent of pleasure itself.[41] The appeal to the quality of pleasures is an illicit way of introducing independent ideals – famously, in the case of Mill, the values of 'human dignity' and of realizing our specifically human capacities. The same point is true in the case of the appeal to the informed and competent agent to defend the preference regarding account of well-being. It serves only to smuggle in criteria that are independent of the preferences themselves. The only plausible reasons for starting from the preferences of the 'informed' and 'competent' are those that refer directly to those independent criteria of excellence. The preferences of the competent and informed ecologist count in virtue of her sensitivity to the objects around her, such that she is better able to make judgements about the value of different habitats.[42]

It might be objected that, as in the case of science, this may give us reasons for moving in an ideal-regarding direction in policy, but that this has nothing to do with well-being. We might value ecologically rich habitats, just as we do beautiful landscapes, and we might be willing to make policy on this basis. However, there is no connection between public commitments to such values and well-being. I have already argued at the end of the last section that many such commitments cannot be separated from well-being. Those arguments apply to the present case also. However, it might be thought that commitments to environmental goods are a special case. After all, what relation could commitments to non-human goods have to *human* well-being?

Environmental commitments are not a special case. Consider again the relation of education and well-being. Education increases the well-being of the agent since it widens her powers to realize significant goods and achievements. The education of the field ecologist develops powers of judgement, discrimination and observation – it renders the agent responsive to the qualities of the object. Here it should be noted again that preferences and desires are themselves educated. Certain desires can distort our perception. A rat appears only as vermin to a person who examines the world from a particular set of desires – for a high crop yield and more wealth. This is not to say that a desire for a good crop is not a proper desire – it is rather to point out the way in which to be moved solely by such desires is to have one's perception of the world distorted. Both science and the arts in contrast are able to develop a disinterested perspective which extends our powers of perception. The ecologist sees not flies, vermin and undrained soil but particular natural beings with particular life histories in a particular habitat. Marx refers to such freeing of perception from the distortion of a particularly narrow utilitarian or commercial set of desires as the 'humanization of the senses'. The term is a good one in so far as it highlights the relation between practices like the sciences and art, and human well-being. To extend our powers of perception from a disinterested perspective *is* to develop characteristically *human* capacities. It is to increase human well-being. A commitment to environmental goods is not independent of a concern with human well-being. I develop this point further in chapter 9.[43]

5.5 IDEALS, PREFERENCES, AND ELITISM

An objection that has been standardly made of arguments of the kind made in the last two sections of this chapter is that they are elitist. My argument has depended on a strategy of assuming that in both scientific and ecological policy questions some preferences should have priority over others since they are supported by good reason and judgement, and by then showing that standard responses to this assumption within want-regarding theories of well-being fail. The assumption might, however, be rejected as 'elitist'. To this charge I respond thus: if it is elitist to say that some judgements are better than others or that some individuals have better powers of observation and judgement than others, then the position *is* elitist. However, 'elitism' in that sense is unobjection-able. 'Elitism' is objectionable when it refers to the claim that different social classes and groups have different natural capacities to make judgements and develop powers of observation and judgement. Elitism in *that* sense is not entailed by the arguments of this chapter – rather the position is compatible with the view that all have the requisite capacities, and since their development increases well-being, all should have the same opportunities to develop them. Hence the demand for literacy programs and the provision of basic goods and health care for all – they are the minimal prerequisites for the development of human capacities. The excessive sensitivity to the charge of 'elitism' is often founded on the fact that within our society it is wealth and status that primarily determine whose judgements and preferences in fact have priority. However, that requires not the denial that some judgements have priority, but conditions of social equality such that wealth and status should not have this role. This argument from authority to equality is developed in chapter 8.

Another charge that might be made against the position developed in this chapter, which is related to that of 'elitism', is that it is paternalist. To say that certain preferences 'have priority' is to license one group imposing its preferences on others on the grounds that 'they know better'. It fails to respect the autonomy of individuals to shape and develop their own lives. That charge again fails. To say that well-being is about developing preferences and capacities, and not simply satisfying whatever desires individuals have, is compatible with non-paternalistic views of politics. It is compatible for example with an educative account of political participation that individuals should engage in political life because this best develops their human capacities and instructs their preferences: that view allows also that autonomy is one component of human well-being. Mill develops just this position. The criticism of the 'paternalism' of ideal regarding principles takes us however away from welfare arguments for cost-benefit analysis towards possible liberal justifications. These I discuss in the next chapter.

6

PLURALISM, LIBERALISM AND THE GOOD LIFE

In the last chapter I noted that both cost-benefit analysis and its neo-classical foundations assume purely want-regarding criteria of optimality and I examined welfare arguments in defence of that assumption. This chapter considers a different liberal justification.

6.1 LIBERALISM AND THE GOOD LIFE

That politics should involve only want-regarding principles of policy has been central to much liberal thought. As Barry notes, one strand of classical liberalism was 'the idea that the state is an instrument for satisfying the wants that men happen to have rather than making good men (e.g. cultivating desirable wants or dispositions in its citizens)'.[1] Some recent accounts of liberalism have been less cautious and identify liberalism simply in terms of the neutrality of politics between different conceptions of the good.[2] Thus, as Dworkin puts it, liberalism asserts that

> political decisions must be, so far as possible, independent of any particular conception of the good life, of what gives value to life. Since the citizens of a society differ in their conceptions the government does not treat them as equals if it prefers one conception to another.[3]

Part of the appeal of cost-benefit analysis lies in the appeal to liberalism and the pluralist society it is taken to foster, and one might defend it in these terms. Thus the proponent of cost-benefit analysis need not appeal to a particular account of human well-being, in the manner outlined in the last chapter, but, rather, might remain agnostic concerning different accounts of well-being. Rather, cost-benefit analysis might be defended on the basis of its *procedural* neutrality between conceptions of the good life. Cost-benefit analysis recognizes that there is a plurality of different conceptions of what it is to lead a good life and the principles of aggregation it incorporates remain procedurally neutral between these. It does not aim to remake citizens, but simply to respond most efficiently to their wants. It is a refined tool of liberal public policy.[4]

In contrast, the account of public policy-making I have defended, it might be argued, is illiberal in its implications. I have assumed that public political debate should be understood as a process through which individuals attempt to come to agreed under-standings of what it is to lead a good life, and hence what wants they ought to have and to educate in others. To engage in debate about environmental goods is to attempt to create in individuals not merely new beliefs but new preferences – and one goal of public education is to develop preferences for environmental goods. To view public policy-making thus as a process in which individuals arrive at public decisions concerning the nature of the good life is incompatible with the possibility of the co-existence of different accounts of the good life. The view of politics it involves is, to use the Rawlsian terminology, perfectionist.[5] Perfectionist political theory is exhibited most clearly in the classical political writing of Plato and Aristotle for whom the purpose of politics is the good life of its citizens: 'the end and purpose of the polis is the good life'[6] where the good life is characterized in terms of the virtues. Hence Aristotle's comment that the best political associa-tion is that which enables every man to act virtuously and to live happily.[7]

The liberal account of the neutrality of politics between con-ceptions of the good life is often characterized in opposition to this classical account of politics. The classical doctrine is taken to be incompatible with the plurality of different conceptions of the good life in modern society. Given such plurality the classical account of politics is neither feasible nor desirable. Typical is the following comment by Larmore who, having rejected Aristotle's 'monist' conception of the good life, writes:

> The ideal of neutrality can be best understood as a response
> to the variety of conceptions of the good life. In modern
> times we have come to recognize a multiplicity of ways in
> which a fulfilled life can be lived ... The state should not

seek to promote any particular conception of the good life because of its presumed *intrinsic* superiority, that is, because it is a *truer* conception.[8]

Liberal neutrality involves a rejection of the 'monism' of classical conceptions of politics. The classical account of politics involves the imposition of a particular conception of public virtues, which modern history has shown to be at best authoritarian in its implications, at worst totalitarian.[9]

In this chapter I counter these claims. I outline and defend the move in Aristotle's *Politics* from the claim that political life exists for the sake of the good life to a pluralist conception of politics. The good life at which politics aims, properly understood, contains a plurality of goods and allows for a diversity of forms of living. I suggest that the problem for those who defend neutrality is that they conflate different senses of 'pluralism' and 'conception of the good', and different accounts of what is good about plurality. I then show that the liberal arguments of J. S. Mill follow broadly Aristotelian lines. I conclude that the definition of liberalism in terms of procedural neutrality between conceptions of the good is unsatisfactory in itself, is false to the history of both classical and liberal political theory, and fails to provide a good foundation for liberal institutions and values.

6.2 ARISTOTLE, THE GOOD LIFE AND SELF-SUFFICIENCY

6.2.1 Self-sufficiency, plurality and the polis

Aristotle's *Politics* has been the major source of the classical conception of politics. For Aristotle the polis exists for the sake of the good life. It is notable, however, that Aristotle combines this doctrine with the claim that plurality is of the very nature of the polis, and a rejection of Plato's attempts to impose an 'excessive unity' on the polis via the common ownership of property and the abolition of the family.[10] I will not enter into a discussion of his defences of the family and private property here.[11] Rather, I want to focus on one general argument for the plurality of the *polis* which is independent of these – that from 'self-sufficiency'.

The argument runs thus:

There is still another consideration which may be used to prove that the policy of attempting an extreme unification of the polis is not a good policy. The household is an institution which attains a greater degree of self-sufficiency than the individual can; and a polis, in turn, is an institution which attains self-sufficiency to a greater degree than a household. But it only attains that goal, and becomes fully a polis, when the association which forms it is large enough to be self-sufficing. On the assumption, therefore, that the higher degree of self-sufficiency is the more desirable thing, the lesser degree of unity is more desirable than the greater.[12]

This argument echoes an earlier discussion of the passage from household through village to polis:

When we come to the final and perfect association formed from a number of villages, we have already reached the polis – an association which may be said to have reached the height of full self-sufficiency; or rather [to speak more exactly] we may say that while it *grows* for the sake of mere life [and so far, and at this stage, still short of full self-sufficiency], it *exists* [when once it is fully grown] for the sake of the good life [and is therefore fully self-sufficient].[13]

The end of the polis is the good life, and hence it is self-sufficient; because it is self-sufficient it must have an internal plurality. The argument as it stands is difficult to follow. To unpack it we need to give a more general account of Aristotle's view of what it is to live well.

6.2.2 Happiness and self-sufficiency[14]

Aristotle claims that *eudaimonia*, happiness or flourishing, is a self-sufficient and complete good.

We regard something as self-sufficient when all by itself it makes a life choiceworthy and lacking nothing; and that is what we think happiness does.

Moreover, [the complete good is most choiceworthy, and] we think happiness is most choiceworthy of all goods, since it is not counted as one good among many. If it were counted as one among many, then, clearly, we think the addition of the smallest of goods would make it more choiceworthy; for

86

[the smallest good] that is added becomes an extra quantity
of goods [so creating a good larger than the original good],
and the larger of two goods is always more choiceworthy.
[But we do not think any addition can make happiness more
choiceworthy, hence it is the most choiceworthy.][15]

Happiness is self-sufficient and complete in that it contains all
those goods pursued for their own sake. It is not one good among
others, but rather includes all intrinsic goods. Since it contains all
such goods – no more could be added – it is the most choiceworthy
of goods. Happiness on this account is an inclusive good. Aristotle
also claims that the goods of human happiness are internally
plural. A flourishing human life contains a variety of intrinsic
goods which cannot be reduced one to another. Thus he writes
elsewhere:

> In fact ... honour, intelligence and pleasure have different
> and dissimilar accounts, precisely in so far as they are goods,
> hence the good is not something common which corres-
> ponds to a single idea.[16]

6.2.3 Self-sufficiency: the individual and the polis

A human being is able to realize this complete and self-sufficient
good only within the polis:

> Not being self-sufficient when they are isolated, all indi-
> viduals are so many parts all equally dependent on the
> whole [which alone can bring about self-sufficiency]. The
> man who is isolated – who is unable to share in the benefits
> of political association or has no need to share because he is
> already self-sufficient – is no part of the polis, and must
> therefore be either a beast or a god.[17]

While within the household or village individuals can possess
those goods necessary for 'mere life', in the polis they can realize
those goods necessary for the 'good life'. Why? First, only in the
polis can an individual realize the full range of those relationships
which are constituents of human well-being:

> What we count as self-sufficient is not what suffices for a
> solitary person by himself, living an isolated life, but what
> suffices also for parents, children, wife and in general for

friends and fellow-citizens, since a human being is naturally a political [animal].[18]

Given the kind of beings we are, friends, family and fellow citizens are goods, and a person without them could not live a flourishing life. Second, these relationships make accessible to us a variety of goods that could not be realized alone or within smaller associations. My concern for the well-being of those for whom I care widens my own interests. This point deserves a little more development.[19]

For any individual there are limits to the goods she can pursue. Individuals face limits of capacity, time and resources which impose on them practical choices in their pursuit of activities that are non-instrumentally good. An individual may not have the capacities to be successful in some pursuits – she may lack a musical ear, the voice for oratory and so on. An individual who is capable of excellence in many activities – in music, mathematics, sport and carpentry – is rarely capable of realizing excellence in all. Pursuit of the good of one will rule out accomplishment in others. Moreover, some groups of activity will make up a form of life that is incompatible with others: one may not be able to lead a life of contemplation and a life of action. Finally, the pursuit of such activities may conflict with calls of other relationships. Such conflicts give rise to the practical dilemmas of individual lives. There is no algorithmic procedure in such cases – rational choice is made on the basis of judgement of one's particular capacities, the possibility of success, the relative merits of the goods of different activities, the pleasures each activity will bring, and so on. Choices may be more or less difficult. However, the limitations of individual lives force such choices upon us.

Choices are forced also on a particular society. However, the boundaries within which choices are made are wider. *I* cannot realize excellence in music, politics, carpentry, sport etc. – *we* can. The goods realizable by the polis are wider than those any member or household can realize. This greater range of the goods realizable within the polis enhances the lives of its members. Through my relations with others, I can have a vicarious interest in these goods. Consider the case of friendship. To have friends with a diversity of interests and pursuits extends me. In caring for the good of my friends, I care for the success of the projects in which they are involved, for their realization of excellence in the

88

activities they pursue. A friend 'shares his friend's distress and enjoyment'.[20] Thus in friendship the ends of another become one's own. Hence, while I may not be involved in such activities, I have a vicarious interest in the achievement of good within them. My concerns are extended by those around me. While there are limits to the goods I can personally achieve, I can retain an interest in their achievement through others for whom I care. Hence, given relations of friendliness of a kind Aristotle assumes in an ideal polis, a community in which the largest number of goods can be realized will enrich the lives of all its members.

We are now in a position to understand Aristotle's argument from self-sufficiency against the excessive unity of Plato's ideal society. Humans can achieve a complete and self-sufficient good only within the polis. This in turn requires that individuals are able to enter a variety of relationships and within different associations pursue diverse and distinct goods. The polis has the comprehensive goal of realizing the good of the 'whole of life' which contains these other goods. On this view, the polis does not replace other partial associations, but is rather a community of communities containing a variety of associations realizing particular ends.[21] The polis is plural in the relationships, goods, and associations that it contains.

Finally it should be noted that to say that the polis has this comprehensive goal and to claim that it is more self-sufficient than the household or individual does not entail that the goods it can pursue are without limit. There are contingent limits on the goods any society can pursue and this entails that the practical conflicts beloved by Berlin and those who follow him[22] still inevitably exist in public as well as individual life. Just as in individual lives we must choose between different goods so also must we make social choices. Health may be a good, but so also are arts – and any community may have to give up resources for those with health needs for the pursuit of arts. Environmental goods must enter into choices with other goods not reducible to them. How much any good should be realized at the expense of others in the end is a matter of practical judgement. As I show in the next chapter there is no algorithmic accounting procedure that can deliver judgements for us.

To view the purpose of politics as the pursuit of the good life is then compatible with a pluralist view of the political community and with the practical dilemmas that are consequent upon such pluralism. The failure to allow this possibility stems not from any necessary connection between the classical conception of politics and the suppression of pluralism, but rather with the particular monist conceptions of the good life itself that have often been associated with attempts to implement the classical conception. The problem lies not in the view of *politics* involved, but rather in the view of what the good life is.

6.3 PLURALISM: GOODS AND BELIEFS

The proponent of liberalism may feel dissatisfied with the Aristotelian defence of pluralism outlined in the last section. An objection might run as follows: Aristotle's account of the good life might be internally plural, it might allow for the flourishing of a variety of activities, but it remains just one conception of the good life which competes with others. Hence, a political society that was committed to the good life for its citizens would still be one which was incompatible with the co-existence of a plurality of ways of life and cultures. Thus Aristotelian pluralism remains illiberal.

This objection I will argue fails. However, it does reveal an important ambiguity in the way in which the term 'pluralism' has been employed in liberal arguments. The term 'value-pluralism' can have at least two distinct sets of meaning which are often conflated.

(1) Value-pluralism can be a thesis about *goods*. (*a*) The pluralist holds that there are a plurality of intrinsic goods which are not reducible one to another. (*b*) Politically, the pluralist holds that the end of politics is the realization of the plurality of goods. These two theses are themselves logically independent.

(2) Value-pluralism can be a thesis about *beliefs* about goods. (*a*) At a descriptive level the thesis is that there are a plurality of beliefs about what is of value. (*b*) At the meta-ethical level it is the thesis that no belief about values is superior to any other in the sense of being 'truer'. (*c*) At the level of political theory it refers to the liberal neutrality thesis that it is not the end of politics to promote one belief about the good because it is assumed to be superior. It should be added again that those three levels are themselves logically independent. For example, one might hold that one account of the good life is superior but deny that politics

should be concerned with its implementation. (Moreover, it is clearly possible to hold consistently 2 (*a*) and 1 (*a*) and 1 (*b*).)

Aristotle's account of the good life and of politics is pluralistic in the first set of senses. The end of the polis is to promote the good life given a pluralist conception of the good life. Politics aims at the realization of a variety of intrinsic goods. In defending these claims he rejects the meta-ethical claim that no belief about value is superior to any other, and the political claim that one belief about the good should not be promoted in virtue of this superiority. Hence for the liberal committed to neutrality Aristotle's account remains illiberal, since politics should be neutral between all beliefs about the good: such beliefs might include both monist and pluralist views of goods.

This reply clarifies the neutrality thesis – but in doing so it also weakens it. In the first place, neutrality between beliefs is not necessary to defend the co-existence of different ways of life and cultures, or, indeed, of different 'conceptions of the good' given the way that term is often employed. The much-used phrase 'conceptions of the good' suffers from a misleading ambiguity. (1) It is sometimes used to refer to individuals' 'life plans'.[23] Thus understood Aristotelian pluralism is committed to the co-existence of different conceptions of the good. The pluralism of the polis depends on different individuals pursuing different life plans each with its own distinct goods. (2) 'Conceptions of the good' is sometimes used interchangeably with 'forms of life' or 'ways of life'. Larmore for example in the passage quoted earlier refers to 'the multiplicity of ways in which a fulfilled life can be lived'.[24] Again Aristotelian pluralism allows that different forms of life – say that of action and that of contemplation – can each have its own internal excellences and virtues. (3) 'Conceptions of the good' is sometimes used to capture differences between different cultures. While Aristotle himself views all cultural difference in terms of a departure from Greek excellence – the peoples of northern Europe have spirit but lack intelligence, those of Asia have intelligence, but no spirit, the Greeks unite the qualities of both[25] – that discussion, for all its undoubted problems, presupposes the possibility that different cultures have their own virtues. It is compatible with his position to allow that different cultures develop different excellences of character. Moreover, the distinctive practices of different cultures provide the settings in which standards of excellence and their realization take place, and hence the precondition for individual achievement. Cultural diversity in the sense that it incorporates differences in artistic, culinary, sporting activities and the like is consistent with a suitably pluralistic conception of the good.

Cultures, however, are more than colourful activities. They incorporate beliefs about the ends of life, the social relations between and virtues of those of different genders, castes and classes, and so on. It is if 'conceptions of the good' is used in the sense of 'belief about what is good' that clear incompatibilities emerge between the general Aristotelian position outlined in the last section and that of the liberal committed to neutrality. The liberal is committed to the co-existence of different beliefs about the good life and of different life plans, ways of life, and cultures that are informed by such beliefs. The Aristotelian position in contrast encourages diversity only in so far as it comes within its specific account of the good.

Is pluralism in beliefs about the good itself a good? Should political processes remain neutral between divergent beliefs and the forms of life associated with them? These two questions are logically independent. One might deny that pluralism in beliefs is a good, but still hold political neutrality. However, much of the rhetorical power of the neutrality thesis relies on the appeal of plurality in beliefs. Surely no one could deny that such plurality is a good. I do so now.[26] In the next section I shall argue that there is nothing *per se* good about pluralism in beliefs and that neutrality between beliefs entails a cramped view of political argument. The virtues appropriate to belief are rather the intellectual virtues exhibited by those able to appreciate the fallibility of their own beliefs and the reasonableness of many of those they may not share, and the related social virtue of tolerance. Pluralism in beliefs may indicate the health of such virtues. However, it is not itself a good. That conclusion should, however, be treated as provisional. In the last section of this chapter I will add some necessary qualifications.

6.4 RATIONAL ARGUMENT, PLURALISM AND CONVERGENCE

Consider what it is to engage in argument with others, be that argument factual or ethical. To argue for a belief sincerely is to seek to convince, to be open to the arguments of others and to allow oneself to be convinced. The activity of argument only makes sense given an ideal of convergence of belief.[27] I am told that much recent post-structuralism seeks to deny this, and that one sometimes finds post-structuralist lecturers opening their talks with a claim that they do not seek to convince. They do so in bad faith. Their explicit utterances contradict felicity conditions of the speech acts in which they are engaged. It is like someone saying 'I want you to believe that I don't want you to believe that I have the want I express in this sentence'. I once heard ascribed to Hobbes the view that 'logic silences quibblers'.[28] Whether or not the phrase captures Hobbes's position, the observation it makes is a good one. Argument is an attempt to silence opinions. What distinguishes argument from other forms of silencing is that it does so legitimately. It seeks to persuade by reference to the impersonal canons of rational discourse, and not personal relations of power. Sincere argument aims not at simple convergence, but at convergence founded on good reason, for this is a condition of paths not simply converging, but converging on truths. Insincere advocacy can play a proper role in argument in virtue of this condition. I may for example play devil's advocate, and in doing so my aim will not be necessarily to convince – the opposing opinion might be one that I share – but rather to ensure that the shared opinion is held for good reasons. I do not do so simply to double the number of views around. Convergence remains the object of discourse. Plurality in belief is not the aim of reasoned argument.

Given that convergence of belief is an end of rational discussion, it appears that if one believes that argument about values plays a proper role in public political debate, then politics cannot remain neutral between beliefs about the good.[29] Neutrality requires not a conception of politics as a rational conversation, but rather a technical conception of political argument of which cost-benefit analysis provides the purest example. If conceptions of the good are not to have a place in the justification of public policy, then politics becomes a method of aggregating whatever ideals people happen to have, without conversation or judgement on those ideals themselves. Ideals are to be treated as wants or preferences. Politics thus becomes a surrogate market place in which substantive normative argument is irrelevant. Cost-benefit analysis provides the clearest example of such technically conceived rationality. If politics is to be a forum that includes rational arguments about ends, then neutrality fails.[30]

However, reasoned argument does presuppose and promote other goods and virtues, which are sometimes associated with liberalism. To engage in argument, as opposed to preaching, instructing and other related speech acts, is normally to accept one's fallibility – that one's own claims may be false – and to have the capacity to comprehend the possible reasonableness of the opposing view – that while the conclusion defended may be false, there are good reasons for holding that conclusion. Here, I make a qualification to my earlier endorsement of Hobbes's claim that 'logic silences quibblers'. Hobbes was appealing to the algorithmic logic of geometry. The silenced, once he has accepted the premise, is 'forced' to accept the conclusion he previously rejected. Most argument is not algorithmic. It leaves room for judgement, and reasonable interlocutors can find themselves at the end of an argument still with their respective positions: dialogue, while seeking to limit the options, may succeed in each comprehending the reasonableness of the opposing view, while remaining committed to their own. Choices between beliefs are often, although not always, underdetermined by the values of rationality. Sincere argument requires, then, particular intellectual virtues, and engagement in argument is the way in which such virtues are developed.

The social virtue argument develops is that of tolerance. Tolerance is a virtue that can be exhibited only towards that which one holds in some way to be less than ideal.[31] With respect to beliefs, it can be exhibited only towards those with which one disagrees. Tolerance is a difficult virtue to nurture precisely because the object is such that one would rather it was otherwise. A virtue of public argument is that it encourages tolerance. It is this point that provides an argument for the Periclean connection between democracy and toleration.[32] In so far as democracy involves political debate that proceeds via rational argument, rather than force or personal authority, it allows individuals to see why other beliefs are to be tolerated, even though one does not share them and seeks to alter them. That politics should aim at the good life of its members – and that politics should involve debate about the good life – is compatible with and indeed encourages the virtue of tolerance. One can recognize that individuals can hold different beliefs that are reasonable, and follow forms of life informed by those different beliefs which are such that they deserve respect, while arguing against both. The classical account is inconsistent only with neutrality. Pluralism in beliefs about the good may indicate the presence of tolerance. To the extent that it does it is an indication that a social good exists. It is not, however, itself a good.

6.5 MILL AND THE CLASSICAL CONCEPTION OF POLITICS

The view that liberalism is to be defined in terms of the political neutrality between different conceptions of the good and in opposition to the classical conception of politics plays no part in the classical liberalism of the nineteenth century. In particular, it is quite foreign to the work of J. S. Mill. Mill's political theory is self-consciously articulated within the classical conception of politics. While he criticizes Plato for holding that the *only* end of political society is to make citizens virtuous, he does not reject the view that it *is* an end,[33] and in *Considerations on Representative Government* he asserts that it is the chief end:

> The first element of good government, therefore, being the virtue and intelligence of the human beings composing the community, the most important point of excellence which any form of government can possess is to promote the virtue and intelligence of the people themselves. The first question in respect to any political institutions is, how far they tend to foster in members of the community the various desirable qualities moral and intellectual.[34]

Mill's arguments for democracy are founded on that classical conception. Participatory democracy is the best form of government since it is that which develops most fully the character of the individual, and in defending that claim Mill explicitly refers back to classical Athens as a model of the public education that democracy can afford.[35]

The classical account of politics also lies at the basis of his arguments in *On Liberty*. Mill's defence of his principle of liberty is founded not on neutrality between conceptions of the good, but on a particular conception of the good. The best life for humans is that which realizes most fully our distinctive human capacities. This point lies at the heart of the distinction between the lower and higher pleasures in *Utilitarianism*[36] and the argument for liberty of action in *On Liberty*:

> to conform to custom, merely *as* custom, does not educate or develop in him any of the qualities which are the distinctive endowments of a human being. The human faculties of perception, judgements, discriminative feeling, mental activity and even moral preference, are exercised only in making a choice.[37]

This defence of liberty is not neutral between different conceptions of the good. If, as some modern defenders of certain religious traditions maintain, reflection undermines faith, then, for the Millian liberal, so much the worse for those traditions.[38] Cultures and religions that are stationary, that do not allow room for reflection and that render individuals alike, are cultures that Mill takes to be incompatible with the liberal society. His politics does not aim at procedural neutrality. Rather, the procedures he defends are aimed at the undermining of certain kinds of culture and the development of others.

Mill's approach to politics is classical. The premises of his arguments are those of Aristotle – that the best life for humans is that which develops their distinctive capacities. He also holds, like Aristotle, a pluralistic account of that best life. It includes a variety of goods, and hence the political must develop such variety. This said, Mill undoubtedly does differ from Aristotle in a number of important details which are critical to his liberalism.[39] In particular, Mill, unlike Aristotle, does tend to praise individuality *as such*. He is less inclined than Aristotle to believe that our distinctive human powers are to be realized in similar ways:

> Different persons require different conditions for their spiritual development. . . . The same things which are helps to one person towards the cultivation of his higher nature are hindrances to another.[40]

Different individuals develop their own distinctive powers in distinctive ways. Similar points apply to culture. Where Aristotle views cultural diversity as a falling away from a Greek perfection, Mill sees in it something valuable. Thus the progress of Europe is taken to reside in their remarkable diversity of character and culture. Individuals, classes, nations, have been extremely unlike one another: they have struck out a great variety of paths, each leading to something valuable.[41]

However, while Mill puts a great deal of stress on diversity, this does not take him outside of the classical conception of politics. Diversity is defended because it assists the person to the development of 'his higher nature' or leads 'to something valuable'. Mill does not claim that we cannot make distinctions of value, that there is not an 'intrinsic superiority' of some conceptions of the good life, or that political arrangements should be neutral between such conceptions. None of the arguments for diversity depends on an assumption about the need for 'neutrality' between conceptions of the good. Rather they presuppose its denial.

Relatedly, nothing in Mill's arguments rules out the possibility or desirability of unforced convergence, in particular of beliefs. Mill rejects the Protagorean relativism defended at his time by Grote, and in ours by Feyerabend and post-modernists:

> Mr Grote says: 'To say that all men recognize one and the same objective distinction between truth and falsehood would be to contradict palpable fact. Each man has a standard, an ideal of truth in his own mind; but different men have different standards.' Of the proof of truth, yes: but not, we apprehend, of truth itself. No one means anything by truth, but the agreement of a belief with the fact which it purports to represent.[42]

The aim of dialogue and discussion is convergence on the truth. Mill's concern is not to deny that convergence, but to distinguish, in a manner similar to that outlined in the last section, between legitimate and illegitimate convergence.[43] Convergence is a mark of truth only if it is achieved through free deliberation where each is open and is able to respond to the opposing argument.

> Truth, in everything but mathematics is not a single but a double question: not what can be said for an opinion, but whether more can be said for it than against it. There is no knowledge, and no assurance of right belief, but with him who can both confute the opposite opinion, and successfully defend his own against confutation.[44]

The 'negative dialectics' exhibited in Plato's dialogues provides Mill with the model of free discussion that informs his defence of liberty of discussion in *On Liberty*. But the test of negative dialectics is meant to issue not in diversity, but in convergence on the truth.[45]

The liberalism of J. S. Mill self-consciously refers back to the classical conception of politics, and takes Athenian democracy as its model. It is founded not on neutrality between conceptions of the good, but on a conception of the good. It sees political participation and liberty as a means to the creation of virtuous citizens who develop their human capacities to the full, and public dialogue as a path to knowledge of what is true. That Mill's liberalism is thus founded in classical conceptions of politics and dialogue is one of its virtues.[46]

The classical account of politics provides the best foundation for those 'liberal' values shared by both socialist and liberal traditions. In starting from that account, and rejecting the want-regarding principles of modern liberalism, the defender of environmental goods is not committed to an illiberal politics.

6.6 SOME QUALIFICATIONS: ECOLOGY, AESTHETICS AND DIVERSITY

My arguments in this chapter have not allowed that pluralism in beliefs about the good can have value of itself. In this section I qualify that position. I review two arguments for the intrinsic value of a plurality of beliefs and of ways of life founded on them. The first, from ecology, I show fails; the second, from aesthetics, succeeds and shows my earlier conclusions in 6.3 to be defective as they stand: I will add some necessary qualifications to the position developed there.

6.6.1 Ecology and diversity

In the literature on environmental ethics and politics, pluralism has received renewed support under the 'principle of diversity'. Thus in his original distinction between 'deep' and 'shallow' ecology, Naess appeals to biological and cultural diversity as if they fall under a single argument:

Principles of diversity and of symbiosis: Diversity enhances potentialities of survival, the chances of new modes of life, the richness of forms. And the so-called struggle of life, and survival of the fittest, should be interpreted in the sense of ability to co-exist and cooperate in complex relationships, rather than ability to kill, exploit and suppress. 'Live and let live' is one more powerful ecological principle than 'Either you or me'.

The latter tends to reduce the multiplicity of forms of life, and also create destruction within communities of the same species. Ecologically inspired attitudes therefore favour diversity of human ways of life, of cultures, of occupation, of economies.[47]

This argument fails.

(1) Biological diversity cannot be taken to be of itself a good. I recently heard a geneticist suggest that worries about the loss of biological diversity were groundless: gene-splicing machines would allow us endlessly to produce new organisms. The real world consequences of this suggestion aside, it appears to me that a diversity of sealed genetic freaks thus produced would have no intrinsic value. It is not simple diversity that is valued, but diversity within particular ecological communities. Biological diversity is a good because it is a necessity for the stability and robustness of ecosystems.

(2) Diversity in that context concerns the spread of different *species* of being. Diversity between species is compatible with, and sometimes requires, a lack of diversity *within* particular species.

(3) Specifically, diversity *within* the human species cannot be defended in terms of its ecological consequences. To call for ecologically sustainable forms of life is necessarily to *narrow* the forms of life open to individuals. A variety of human ways of life are removed. Most notably the unsustainable consumerist economies and cultures of the west are ruled out by such arguments. So also are many cultures in Africa in which the cattle destructive of local ecologies have a central social significance. Ecological problems call not for a widening of cultural and economic possibilities, but, rather, for new constraints on human ways of life. The arguments from natural to social diversity of the kind to which Naess appeals fail.

6.6.2 Aesthetics and diversity

There is, however, another kind of argument which does support both natural and social diversity – namely that which appeals to our aesthetic responses to diversity. Part of our aesthetic interest in natural beauty is founded on responses to diversity – and part of the problem conservationists often have, with respect to wetlands for example, is that an uneducated eye may fail to see diversity that is present. Similarly, part of the response to the diversity in human cultures and ways of life is aesthetic in nature. A city with different ethnic quarters is more attractive than one without, and the attraction of travel often lies in the taste for difference. The language used to describe social plurality often draws on visual and musical metaphors: cultures are described as 'colourful' and 'vibrant', for example. Such aesthetic considerations form a part of Aristotle's case against Plato. Thus he remarks of excessive unity in society: 'It is as if you were to turn harmony into mere unison, or to reduce a theme to a single beat'.[48] Similar remarks run through Mill's defences of individuality: 'Among the works of man, which human life is rightly employed in perfecting and beautifying, the first in importance is man himself'.[49] The appeal to 'diversity' in green thought probably owes more to such aesthetic considerations than it does to any specifically 'ecological' principle.

Promotion of such aesthetic goods is compatible with the view that the purpose of politics is the good life of its citizens. Aesthetic goods are a component of the good life, and there are good aesthetic reasons to encourage a cultural variety. Likewise with respect to beliefs, a world with diverse beliefs is certainly more interesting than one without. Here I need to qualify my earlier conclusion that plurality of beliefs is not a good. This is the case only if one assumes, as I did in 6.3, that truth is not only the chief value with respect to belief, but the sole value. That assumption is false. Truth is but one value amongst others. While truth might entail the narrowing of the range of beliefs, other values, notably aesthetic values, require its broadening.

However, as I noted earlier, beliefs do not exist in a social-vacuum and cultures are more than colourful activities. They incorporate positions about the ends of life, the social relations between gender, caste and class, and so on. In so far as a culture incorporates such elements any aesthetic good in diversity needs

to be subordinate to other considerations about what life best
befits humans. Cultures are often oppressive to those within
them, and individual men and women can find themselves
against an alliance of conservatives from within and 'cultural
liberals' from without.[50] Similarly, the traveller who delights in
'unspoilt' cultures often desires the spectacle of cultural monu-
ments that, however attractive from the outside, are a weight on
those within. Cultural diversity may form the basis of the
upmarket tourist trade, but, whatever its undoubted pleasures,
there are other goods in human life that often take precedence
over such aesthetic considerations. Diversity as an aesthetic good
needs to take its place amongst other goods.

7

PLURALISM, INCOMMENSURABILITY, JUDGEMENT

The appeal of cost-benefit analysis, like that of its parent, utilitarianism, is that it promises a decision procedure that gives a rational resolution of apparently conflicting preferences and appraisals. It does so by the use of algorithmic procedures which give determinate answers to any problem. There is, in the economic literature, a widespread assumption that nothing else could provide a rational solution. In this chapter I argue that the existence of plural and incommensurable values in environmental appraisal reveals that the promise of cost-benefit analysis is illusory. Moreover its problems raise deeper difficulties for its foundations in neo-classical economics. The appeal of cost-benefit analysis depends on a cramped and mistaken account of rationality – one that misidentifies rational choices with those that can be arrived at by way of algorithmic procedures. In the final two sections I examine the implications for political economy of this mistaken account of practical rationality.

7.1 VALUES: INCOMMENSURABILITY, INCOMPARABILITY, INDETERMINACY

Cost-benefit analysis assumes that there is a single measure of value – affected agents' willingness to pay at the margin for the satisfaction of preferences – through which one can arrive at a unique ranking of the value of different policy options. It assumes value commensurability. Is that assumption of value commensurability defensible? An immediate problem in answering that question lies in ambiguities in the way the terms 'commensurability' and its contrary 'incommensurability' have been used in philosophical discussion. The term 'incommensurability' has prob-

102

ably led to more confusion in discussion of both ethics and science than any other single word in the philosophical vocabulary. In its root sense, to say that two entities are commensurable is simply to say that there exists a common measure by which to compare them: in evaluative appraisal of objects, value commensurability entails that there is a 'measure' of value in terms of which one can uniquely rank the objects evaluated. Commensurability can, however, take strong or weak forms depending on whether one takes the measure to have a cardinal interpretation, or merely an ordinal one. Weak commensurability needs in turn to be distinguished from weak comparability, that is from the claim that one can rationally choose between items without being able to produce a general ranking of different items. Finally, weak comparability needs to be distinguished from incomparability – the claim that no rational choice between items is possible – and value indeterminacy – the claim that values underdetermine choice. This section aims merely to clarify these different terms.[1] In 7.2 I will argue that in environmental policy-making one cannot, as the cost-benefit analyst does, assume value commensurability in either its strong or its weak forms. Weak comparability is all that we can reasonably expect.

7.1.1 Strong commensurability

Cardinality is the mark of strong commensurability. To hold that values are strongly commensurable is to hold not only that the measure ranks objects, but that there is a particular single property that all objects possess which is the source of their value, and that our evaluative measure indicates the amount or degree to which that property is present. Strong commensurability presupposes value-monism, that apparently different kinds of value can be seen as instances of a single super-value which provides a unique best ranking of a set of values. Our evaluative measure indicates the degree to which an object exhibits or produces that super-value.[2]

7.1.2 Weak commensurability/strong comparability

Commensurability need not involve a commitment to a cardinal measure; an ordinal measure will suffice. Our measure ranks objects, 1st, 2nd, 3rd, etc., but does no more than that. Commensurability in this sense I term weak commensurability. Weak commensurability, however, requires the strong comparability of values. To hold strong value comparability is to hold that while there may be no single value in terms of which all states of affairs and objects can be ranked, there does exist a single comparative term in terms of which they can be ordered. The Ramsey Centre Report on Environmental Ethics characterizes commensurability in terms of strong comparability: 'All that commensurability of values requires is that one be able to make judgements such as "This is more valuable than that".[3] They defend the commensurability of environmental values thus defined: 'the values that enter environmental disputes are commensurable, in our view, because they can enter judgements of the form "This is more valuable than that"'.[4] Such comparability is consistent with value-pluralism, that there are different values that are not reducible one to another.

7.1.3 Weak comparability

Strong comparability needs to be distinguished from weak comparability. One can make the distinction by reference to an unsound argument that the Ramsey Centre Report presents for strong comparability:

> Let us take just one typical case: comparing enjoyment of art or natural beauty with saving lives. It may look as if one could not say that a certain amount of aesthetic enjoyment was more or less valuable than one life: that such a comparison did not even make sense. But governments do make such comparisons, and it is hard to deny they make sense. For instance, the government of the United Kingdom has decided that it is justified in subsidising the Covent Garden Opera, even though it knows perfectly well that the money it spends could save a certain number of lives if it were transferred to the N.H.S. cancer-screening programme.[5]

This argument assumes that the claim that we can and must make choices between different objects and states of affairs, and that we can do so sensibly and rationally, entails that we are committed to saying that one state of affairs is more valuable than another. It is far from clear that this is the case. One might refuse to accept the statement 'X is more valuable than Y' while choosing X over Y where choice is required. Thus refusal stems not from moral squeamishness – that one does not want to accept that one really does find so much art better than so many lives – but, rather, from the vacuity of the comparative given a plurality of values. To say 'X is more valuable than Y' is to invite a response 'in what respect?', and given value plurality there may be no respect in terms of which the comparative statement can be grounded.

The difference between strong and weak comparability, and one defence of weak comparability, can be expressed in terms of Geach's distinction between attributive and predicative adjectives.[6] An adjective A is predicative if it passes the following logical tests:

(1) If x is AY, then x is A and x is Y;
(2) If x is AY and all Ys are Zs then x is AZ.

Adjectives that fail such tests are attributive. 'Red' is, in its standard uses, predicative.[7] Thus if x is a red car it follows that x is red, and, since all cars are vehicles, that x is a red vehicle. 'Small' is attributive. That x is a small blue whale does not entail that, since all blue whales are mammals, x is a small mammal. Geach claims that 'good' is an attributive adjective. In many of its uses it clearly fails (2): 'X is a good golfer, all golfers are persons, therefore X is a good person' is an invalid argument. Correspondingly, statements of the form 'X is good' need to be understood as elliptical. They invite the response 'X is a good what?'.[8] If 'good' is attributive, then its comparative form will have its scope limited by the particular noun it qualifies. 'X is a better golfer then Y, all golfers are persons, therefore X is a better person than Y' is an invalid argument. That a comparative holds in one range of objects does not entail that it holds in the wider range. Given a claim that 'X is better then Y' a proper response is 'X is a better what than Y?'. Similar points can be made about the adjectives 'valuable' and 'is more valuable than'. If evaluative adjectives like 'good' and 'valuable' are attributive in standard uses, it follows that their comparative forms have a limited range. That does not, however, preclude the possibility of rational choices between objects that do not fall under the range of a single comparative. Weak comparability is compatible with the existence of such limited ranges. In 7.2 I show that for some environmental choices only weak comparability is possible.

7.1.4 Incomparability

To hold that one can make rational choices between objects and states of affairs without holding that there is a comparative term that orders them is to hold the weak comparability of values. This needs to be distinguished from claims concerning the incomparability of goods. Consider Kierkegaard's claims concerning the choice between the aesthetic, moral and religious lives.[9] The choice, he claims, is not open to rational appraisal at all. There is no place for reasoned judgement in adjudication between them – each has its own distinct criteria of choice. Whatever the truth or falsity of Kierkegaard's position – and I believe it is false – the defender of weak comparability is committed to no such radical choice: the choice *is* made on the basis of rational judgements of the relative goods in question. No leap of faith is required, and neither is it replaced by a non-rational procedure – the tossing of a coin, for example.

7.1.5 Indeterminacy

Finally it should be noted that problems of value-commensurability and comparability need to be kept distinct from problems of determinacy. It is often the case that choices are underdetermined by values. Thus, for example, in the sciences, the values to which appeal is made in theory choice – consistency with evidence, internal consistency, simplicity and so on – often, although not always, underdetermine theory choice. Two or more theories might all satisfy such values. The values might not determine a unique 'best' theory. Hence, reasonable individuals might disagree by reference to the same values. That this is the case is quite consistent with the strong comparability of such theories. All theories might belong to the same 'comparability space': disputants agree that it makes sense to say one theory is better than another. They disagree as to which theory holds that position, and they may do so on the basis of identical values. Indeed, underdetermination is compatible with strong commensurability. Even given just one value that ordered all objects – say pleasure – it might still be the case that this supervalue did not determine a unique best answer. Questions of indeterminacy are then independent of questions of commensurability and comparability.[10]

7.2 ENVIRONMENTAL VALUES: DESCRIPTION, APPRAISAL AND PLURALISM

Environmental objects and states, like any others, are evaluated under different descriptions. A particular location can be characterized as a particular kind of ecosystem, as a wetland of a certain variety, as a landscape, as a dump, as a place that is inhabited by some community, as an industrial wasteland, as a soil type suitable for a specific kind of agriculture, as a feeding ground for certain migratory birds, as the habitat for a certain species of plant or beast, and so on. Similarly, a particular being can be characterized under different descriptions – as a member of a certain species, as a member of an ecological system, as an entity with particular powers and capacities, as an entity standing in specified relations to others – a mother, father, child, etc., and so on. It is under such descriptions that evaluation takes place. A location is not evaluated as good or bad as such, beautiful or ugly as such, but, rather, as good, bad, beautiful or ugly under different descriptions. It can be at one and the same time a 'good A' and a 'bad B', a 'beautiful C' and an 'ugly D'. A location may have considerable worth as a place – it may embody in a particularly powerful way the work of a community – but little worth as a habitat, an ecological system or as a landscape: the old slate workings in Dinorwic, near Llanberis, North Wales, are of this kind. A wetland might be of considerable worth as a habitat and as an ecosystem, but at the same time have little value as a landscape: consider the example of Rainham Marshes discussed in chapter 5. The use of these value terms in such contexts is attributive, not predicative. Relatedly, one often employs more specific evaluative terms that do not transfer across descriptions. It makes sense for example to talk of an 'evocative place' or an 'evocative landscape'; one would be less likely to talk of an 'evocative habitat' or an 'evocative ecosystem'. Evaluation of objects, then, occurs under a particular description.

Such descriptions often invoke quite different practices and perspectives from which evaluation is made.[11] To evaluate a location as a landscape is to invoke a set of aesthetic practices of landscape painting and poetry and kindred practices including, for example, that of hiking or walking for its own sake. To evaluate a location as a habitat is to invoke a set of scientific practices. To evaluate a location in terms of its soil may invoke either the disinterested practice of science or the interested practices of agriculture and industry. To evaluate a location as a place is to invoke the relation a particular community has had and continues to have with it.

Evaluation of objects under different descriptions invokes not just different practices and perspectives, but also different criteria and standards for evaluation associated with these. It presupposes value-pluralism. Appeal to different standards often results in conflicting appraisals of an object: as noted above, an object can have considerable worth as an A, B and C, but little as a D, E and F. Given such value-pluralism, can one expect commensurability in the form of strong comparability, or must we be content with weak comparability? The answer depends in part on whether one is comparing objects within a perspective or across different perspectives.

Problems of commensurability and comparability sometimes arise within a particular practice or perspective. They do so in virtue of the plurality internal to those perspectives. Consider aesthetic or, more particularly, landscape evaluation. It might be the case that what I value in one mountain landscape is its dramatic qualities, while in another wooded landscape it is the variety and blend of colours. That same wooded landscape I might love for the striking contrasts of reds in autumn and for the subtle contrasts of greens in spring. In making comparisons in the aesthetic merits of the landscapes, a plurality of values already exists and there is no aesthetic super-value, in terms of which the choice can be made. There is, however, a common set of aesthetic comparatives one might sensibly use to rank the different landscapes: the appraisal takes place within the same comparative space. In virtue of this strong comparability, while it is not assured within such a perspective, is at least possible.

When one moves across practices and perspectives, one often moves into quite distinct comparative spaces. Consider again the appraisal of habitat. It may be unusual, but it is possible to refer to a beautiful habitat. However, the evaluation is irrelevant to the appraisal of the habitat *as* a habitat. A quite distinct set of goods and comparative terms is relevant – species richness, the degree to which it has been modified by human action, its fragility, its particular history, and so on.[12] Comparatives about a particular habitat appeal to a plurality of goods, as with the aesthetic case. However, there is a set of comparative terms which apply across habitats: habitats belong to the same comparative space. Landscapes and habitats do not: under its description as a habitat a place requires a quite distinct evaluative language from that used under its description as a landscape. While it may be possible to refer to a 'beautiful habitat' such descriptions are irrelevant for the appraisal of a habitat *as* habitat. Given such a strong disjunction, weak comparability is all that one can reasonably expect for evaluations that cross perspectives or practices.[13]

Thus assume the following:

'Landscape A is more beautiful than landscape B';

'Habitat B is richer than habitat A'

where landscape A and habitat A are identical and so also are landscape B and habitat B. One must, let it be assumed, make a choice between them. What is involved in such a choice? In part it is the significance or importance one gives to the different kinds of value in that context. One may allow that aesthetic values are here important but not as important, say, as those of habitat value, or human life. In part it depends on the degree to which A is more beautiful than B and B richer than A. It may depend on the rarity of the habitat. (Rarity itself cannot be a value, since everything is rare under some description. It is, however, an amplifier of value. If an object has value under some description, and is also rare under that description, then its value has greater significance.) In making a choice one will have to resort to a higher level judgement. What is involved in making such a judgement is not an appeal to some other value in terms of which significance is made or in terms of which relative differences between different values are based on one scale. Rather, one considers what, given the different values to which appeal is being made, one should do with them. Assume a judgement for A over B in this particular context. Does it make sense to say 'A is more valuable than B'? There is a good case for saying that it does not. One wants to say that 'landscape A is more beautiful than landscape B' and 'habitat B is richer than habitat A' but that, given those differences in values, all things considered we should choose A. No further comparative statement need be denied or assented to. All the relevant questions of relative values have already been answered. One makes a rational judgement in the context and that is it. If someone persists in asking 'but is A more valuable than B then?' the proper response is 'well, it's more beautiful as a landscape, although B is a richer habitat'. Weak comparability is all one can expect.

7.3 COST-BENEFIT ANALYSIS AND INCOMMENSURABILITY

Cost-benefit analysis is committed to the existence of a single measure that orders all objects and states – persons' willingness to pay at the margin for the satisfaction of preferences. Hence, it is committed to weak commensurability. Under some welfare interpretations it is understood to involve strong commensurability – that is, it is taken to presuppose that there is a single source of value, and willingness to pay provides a cardinal measure of different amounts of that value. The measure is a cardinal measure. It not only orders objects and states of affairs but tells us a unique amount of value they possess. What then does it measure? One possible answer is a classical hedonistic utilitarian one. In classical utilitarianism it is units of pleasure and pain that provide the super-value for ranking different objects and states of affairs. Individuals have preferences for different objects and states of affair, and willingness to pay for the satisfaction of a preference will then be taken to correspond to a person's estimate of the pleasure they expect from that satisfaction.[14] Alternatively, one might answer with modern preference utilitarianism that it is preference satisfaction as such that provides the value through which all objects and states of affairs can be ranked. Willingness to pay measures the precise strength of a person's preference for a good. Both answers provide a case for strong commensurability, and provide a possible justification for treating willingness to pay as a cardinal measure of value.

Neither justification is satisfactory, since neither pleasure nor preference will however do the trick of reducing a plurality of values to a single value which provides a unique ordering of objects and states of affairs. Even if pleasure were the ultimate and only intrinsic value, it could not provide a single value to order goods, since pleasures themselves are plural in character: the pleasure of drinking beer and that of good conversation are different in kind and are not measurable on a single scale.[15] Preferences, on the other hand, answer to values – not values to preferences. I prefer A because of its value, I do not value it because it is preferred. Hence, given plurality of values, our preferences merely record our judgements in resolving conflicts between them. They do not provide the supreme value through which they are to be resolved.

Cost-benefit analysis does not provide a way of resolving value plurality. Its problems are not, however, local ones. The existence of incommensurable values raises more general difficulties for both neo-classical and Austrian economics. Both rely on similar misconceptions about practical rationality and market exchange. The assumptions they make about practical rationality I discuss in 7.4 and 7.5, those about market exchange in section 7.6.

7.4 INCOMMENSURABILITY, TRANSITIVITY AND JUDGEMENT

The existence of plural and incommensurable values raises problems of practical conflict. Agents can find themselves in situations in which different values pull them in different directions. That this is the case has been defended widely in recent literature.[16] A striking form in which practical conflict can reveal itself and which is of particular significance for neo-classical economics is in apparently intransitive preference orders. A central assumption of neo-classical economics is that intransitive preference orders are irrational. Thus, for the 'rational' neo-classical agent given three goods, x, y and z, if the agent prefers x to y and y to z, then she prefers x to z.[17] However, the existence of incommensurable and plural values raises difficulties for this assumption.[18] Given an irreducible plurality of values, it is possible for a single individual to have a preference structure parallel to that which Arrow outlines for social choice.[19] Given three values u, v and w, and three objects or states of affairs, A, B and C, it is possible that the following value-assignments hold:

	u	v	w
A	1st	3rd	2nd
B	2nd	1st	3rd
C	3rd	2nd	1st

Given that equal weights are assigned to the different values, it appears to be the case that A is to be preferred to B, and B is to be preferred to C, but C is to be preferred to A. Suppose, for example, that I have a choice between three jobs A, B and C, and I am comparing them across three value dimensions, u, the intrinsic interest of the job itself, v, the location of the job, and w, the friendliness of the colleagues. It is possible that the value rankings will be as in the matrix above: I prefer A to B, because although the job location of B is better than A, job A is itself the most interesting and the colleagues will be friendlier than those in B; I prefer B to C, because while C has the most friendly colleagues, B is in the best location and the job itself is more interesting than C; when I compare C to A, I find that I prefer C, for while A is the most interesting job, C has the friendliest colleagues and is in a better location than A. Given that equal weight is assigned to the different value dimensions and that those dimensions are themselves separable, and given that I assign equal probabilities that my judgements about the jobs turn out to be correct, it follows that my preferences will be intransitive. Moreover, they are so without any failure of rationality. 'Rational agents' can find themselves in a situation in which, whatever they choose, there is an alternative which should be chosen above it. This possibility reveals in a strong form the relation between value plurality and practical conflict. Finally it provides a basis for a possible failure of transitivity in social choices which is independent of that outlined by Arrow. Consider, for example, a choice between three environmental sites A, B and C, on three values, u, landscape value, v, scientific interest, and w, amenity value. Given the value orderings and assumptions noted above, it is possible that a dictator or unanimous assembly would, if presented with pairwise choices, choose A over B, B over C and C over A.

Given a plurality of values, can such conflicts be resolved? If so, how? If a rational resolution is to be possible, then the obvious place to begin would be with the assumption that the different values have equal weight. Thus a conflict over different jobs of the kind outlined above might compel one to reconsider the weight or significance one placed on the different values involved. Do they really pull with equal force? This kind of consideration has led some prominent theorists to introduce general priority rules that state a ranking order amongst values themselves. Rawls's rules introducing a lexical ordering amongst values provide perhaps the best-known example.[20] Values are ranked in an order of priority, $v_1, v_2, v_3 \ldots v_n$, such that only when v_1 has been satisfied does one consider v_2, only when v_2 has been satisfied does one consider v_3 and so on. In the context of value conflict a lexical ordering entails that the option that is best in the category of value with greatest priority – say 'liberty' or 'rights' – is to be chosen. This rule-based approach to the resolution of practical conflicts is, however, unsatisfactory. While it may be true that resolution of practical conflicts requires second-order consideration of the significance and weight of different values, it is implausible to assume that there exists a priority rule which will sort out such conflicts in advance. For any putative priority rule there are contexts in which it will fail to provide a satisfactory solution to practical conflicts.[21]

That such priority rules are implausible is not simply a result of the failure of particular theorists to do the job properly. The rule-based approach to the resolution of practical conflict that they represent is misconceived. Rawls introduces his priority principles in opposition to what he calls 'intuitionism':

> intuitionist theories have two features: first, they consist of a plurality of first principles which may conflict to give contrary directives in particular types of cases; and, second, they include no explicit method, no priority rules, for weighing these principles against one another: we are simply to strike a balance by intuition, by what seems to us most nearly right.[22]

The key characteristics of 'intuitionism' as Rawls describes it are value-pluralism and a requirement that practical judgement plays a necessary role in the resolution of conflicts between values. That doctrine appears to me to be entirely correct. To appeal to the necessity of priority rules to adjudicate value conflict and to reject judgement commits two fallacies – (1) the fallacy of interpreting rules by rules, and (2) the fallacy of the separability of values.

(1) The fallacy of interpreting rules by rules. Practical dilemmas arise for rational agents when general principles which are themselves consistent are placed in conflict when applied in a particular situation.[23] The problem of practical conflict is in one sense just a striking example of a more general problem of how to apply general principles to particular cases. It is a problem lawyers face when two statutes conflict in a particular case. It is a misconceived solution to this problem to introduce *another* general principle to resolve a difficulty in the application of general principles to particular cases. Problems in the application of general principles to particular cases cannot be resolved by appeal to other general principles, for those principles themselves raise the same problems of application. The process of reasoned application of general principles cannot itself be a case of applying a general principle. Rather, what it requires is the exercise of practical judgement –

'Intelligence is [not] about universals only, it must also come to know particulars, since it is concerned with action and action is about particulars'.[24] On this point at least Kant concurs with Aristotle.[25] Practical judgement cannot itself consist of knowledge of general principles of value.[26]

(2) The fallacy of the separability of values. To use a priority principle to adjudicate value-conflicts is to assume that each value can be treated like a discrete item on a list, its contribution to the final appraisal of a particular item's worth being separable from that of others. Such discreteness must be assumed if one is to engage in a lexical ordering of values. That assumption is false.

Consider aesthetic appreciation. It would be odd to go about the appreciation of a novel by treating the different components – plot, characterization, use of imagery and so on – as entirely discrete items which are open to an ordering principle. Our appreciation of a plot cannot be entirely disconnected from the characterization; a good plot works only with good characterization. This is true also of much political and ethical judgement. In ethics, the denial of the separability of value is a defensible component of the unity of the virtues thesis defended to different degrees by Plato, Aristotle and Aquinas.[27] While it would be false to argue that there is but one virtue – intelligence – and all other virtues are instances of it, and too strong to assert that an individual cannot have one virtue unless she has them all, it is true that a virtue often cannot be treated apart from the company it keeps. Courage is not an excellence when it appears amid vices – for example as a disposition of the dedicated Nazi. Correspondingly, some vices take the appearance of virtues when they are found among vices. Cowardice and laziness are qualities that one hopes to see in the character of some rulers. One of Ronald Reagan's saving graces was that he slept a lot. Similar points apply to political values. For example, one's appreciation of the value of freedom, 'positive' or 'negative', in a particular society, cannot be simply treated as separable from what individuals realize with that freedom. Different political and ethical values when applied in a particular context cannot be applied in isolation from one another. Judgement is required to assess the particular mix of value. To use a priority principle is necessarily to assume the separability of values. Hence the implausibility of priority principles when applied.

Practical judgement plays then a necessary role in resolving practical dilemmas. That role goes unrecognized in mainstream economic analysis for reasons outlined in the next section.

7.5 TWO ACCOUNTS OF PRACTICAL REASON

Cost-benefit analysis owes its appeal to a particular algorithmic conception of practical rationality. According to that conception, for a decision-making process to be rational it must be the case that there exists (1) a set of technical rules which are such that (2) when given a suitable description of a different object or state of affairs they yield (3) by a mechanical procedure (4) a unique and determinate decision. Cost-benefit analysis provides the example *par excellence* of such a procedure. Its efficiency criteria provide a set of rules that, given a quantitative description of weighted preference satisfaction in different states of affairs, yield by purely algorithmic procedures a unique best answer.

This conception of rationality is not a local affair of cost-benefit analysis, but is central to a much wider range of forms of economic theory. In particular, a central assumption in most is that one must have monetary measures of different states of affairs since without them no rational comparison is possible. While that assumption has been largely unquestioned, it was a subject of critical discussion in the socialist calculation debates of the 1920s and 1930s, although this chapter of the debate has largely been ignored in subsequent discussions. The debate now is normally presented in terms of a conflict between the Austrian critics of socialism, von Mises and Hayek, and the defenders of a form of market socialism, Lange and Taylor, different sides being presented with the laurels of victory.[28] The disputants in that later debate, however, shared an assumption that was at the heart of von Mises's own earlier defence of capitalism and which had been criticized by Austrian Marxists, notably the positivist Otto Neurath.

Von Mises's earlier arguments against socialist planning turned on an assumption about commensurability.[29] His central argument was that rational economic decision-making required a single measure on the basis of which the worth of alternative states of affairs could be calculated and compared. He makes the point thus in his later *Human Action*:

> The practical man . . . must know whether what he wants to achieve will be an improvement when compared with the

present state of affairs and with the advantages to be expected from the execution of other technically realizable projects which cannot be put into execution if the project he has in mind absorbs the available means. Such comparisons can only be made by the use of money prices.[30]

The position that von Mises is defending here – that comparability requires monetary prices that measure exchange values – was one that had been rejected by Neurath. For Neurath, a socialist economy, since it was to consider the use-value of goods only, would have to be an 'economy in kind'. In such an economy, while physical statistics about energy use, material use and so on would be required, there would be no need for a *single* unit of comparison. Thus in 1919 he wrote in a report to the Munich Workers' Council that, in considering alternative projects: 'There are no units that can be used as the basis of a decision, neither units of money nor hours of work. One must directly judge the desirability of the two possibilities.'[31] Such direct comparison will need to appeal directly to political and ethical judgements, including concern for future generations:

> The question might arise, should one protect coal mines or put greater strain on men? The answer depends for example on whether one thinks that hydraulic power may be suffi-ciently developed or that solar heat might come to be better used, etc. If one believes the latter, one may 'spend' coal more freely and will hardly waste human effort where coal can be used. If however one is afraid that when one generation uses too much coal thousands will freeze to death in the future, one might use more human power and save coal. Such and many other non-technical matters determine the choice of a technically calculable plan . . . we can see no possibility of reducing the production plan to some kind of unit and then to compare the various plans in terms of such units.[32]

Neurath rightly allowed that comparability need not presuppose commensurability. Non-technical practical judgement plays a necessary role in policy choices.[33]

Von Mises's assumption of the necessity of a single measure, and the view of practical rationality it assumes, continues to be that standard in modern economics, including environmental economics. Consider for example the comment of Pearce *et al.* on physical descriptions of environmental goods:

> Physical accounts *are* useful in answering ecological questions of interest and in linking environment to economy . . . However, physical accounts are limited because they lack a common unit of measurement and it is not possible to gauge their importance relative to each other and to the non-environmental goods and services.[34]

The need for a common measure is required for Pearce *et al.* because to compare different options on their approach *is* to apply the general technical rules of cost-benefit analysis to states of affairs thus measured. Given the account of practical rationality assumed in the Pearce report no comparison is possible without a single monetary unit. They allow no place for practical judgement.

The plausibility of cost-benefit analysis and a purely 'economic' approach to environmental evaluation generally relies on this cramped algorithmic conception of practical rationality. On this view to reject the world of monetary descriptions of different states of affairs, efficiency principles and mathematical algorithms is to reject reason. That view of practical rationality is quite mistaken. It fails to allow for the proper place of good practical judgement in decision-making outlined in the last section.

It should be noted that to appeal to practical judgement is not to appeal to untutored intuition.[35] Judgement of the worth of particular states of affairs can be informed or uninformed, competent or incompetent, tutored or untutored. Good judgement is founded on the existence of capacities of perception[36] and of knowledge based in education and experience. For example, to be able to compare the value of different ecological systems is to be informed, and to have the capacities to discriminate the particular features to be perceived: a well-trained and experienced field-worker may in that sense be in a better position to evaluate a site than a person with a deeper theoretical grasp of the principles of ecology. To appeal to good judgement is not then merely to appeal to intuition, but to appeal to judgements properly informed and educated.

It should also be noted that to make an appeal to a necessary role for practical judgements in decision-making is *not* to deny any role to general principles. Neither, it should be stressed, does it deny a place for the use of technical rules and algorithmic procedures. One of the mistakes of defenders of practical judgement is to set up an *opposition* between 'moral and aesthetic judgements' and the 'technical' rule-governed rationality of science.[37] Moreover, there is a necessary role for rules of thumb, standard procedures, the default procedures and institutional arrangements that can be followed unreflectively and which *reduce* the scope for *explicit* judgements comparing different states of affairs. We cannot be exercising ethical and political judgements in a reflective way all the time. There are limits on time, efficient use of resources and the dispersal of knowledge which require rules and institutions. Such rules and institutions can free us for space and time for reflective judgements where they matter most.[38] Rules and institutions need, however, to be open to critical appraisal. Institutional practices may embody a practical knowledge – they may also simply serve powerful groups, or be procedures with environmentally damaging consequences. Likewise the market may be *one* way in which dispersed knowledge can be put to good effect. It is not *pace* Hayek the only way – and if its consequences are ecologically damaging there is a case for putting severe limits on its use or, more radically, with Neurath, replacing it with a quite different set of institutions.[39] That we require *some* rules and institutions to free us for making judgements about what matters does not entail that we require *any* institution, still less current institutions. Nor does it disallow the possibility of radical institutional changes.

7.6 WILLINGNESS TO PAY: COMMODITIES AND COMMENSURABILITY

Why is the assumption of value commensurability so widespread in neo-classical and Austrian economics? The answer lies in deep-seated assumptions about the relation between the exchange value of goods and their value *per se*. What these assumptions are and what is wrong with them become apparent if we consider an objection about the use of 'willingness to pay' measures of value which, although logically independent of those thus far considered, is related and of importance in its own right. The objection turns on the way those measures are often treated as if they existed in a social vacuum, divorced of a social meaning. That socially neutral view of the measures cannot be sustained.

Sagoff in *The Economy of the Earth*[40] makes much of the fact that respondents to willingness-to-pay surveys often do not co-operate. They either refuse to put a price on an environmental good when asked how much they would be willing to pay for it, or they put an infinite price on it. Sagoff argues that these protest bids reveal that the preferences individuals display in the market as consumers are distinct from the values they operate with as citizens, a distinction I will discuss in more detail in the final chapter. Now while I believe Sagoff is right that individuals reveal different preferences in different institutional contexts, I do not believe it adequately explains the existence of protest bids. There is a much simpler explanation of the bids which concerns the social meaning of acts of monetary evaluation.

Both Austrian and neo-classical economics assume that price is simply a neutral 'measuring rod'[41] of the marginal utility a person expects to receive from an object. In defending this they commonly assert that to put a money value on an object is not to say that money is a supreme value.[42] This may be true but it rather misses the point of those who object to treating all goods as if they could have a price. To treat price as a neutral measuring device and acts of buying and selling like exercises in the use of a tape measure is to fail to appreciate that acts of exchange are social acts with social meanings. Consider the most famous example of assignments of 'willingness to pay' – that of Judas accepting a price of thirty pieces of silver for taking soldiers to Christ (Matthew. 26, 14–16). The act of so putting a price on Christ is not merely an act of measuring badly done – what is wrong with the act is not that thirty pieces of silver was a poor evaluation, that he should have gone for more. What is wrong with it is that it is an act of *betrayal* – that a person's commitment to another is treated as something that can be bought or sold. The act of betrayal would have looked no better, but possibly worse, had Judas put in a higher bid. Neither does the fact of betrayal depend on the assumption that money is the supreme value. One can make Judas as benign as one likes. Assume the money was for the poor, for whom, after all, he had previously expressed concern (John 12, 4–5). Or to make him more benign still, let us assume with Borges a Judas of incredible benevolence, one who knows that for the redemption of humankind to take place Christ must be betrayed and die in consequence of that betrayal.[43] How could he betray him? By acting just as he did. Whatever Judas's values, however noble and non-pecuniary were his reasons, the act of accepting a price on one's friend is an act of betrayal.

Commitments to others – to friends, family and to items one values, to the preservation of particular landscapes, species and so on – are constituted by a refusal to treat them as commodities that can be bought or sold. To treat them as such is to betray that commitment. A person who would be willing to put a price on a friend simply has not understood what it is to be a friend. The commitment of friendship is constituted in part by a refusal to treat the friendship thus. A person who could thus price friendship would have no sense of the loyalties that are involved in that relationship. This is true of commitments in general, including those to non-human goods. Such considerations underlie the refusal of respondents to answer questions concerning their willingness to pay for environmental goods. They display commitments via just such refusals.

Raz puts the point made above by saying that incommensurability is constitutive of certain relations.[44] While my discussion above owes much to Raz's account of 'constitutive incommensurability,' that term may be misleading. Incommensurability as such is not the question at issue but, rather, the *particular* social form of commensurability involved, namely that expressed in monetary relations, a point that Raz himself allows.[45] An individual might be willing to say 'I value my friendship with Mary more than my friendship with Martha', and might exchange several days she might have spent with Martha for just a few hours with Mary, without being willing to put a price on either – or on how much they would accept in compensation for spending less time with Mary for time with Martha or would pay to get Martha away for time with Mary. If the friendship with Martha was in order one would refuse regardless of the other friendships one had. Individuals can and do refuse to make monetary comparisons about goods of which they are willing to make value comparisons. The issue of 'willingness to pay' is to that extent independent of that commensurability. However, the existence of such social meanings does raise some major independent problems with cost-benefit analysis. The existence of protest bids shows individuals to have a healthy commitment to certain goods and an understanding of the limits of markets. Protests reveal neither irrationality nor strategic rationality, but decent ethical commitments.

Moreover, that economists fail or refuse to recognize this does highlight a looser connection between the use of monetary measures and the assumption of commensurability within economic theory itself. Marx in *The German Ideology* notes that the presumption in classical utilitarianism that there is a single value to which all others are reducible gains its apparent plausibility from the existence of a single monetary measure for all goods. The apparent plurality of different goods is in practice treated as if they were reducible to a single value.

> The apparent stupidity of merging all the manifold relationships of people in the *one* relation of usefulness, this apparently metaphysical abstraction arises from the fact that, in modern bourgeois society, all relations are subordinated in practice to the one abstract monetary–commercial relation.[46]

The assumption in neo-classical economics that all goods are strongly comparable has a similar foundation. The fact that in the market place individuals are forced to make a judgement of the form 'how much would you be willing to pay for x' and have to engage in monetary comparisons of different goods is taken to entail the existence of a single preference order. For any pair of goods x and y an individual is supposed to be able to say 'I'd spend more, less or the same on x than on y'. In the exchange of commodities there is a comparative that orders them all. Hence the completeness axiom in the neo-classical definition of the rational agent. However to deduce strong comparability in value on the basis of the existence of prices is a mistake. As Aristotle notes, through exchange, objects which 'cannot become commensurate in reality'[47] are made to appear commensurable. Likewise Marx's argument that, through money, goods and relationships that are often incommensurable in their *use-value* are treated as if they were commensurable in exchange is sound.[48] It is because both neo-classical and Austrian economics refuse to accept that exchange value is anything except a measure of expected marginal use-value that they make the illicit move from price commensurability to value commensurability. It is also why they tend to be blind to the social meanings of exchange and of the refusal to put a price on a good. Commensurability in exchange does not entail commensurability of value. Value commensurability is not required for rational decision-making.

In this chapter I have argued for a role for good practical judgement about particulars in policy choice. Cost-benefit analysis relies on a cramped and false conception of practical rationality. To defend a role for good judgement raises, however, another problem. Isn't the distinction in capacities of judgement inegalitarian? Doesn't it allow for a role of authoritative judgement that is incompatible with democracy? These questions raise important issues about the justifiability of rational authority in modern political life. I address these in the next chapter.

8

AUTHORITY, DEMOCRACY AND THE ENVIRONMENT

I begin with a problem of practical epistemology which has become increasingly acute in recent years. There has been a growth of a sceptical attitude to the claims made by scientists – in particular those made by the scientific experts wheeled out by governments and industrial companies to reassure the public that some apparent harm, say a pollutant in the water, is not really that damaging to themselves or to the natural world. Such scepticism is often rational. However, if as sometimes happens, it results in a quite *general* disbelief in *any* claim made by science, such scepticism becomes dangerous. A rational environmental policy depends on taking seriously scientific claims about acidity in water, the depletion of ozone, global warming and so on. A general scepticism about science undermines the possibility of rational and well-informed action in response to these.[1] The central place of science in decision-making about the environment raises a related long-standing and important problem concerning the role of authority in democracy. When is it rational and defensible for citizens to accept the judgement of another individual, the grounds for which they are not in a position to appraise? In what conditions, if any, is deference to an authority rational and ethically defensible? When is scepticism justified, and what are the limits of rational scepticism?

These problems, it should be noted, are not confined to science. They apply as well to most other practices in which authoritative judgements are central, for example in the arts. Proper scepticism about some aesthetic judgements, say of a modernist architect who seems to have no sense of how his concrete block of offices blends ill with other buildings, can produce a crude subjectivist account of aesthetic value which allows of no distinction between

'I like x' and 'x is good'. Neither is the problem of authority confined to environmental problems. There are very few beliefs and judgements that we make which are *not* founded on the acceptance of the authoritative judgements of others. The problem of when it is rational to defer to an authority is a problem that lies in the background of most of our decisions and judgements, private and public. The role of scientific authority in environmental policy merely raises it in a particularly acute form. In the next section of this chapter I will attempt to define more clearly just what the problem is.

8.1 AUTHORITY: BETWEEN 'RATIONALISM' AND IRRATIONALITY

The importance of authority in public life has been a central component of conservative thought from Burke through to Oakeshott and Hayek. It informs, in particular, their critique of 'rationalism'. Consider Oakeshott's sketch of the 'rationalist':

> At bottom he stands ... for independence of mind on all occasions, for thought free from obligation to any authority save the authority of 'reason' ... he is the *enemy* of authority, of prejudice, of the merely traditional, customary or habitual. His mental attitude is at once sceptical and optimistic: sceptical, because there is no opinion, no habit, no belief, nothing so firmly rooted or so widely held that he hesitates to question it, and to judge it by what he calls his 'reason'; optimistic, because the Rationalist never doubts the power of his 'reason' (when properly applied) to determine the worth of a thing, the truth of an opinion, or the propriety of an action. Moreover, he is fortified by a belief in a 'reason' common to all mankind, a common power of rational consideration, which is the ground and inspiration of argument.[2]

The position of the 'rationalist' thus described is untenable. It is so, not least, in virtue of the division of knowledge in society.[3] No one can rely on his own 'reason' to judge any proposition. To judge the truth or falsity of a statement in ecology, for example, requires a background of quite specific knowledge. We rely on knowledge that is distributed across our society, both for our own opinions and to guide action in spheres in which we have no opinion. Oakeshott's critique of the rationalist, however, does not rely simply on the division of knowledge of society. Were it to do so, there would be few who would be 'rationalists'. The very project of the encyclopaedia of the Enlightenment depends on the existence of dispersed knowledge – and recognizes the necessity that we have to accept the testimony of others. The belief that an individual can by their individual reason and experience alone judge any proposition cannot of itself be the defining characteristic of 'rationalism'.

What distinguishes the 'rationalist' is not that he does not accept the need to rely on the testimony of others, but his view that the testimony could be recorded in an encyclopaedia. All there is to any specific body of knowledge can be articulated in propositional form. The central move in Oakeshott's critique of the rationalist is in his rejection of the transparency and vocalizability of knowledge. Hence the centrality of the distinction between technical and practical knowledge in his critique of rationalism. Technical knowledge is knowledge that can be 'formulated into rules which are, or may be, deliberately learned, remembered and ... put into practice; its chief characteristic is that it is susceptible of precise formulation ...'.[4] In contrast, practical knowledge 'exists only in use, is not reflective and cannot be formulated in rules'.[5] Practical knowledge requires capacities of judgement and perception of particular cases that can be learned only by habituation and which cannot, like technical knowledge, be found in books. Such practical knowledge makes the appeal to authority stronger than that which follows from the intellectual division of labour. The statements of those whom we take to be authorities we accept not simply because we have not the time to corroborate the grounds for their utterances, but because we lack the capacities to make the relevant judgements in the absence of an apprenticeship in the practice.

The assumption that different practices develop different capacities of judgement and perception is one that I have already accepted in the last chapter. However, given this radical opacity of authority, it is still possible to ask the question 'when is it rational to defer to an authority?'. The Enlightenment critique of unfounded authority can still be rescued. Oakeshott's account of the 'rationalist' position is something of a caricature. It sets up a choice between believing only in the authority of 'individual reason' and believing only in the authority of tradition. That choice is a quite false one. The conservative's Enlightenment 'rationalist' who accepts only his individual reason is a straw man against which the defence of quite irrational forms of authority can be mounted. The Enlightenment project of subjecting authority to rational scepticism can proceed without an individualist picture of human reason or the assumption that all knowledge can be articulated. Thus it is not the case that because an individual, following only his own educated reason, cannot judge any and every matter, the individual must thereby defer to any and every authority. There are occasions when it is rational to defer to an authority and occasions when it is not. Just because there exists a long-standing tradition in the study of the effects of stars on our fate is no reason not to doubt the truth of the claims the astrological tradition makes. There are tools of suspicion[6] the ordinary citizen is able to apply to authorities to test the reliability of their claims. There are also social conditions which make it more reasonable to accept the judgements of an authority and social conditions where it is less reasonable to do so. Some positions of authority appear to be founded ultimately on simple wealth or power. Other positions of authority appear to be better founded on requisite capacities developed through training in a rational set of practices. The problem of authority is *not* the problem of 'reason' or 'authority' but, rather, the question: when is it rational to accept as authoritative the judgements of others? This question I address in the remaining sections of this chapter.

8.2 TWO FORMS OF AUTHORITY

Most of us in the course of our education have had teachers who, while they hold a position of authority in the classroom, lack authority. They might lack authority in one of two ways. They may not have an authoritative personality – some teachers enter a classroom and are able to control it without trying, while others enter and, despite their best efforts, find that the classroom is soon in mayhem. Teachers can also lack authority in another sense – one may simply not believe that they are competent in the subject: they make obvious inaccurate statements, their accounts of some theory or phenomenon appear confused, they do not seem able to answer simple questions and so on. While they may be in authority in the classroom they do not seem to be an authority in the subject they teach. They may have personal authority but lack intellectual authority. The difference between these is often more apparent to peers than to a student. Thus peers may say of a colleague that he gives a good performance, but that he lacks a grasp of the subject; whereas another teacher, they might add, while she is clearly an authority is unable to teach with authority. In this section I clarify the distinctions between these senses of authority, between being in authority, having authority, and being an authority, in particular, between the last sense and the first two. I do so in terms of a distinction MacIntyre makes between practices and institutions and a related contrast I will draw between 'authority that is internal to a practice' and 'authority that is external to a practice'.

MacIntyre characterizes a practice thus:

> By a 'practice' I am going to mean any coherent and complex form of socially established cooperative human activity through which goods internal to that form of activity are realized in the course of trying to achieve those standards of excellence which are appropriate to and partially definitive of, that form of activity, with the result that human powers to achieve excellence, and human conceptions of the ends and goods involved are systematically extended.[7]

A *practice* is characterized in part in terms of its possessing internal standards of excellence – in both the performance and the product of the activity – and relatedly of *internal goods* – that is, those goods which cannot be specified without reference to the kind of activity it is. Thus, in chess, for example, particular kinds of positional skills and strategic and analytical powers will be characteristic internal goods. The recognition of internal goods requires participation in the practice: 'Those who lack the relevant experiences are incompetent thereby as judges of internal goods.'[8] External goods in contrast are goods such as material wealth, power and status which can be specified independently of any particular activity and can be recognized by those who do not engage in that practice. The *institutions* which form the organizational background necessary for the existence of practices – clubs, universities, professional organizations and so on – are concerned with the acquisition and distribution of such external goods. Institutions, however, not only sustain practices, they can also corrupt them. The pursuit of external goods – wealth, power and status – may come into conflict with the pursuit of the internal goods of practices.

To enter into a practice is to accept the authority of the standards of excellence of that practice, and to allow them initially at least to govern one's own judgements, preferences and choices. Only given such initial deference to the standards will one be able to reject some of them later for the purposes of the further development of a practice. Acceptance of the authority of the standards of a practice cannot, however, occur in some disembodied way. Deferring to the authority of a practice's standards necessarily entails deferring, initially at least, to the judgements of a person trained within that practice. That person is an authority – and in accepting her judgements concerning the goods and excellences of a practice one necessarily does so without, as yet, being able to appraise the grounds of her judgements. Education in any practice entails deference to an authority. Authority of this kind I will call 'authority internal to a practice', or 'internal authority'.[9]

An important point to note about this authority is that it is *impersonal*. Where a practice is in order the authority of that person resides in her *embodying* the historically developed standards of the practice that are independent of herself. It is in virtue of her capacities to recognize the independent excellences and goods of a practice that one defers to her authority. In calling such authority impersonal I do not mean that the person's individual character and capacities are irrelevant to one's deference to them. A person can embody a set of standards only if she has a particular set of powers, a background of knowledge and a number of excellences of character which, in part, make her the person she is. Rather, in calling the authority impersonal I want to distinguish it from two forms of 'personal' authority. First, her authority cannot be said to be founded on the basis of 'her personality' as such. The authority she has is not a consequence of her having a 'forceful' personality, and the like. Internal authority is that authority a person has only in so far as her character is one that embodies the standards of a practice. Second, the authority she has is impersonal in that it does not depend merely on any particular institutional position or status she may hold.[10] The felicity conditions of her speech acts cannot depend simply on her position in an institution as such, but rather in standards that are independent of that institutional position.

Consider an imperative 'Do X'. There are two answers that a person might make to the response 'Why?': (1) 'Because I am your teacher, your manager, your priest, paying you, etc.'; and (2) 'Because X would be the right thing to do, is the best thing to do, is a valid inference, would give balance to the picture, etc.'. The second set of responses makes no call on institutional positions of authority, but, rather, on standards independent of institutional positions and personal qualities. The felicity of the speech act calls only on such impersonal standards. One accepts the answers only if one believes the person has the capacities of judgement to make such a call on these standards. In contrast, the first set of responses makes essential reference to the individual's occupancy of a particular institutional position or status. If it turned out that the individual did not have that position, or that the addressee was not within the range of that institutional authority, for example, that a teacher's imperative was not addressed to a pupil, then the imperative is unfelicitous. On its own terms there is no backing for its authority. Authority which thus resides in institutional position or has its source in purely personal qualities I will term 'authority external to a practice' or 'external authority'.

Internal and external authority can often come apart. In particular, the positions of authority and power that form the background to social practices might be filled with individuals who lack internal authority. A person who holds such positions may have in this sense no authority: they may not embody the standards of a practice. Vice versa, a person who lacks a position may still have considerable authority. Where the institutions of a practice are filled with those who lack internal authority, the institution is in a state of disarray. This points to a qualification that needs to be made to the simple demarcation of external and internal authority made thus far. Some external goods bear a closer relation to internal goods than others. Consider the difference between wealth and honour. Honour has an intrinsic relationship to any internal goods that wealth lacks. Thus, to honour someone is to recognize them for something good they have done or some capacity of excellence they possess. Honour is thus derivative on the existence of some good for which recognition is due.[11] Honour cannot be disassociated from reference to recognition of goods. Where it is, it has been confused with 'fame' or 'status'. Within particular institutional contexts, for example where recognition by peers in a practice determines institutional position and other external goods, these can have a contingent relationship with an internal good. Thus institutional positions –

say a 'professorship' – often combine honour and other goods. Where an institution is in order there may exist a relationship between some external goods and internal goods. One might therefore defer to a person's judgement in virtue of her holding some position, say a research post in biology. Position in such circumstances may be the best *indicator* one has that judgements are authoritative. However, the only rational *grounds* for deferring to the judgement is the internal authority that is taken to be correlative with that position.

The distinction between internal and external authority takes us some way towards an account of rational authority. Internal authority is a necessary condition for the rational acceptance of a person's authority. That is, deference to the judgements of a person the grounds of which one is not oneself able to appraise is rational only if there are good reasons for believing that the person's judgements meet the internal standards of excellence of a practice. Or to make the same point in a negative way, persons' possessions of external goods *as such* – their occupancy of institutional positions, their possession of wealth – are never good grounds for yielding one's own judgement to theirs. Neither is the force of their personality, except in so far as the personal qualities are those which embody the virtues and excellences of a practice. To defer to an authority on these grounds is to surrender one's autonomy. To defer to internal authority is a necessary condition for the exercise of autonomous choices. Someone who relied purely on her own 'reason' could make few rational choices.[12]

Internal authority is, then, a necessary condition of rational deference to an authority. However, it is not a sufficient condition. That persons' authority is internal to a practice does not justify their judgements or make it rational to accept them. Practices themselves are often 'bogus'. They issue in claims which are false, develop ways of 'seeing' which are forms of blindness, develop dispositions of character which are vices. It is this that provides the component of the Enlightenment legacy that ought to be accepted. That the Enlightenment theorist might have appealed to individual reason and a false egalitarianism in judgement, in the fashion of Oakeshott's rationalist, does not entail that much of the Enlightenment critique of superstition and of the bogus forms of authority it supported was not in order. For example, a religion might claim to develop knowledge of God's universe, and to inculcate the virtues. It might issue in systematic falsehood and systematic vices – not because of the failure of its priests to follow its precepts but in virtue of the fact that they do. The external authority of its priests might be founded in the internal authority of religious practice. However, that internal authority itself may lack legitimacy. This Enlightenment critique of particular social practices and traditions is itself proper. So also are some of the tools and skills of suspicion it employed, not least their universal tools of logic and the analytical skills required for their employment. Practices themselves form quite proper objects of criticism. They can, and often do, act as masks for particular interests – for arbitrary power and unfounded barriers to professions.

To accept an individual's authority simply in virtue of the existence of a practice which supported it would be irrational. The practice itself must be subject to appropriate scepticism. The foundation and limits of rational scepticism of practices I discuss in detail in 8.4. Before doing so, however, I clarify in 8.3 the troubled relationship between authority and democracy. Historically, there have been two quite distinct problems of the acceptability of rational authority – one of which I have begun to outline in this section, and another, which is to be found in the work of classical utilitarians and continues to lie at the heart of problems concerning the justifiability of the utilitarian's modern successor, cost-benefit analysis.

8.3 TWO PROBLEMS OF AUTHORITY

8.3.1 Utilitarianism and authority

The problem of authority, and its relation to democracy have been central to the utilitarian tradition.[13] The problem has its foundations in the familiar difficulties of a radical act-utilitarianism – we have neither the time nor the means to calculate the probable outcome of each and every action; hence, the individual must rely on general 'rules' and 'sentiments associated with rules' to guide their actions: 'If our conduct were truly adjusted to the principle of general utility, our conduct would seldom be determined by an immediate or direct resource to it'.[14] However, not only is it not possible for most of us to have the time and means to calculate the consequences of our actions, neither is it possible to calculate the consequences of different kinds of actions and hence of the rules that ought to govern our actions. The scientific investigation of the consequence of kinds of actions is not open to us. Hence, one must defer to the authority of those who are able to study the consequences of action. Thus Austin writes:

> If ethical science must be gotten by consulting the principle of utility, if it rests upon observation and induction applied to the tendencies of actions, if it is a matter of acquired knowledge and not of immediate consciousness much of it (I admit) will be ever hidden from the multitude or will be ever taken by the multitude on authority, testimony, or trust. For an inquiry into the consequences of actions embraces so spacious a field, that none but the comparatively few, who study the science assiduously, can apply the principle extensively.[15]

The problem of political authority lies in the absence of agreement in ethical matters: how is it possible for individuals to defer to any authority, given that 'there is not *that concurrence or agreement of numerous and impartial inquirers* to which the most cautious and erect understanding readily and wisely defers'?[16] The solution to the problem is the progress of the science of ethics, which would bring with it the disappearance of disagreement. Impartial scientific inquiry would converge on a single view: '*In the unanimous or general consent of numerous and impartial inquirers*, they [the multitude] would find that mark of trustworthiness which justifies reliance on authority.'[17] This account of the role of authority in political life is a good example of a theory that falls under Oakeshott's label of 'rationalism'. The ethical principles on which policies are made are clear and simple – those of the utilitarian. The best action is that which maximizes utility – what is required is inductive knowledge about the tendency of actions to realize that end. The authority it defends does not depend on any special capacities of judgement or 'practical knowledge', but only on the dispersal of knowledge in society.[18] The result is a form of what Williams has called 'government house Utilitarianism'.[19] The problem of authority is one of justifying deference to the authority of an elite who are able to calculate the utility of different kinds of action, and providing a mark of when their judgements can be relied upon. Impartial and disinterested application of the tools of scientific analysis will issue in convergence on rational solutions to political and economic problems.

What is the role of democracy given this view? The utilitarian defence of authority is not one that is blind to partiality and self-interest among those who govern. The role for democracy on this conception is to act as a check on this authority. Since those in power have a tendency to pursue their own interests, democracy acts as a means to protect the citizen and ensure that those who have authority do pursue the interests of the citizen. The utilitarian defence of authority has its counterpart in the protective model of democracy also rooted in the utilitarian tradition.[20]

This picture of authority and the related role of democracy continues to inform the defence of 'policy science' in general and cost-benefit analysis in particular. The purpose of politics is to maximize happiness or welfare. The policy scientist does so with the use of mathematically well-defined techniques and rules which yield the maximum satisfaction of preferences. The authority of the policy scientist is founded in this possession of technical knowledge. Divergence of opinion is, given this picture, an indication of the incursion of ideology into the space for technical decision-making. The role of democracy is to protect the citizen from the partiality of the analyst. This account of the authority of the policy analyst is at one level egalitarian. By taking individuals' preferences as given, it makes no distinctions in the quality of judgements of individuals about the objects of preference. All judgements and preferences count equally, the job of the analyst being merely their best aggregation. Moreover, the opacity of authority of the policy scientist is superficial. It is only in virtue of the absence of time and technical knowledge that we cannot ascertain the grounds on which judgements are made. Contrast this problem of authority with that raised by Aristotle.

8.3.2 Aristotle: authority, democracy and judgement

But this arrangement of the constitution [which gives the people deliberative and judicial functions] presents some difficulties. The first difficulty is that it may well be held that the function of judging when medical attendance has been properly given should belong . . . to members of the medical profession. The same may be held to be true of all other professions and arts; and just as doctors should have their conduct examined before a body of doctors, so, too, should those who follow other professions have theirs examined before a body of members of their own profession . . . . When

133

we turn to consider the matter of election, the same principle should apply. To make a proper election, it may be argued, is equally the work of experts . . . It would thus appear . . . that the people should not be made sovereign either in the matter of the election of magistrates or in their examination.[21]

The possible problem that Aristotle raises concerning the relation of authority and democracy looks more radical and insurmountable than that of classical utilitarianism. The opacity of authority is deeper. For Aristotle the knowledge of the member of a profession or art is not only knowledge of universals, but involves the capacity to judge appropriately in particular cases. Hence, the grounds for judgements are not accessible to those who lack experience and apprenticeship within the art.[22] It is inegalitarian about the actual capacities of individuals to make judgements: good judgement requires apprenticeship. Moreover, the role of authoritative judgement is extended from professions and arts to politics. Just as only those trained within a craft can make the requisite judgements about the performance and products of those involved in the craft, so also only those who are politically active and experienced can judge the performance and products of political actors.[23] There does not even appear to be a protective role for democracy. The upshot seems to be the brand of conservatism defended by Oakeshott, which views rationalism as the ideology of the politically inept.

What response might be made to this more radical problem of democracy? I will discuss Aristotle's own response in the next section. With respect to the specific problem of *political* authority, Aristotle's premises yield the standard educative argument for participatory democracy. The premise of the objection to democracy is accepted: political judgement depends upon engagement in political activity. A different conclusion is drawn: all citizens should participate in those activities that develop political judgement. Since the capacity of political judgement is a good and one that has as its object other goods pursued in a society, and since participation in the practice of politics and kindred activities develops political judgement, democracy is the best form of political life. The inegalitarianism about judgement – that not all capacities of judgement are the same, since good judgement is a consequence of involvement in a practice – yields a more egalitarian solution: let all be able to participate. Preferences are not thus simply taken to be of equal validity. Rather, it is through participation in public debate that the best preferences are formed. The result also transforms the citizen from an *object* of analysis, as he is within the utilitarian tradition that informs 'policy science', into a subject who deliberates about policy and whose preferences are formed by deliberation.

However, while this response might give an answer to the problem of *political* judgement, albeit with problems that need to be addressed,[24] it does not solve the problem of authority I outlined at the end of the last section. Participation in activities that develop political judgement may be open to all, but participation in all the practices that inform political choices is not. The capacities of political judgement might be within the reach of all citizens, but not the capacities of, for example, scientific judgement, medical judgement and perhaps also some forms of aesthetic judgement. The problem of authority with which this chapter is concerned has not yet been answered. Rather, it serves only to re-state the problem. What capacities and tools must citizens have if they are to know when and where it is rational to defer to an authority, and how to adjudicate conflicts between authorities?

8.4 THE LIMITS OF AUTHORITY AND THE TOOLS OF SCEPTICISM

When is it rational or reasonable to defer to an authority? What are the grounds for justifiable suspicion and scepticism of authority? In this section I outline some of the more important tools of rational suspicion and the social conditions for their employment.

8.4.1 External authority

At the end of 8.2 I suggested that authority founded on the possession of external goods alone is never rationally defensible. To defer to a person's judgement simply because that person has a great deal of wealth, power or traditional status is mere sycophancy: it cannot be justified. Reference to some internal good is a necessary although not a sufficient condition for rational authority. The problem of authority in existing societies is that power, wealth and status often bring with them special powers to call on internal authority. They bring with them privileged access to internal sources of authority – education and access to cultural goods – or the ability to buy, through either money or patronage, the employment of most of those trained within practices to speak on their behalf – both industries and governments have their 'scientific spokesmen'.[25]

Consider the following comment on the dispute about Rainham Marshes discussed in chapter 5.

> Nature conservation in its practice and in its presentation in the media is still experienced by 'ordinary' people as a dominant form of distant-public discourse – the voice of a scientific and elite culture opposed to their concerns at the local-public level.[26]

To the extent that this is true, it cannot be divorced from the greater wealth, power, social status and access to the public media and education that those within 'scientific elite culture' normally have. Claims to knowledge, aesthetic sensibility and so forth can thus be experienced simply as other forms through which such unjustified power is exercised. In such circumstances, justified scepticism about one source of 'authority' is transferred not surprisingly to scepticism about authority *per se*. The use of scientific experts by governments and industries is likewise treated with suspicion. The 'internal authority' of the expert is compromised by its association with the possession of external goods. Hence the problem outlined at the outset of this chapter: justifiable scepticism of the external source of authority infects the credentials of the internal source and can lead to scepticism about all authoritative judgements. It follows that the social condition best suited for rational authority is one in which internal and external sources of authority are separated.

The need for separation provides a strong argument for social equality, voiced by Tawney:

> Progress depends, indeed, on a willingness on the part of the mass of mankind – and we all, in nine-tenths of our nature, belong to the mass – to recognize genuine superiority, and to submit themselves to its influence. But the condition of recognizing genuine superiority is a contempt for unfounded pretensions to it. Where the treasure is, there will the heart be also, and, if men are to respect each other for what they are, they must cease to respect each other for what they own.[27]

A rough equality in status, wealth and power is a social condition for rational submission to an authority, for only in such conditions can internal authority be clearly separated from external sources of authority. Social equality provides the best conditions for rational deference to the authoritative claims of others.

That argument for equality does little, however, to provide an account of the limits of scepticism in current conditions of inequality. Moreover, even given conditions of equality, one cannot expect special pleading in defence of special interests to disappear. In such conditions, how should the citizen proceed? The existence of a strong link between power, wealth, and special interests and particular authoritative judgements does provide *prima facie* grounds for scepticism about their claims. What is often presented in logic books as an example of the 'fallacy of relevance' – questioning a person's judgement by reference to her having an interest in saying it – is a legitimate tool in the practical art of suspicion. It is quite true that the argument 'since you have a special interest in believing A, A is false' is an invalid argument. Autobiographical utterances aside, statements about a person's interests are logically independent of most of the propositions she is likely to make. However, given the *practical* problem – When is it rational to defer to a claim the grounds of which I am not in a position to judge? – the existence of a special interest is a sound basis of scepticism. Where wealth and power call on internal sources of authority, such sources become legitimate targets of suspicion.

This point provides one of the most important arguments against the commercialization of the academic institutions. If the authoritative judgements of those trained within academic disciplines is to provide the basis for democratic policy debate, it must be independent of both wealth and power – and hence the institutions through which these are distributed in existing society, the market and the state:

> Academic science has been a public resource, a repository for ideas and a source of relatively unbiased information. Industrial connections blur the distinctions between corporations and the university, establishing private control over a public resource. Problems of secrecy and proprietory rights are inherent in these new relationships, and hold serious implications for both academic science and the public interest.[28]

Commerce disrupts the relation between academic science and democratic argument.

8.4.2 Internal authority and universal principles

That individuals have been apprenticed within some practice does not entail that it is rational to defer to their judgements. The practice in which they are trained may not issue in excellence of judgement – it may be bogus or in disorder; or an individual for all her training might be a poor practitioner within her field. Finally, even the best practioners can disagree with each other: the citizen is often presented with two or more opposing judgements. How are citizens not trained within the practice to judge the reliability of a person's judgement?

Among the main sources of rational criticism of authority are the universal principles of rationality that govern all cognitive practices – the formal principles of consistency and of valid argument. The principles of logic are able to take one surprisingly far in the puncturing of claims without authority. Thus if an expert tells us that we needn't worry about industrial emissions of greenhouse gases, since the sources of most greenhouse gases are predominantly natural and not industrial, then we needn't have any knowledge about greenhouse gases to see that there is something wrong. Formal principles of logic will suffice. The same form of argument would show that given a bucket filled with rain water, we needn't worry about spillages from small additions of water by ourselves. No amount of special judgement developed in a discipline excuses an expert from invalid argument.

The principles of logic, like any other principle, require for their application principles of good judgement – forensic skills that any cognitive practice in good order should develop: the analytic capacity to disambiguate the terms employed in an argument, an eye for gaps between premises and conclusion and so on.[29] Such forensic skills have been exemplified by the Socrates of Plato's early dialogues and they are exhibited too in the forms of interrogation employed by a good lawyer. Indeed, it is interesting to note just how far lawyers are sometimes able to reveal the inadequacies in a shoddy piece of science.[30]

8.4.3 Limits of authority

'Experts' often speak as if they were authorities in domains foreign to their own field. This is often quite obvious – as when physicists are called upon as authorities in matters of religion, ethics and politics. Weber's arguments for value-free social science were in part a response to this problem – specifically, the way that experts in a field make policy judgements where their authority is no different from that of the common citizen.[31] The value utterances of experts are often not supported by any capacities or knowledge developed in their field; their authority is thus quite spurious. Such problems are relatively well known.

However, authority beyond its field often takes another, more subtle, form that lies at the basis of much of the misuse of science in policy. I mean here the failure to distinguish abstract and universal knowledge developed within a discipline and the concrete and particular settings in which action informed by such knowledge necessarily occurs. Consider for example the biochemist who claims that, since all biological processes are ultimately chemical, there can be no difference between the use of artificial and natural chemicals in farming, nor between inorganic and organic agriculture. The judgement appears to be one that the biochemist is able to make – it calls on knowledge of his field – and it is true that such knowledge is relevant to the merits of different forms of agriculture. However, the judgement he makes about their respective merits calls on fields beyond his authority. The abstract and general principles of biochemistry cannot of themselves deliver the more specific knowledge required to answer questions about different kinds of agriculture. It fails to allow that judgements about particular kinds of agriculture need to appeal to other disciplines – to ecology and geography, for example. A call must also be made on judgements which are not about the soil at all, but about the institutional and social context in which agriculture takes place. The introduction of fertilizers has economic and social implications on which no natural science could provide judgement. A fault of purely 'technical' solutions to environmental problems in the past has been a kind of 'technical utopianism' which ignores such considerations.[32]

Policy decisions normally occur on the overlap of several disciplines. Recognition of this point lay behind the positivists' call for a 'unified science' – a call that has been misunderstood in

139

the recent caricatures of positivism.[33] The defensible core of the programme lay in a call for the 'orchestration of the sciences':[34] the problem was that of integrating the findings of different disciplines each with its own aims and possibly its own language and techniques, so that, on any specific problem, all relevant sciences could be called upon. The aim was an encyclopaedia in which all the different sciences would be co-ordinated and incompatibilities addressed, a project that represents a modern form of Enlightenment encyclopaedic ambitions.

8.4.4 Practical judgement and democracy

The positivist's project of an orchestrated science certainly highlights the limits of authoritative judgements of any 'expert' in a single discipline about particular matters. However, it could not in itself solve the problems of moving from universal scientific principles to particular applications. Not all knowledge can be articulated in encyclopaedic form, and even given a unified body of articulated knowledge, there is no reason to suppose that it can deliver 'authoritative' judgements on any particular case. The gap between the general principles of science and the particular contexts in which they have to be implemented remains to be bridged. In particular, individuals often have local practical knowledge relevant to the application of general principles: farmers and peasants are *sometimes* quite properly sceptical about the self-confidence of the advice offered by newly trained university graduates – their own everyday knowledge of the soils they work with often provides a useful corrective to scientific authority. This is not because there is not a role for theory, but because the application of abstract theoretical knowledge in concrete contexts requires good practical judgement and needs to be corrected by practical experience. Hence Aristotle's claim noted earlier:

> Nor is intelligence about universals only. It must also come to know particulars, since it is concerned with action and action is about particulars. Hence in other areas also some people who lack knowledge but have experience are better in action than others who have knowledge.[35]

This last point is at the heart of Aristotle's reluctant defence of democracy against the objection quoted in 8.3.2:

There is this to be said for the Many. Each of them by himself may not be of a good quality; but when they all come together it is possible that they may surpass – collectively and as a body, although not individually – the quality of the few best. Feasts to which the many contribute may excel those provided at one man's expense. In the same way when there are many each can bring his share of goodness and moral prudence; and when all meet together the people may then become something in the nature of a single person, who – as he has many feet, many hands and many senses – may also have many qualities of character and intelligence.[36]

Through common deliberation, the citizens may show better sense than the best of individuals.[37] Such common deliberation is a necessity in the modern world. Given that a variety of knowledge and practices inform many choices, it is only through such common deliberation that rational policy is possible. Moreover, good practical judgement, the product of local and concrete experience as well as training in theoretical and abstract disciplines, are requirements of rational ecological policy.

8.4.5 Producers and users

Aristotle also has another argument in defence of democracy which provides an important correction both to MacIntyre's account of practices and to the use I made of it in outlining internal authority:

There are a number of arts in which the creative artist is not the only, or even the best, judge. These are the arts whose products can be understood and judged even by those who do not possess any skill in the art. A house, for instance, is something which can be understood by others besides the builder; indeed, the user of a house – or in other words the householder – will judge it better than he does. In the same way a pilot will judge a rudder better than a shipwright does; and the diner – not the cook – will be the best judge of a feast.[38]

MacIntyre's account of judgement fails to acknowledge this point. Thus he writes of 'internal goods' that they are internal 'because they can only be identified by the experience of participating in the practice in question. Those who lack relevant experience are incompetent thereby as judges of internal goods.'[39] This is false. As Aristotle notes, there are many practices in which it is not the participant but the user who is the best judge of its products. This is true of many environmental goods: the inhabitant of a city is normally a better judge of her city than the planner; the householder a better judge of her house than the architect. This is not to say that there is no room for the education of preferences in such matters but rather that education need not take the form of 'participation'. Indeed internal practitioners often have their judgements distorted by their appreciation of the qualities of performance as against the product. For example, an architect may admire the work of another for the way it solves problems in the use of a new material, but in doing so lose sight of other features of the building, for example the way it blends with its surroundings.

Those practices in which the user's judgement is important are in good order only if there is some means by which the practice answers to the users. The market is often defended on these grounds. Its much-fêted informational virtues[40] are supposed to be in the way that consumer choice determines the outcome of production. Consumer sovereignty in the market ensures that information is passed back to the producers. There are, however, real problems with the market. It informs by 'exit' – some products find a market, others do not – 'voice' is absent.[41] This has two consequences – one distributional, the other educational. The first is based in the fact that the exercise of 'exit' rather than 'voice' leaves behind those without power in the market place. The wealthy exit from the city and leave the poor with the environment they leave behind. The wealthy do not buy food poisoned by additives – the poor consume it. The polluting industries of wealthy nations are exported to those poor enough to accept them. A division grows between two environments, that inhabited by those with wealth, that inhabited by those without.

The second is the result of the lack of dialogue between producer and consumer. Hayek celebrates this: the market communicates, via the price mechanism, only that information which is relevant to the co-ordination of the plans of actors.[42] But this represents an informational failing of markets, not a virtue. A practice is in order where a dialogue exists between producer and users. The consumer's preferences are not uninformed but are rather educated by acquaintance with a practice. The producer in turn needs the critical comment of educated users. There are contexts in which such relationships exist, but they exist not in virtue of the market, but rather through a network of non-market institutions that exist alongside the market. Thus, for example, the professional arts rely on the existence of a body of knowledgeable audiences, educated – significantly – within public education, but also by informal organizations that surround the arts. That body provides the audience also for the public critic. It is only against the background of such non-market institutions that the arts can thrive. They provide a network in which both the artists and an educated audience can meet. Similarly, public education about the urban environment exists only through informal associations that range from environmental groups, heritage associations to some trade unions. The market, as Hayek notes, distributes little information and – as I have argued elsewhere – blocks the distribution of a great deal.[43] The kind of feedback it provides from consumers to producers neither ensures that all receive the goods in question nor issues in an educative dialogue. The educative dialogue exists not through the market, but alongside of it.

The significance of the existence of a citizenry with educated preferences – through a public education system and public associations together with the media that address that audience – is raised by another component in Aristotle's account of the problem of authority. Thus, in noting that professions best answer to members of a profession, Aristotle comments:

> The term 'doctor' is used in three different senses. It is applied to the ordinary practitioner; it is applied to the specialist who directs the course of treatment; and it is also applied to the man who has some general knowledge of the art of medicine. (There are men of this last type to be found in connexion with nearly all the arts; and we credit them with the powers of judging as much as we do the experts – i.e., the practitioners and specialists.)[44]

The background of a general training in the arts and sciences and other practices, the components of the traditional liberal education which is being threatened by 'vocational' education, develop a capacity to think critically about the judgements of trained professionals. The existence of a general and increasing knowledge of natural history – through natural history associations, conservation groups and environmental groups, as well as public education – provides the basis of much of the proper scepticism of the scientific spokesperson of special interest groups. Within existing society the continued existence of such associations and institutions, independent of both state and market, is a necessary requirement for rational scepticism about authority.

Deference to scientific authority and authority internal to other practices is rational if guided by the skilful use of the tools of suspicion in the right social conditions. However, some green critics of science may remain unconvinced, not because of the problem of authority as such, but because science itself is seen as an unreliable ally, or worse a foe, of environmental concern. This position I consider in the following chapter.

9

SCIENCE, POLICY AND ENVIRONMENTAL VALUE

What role does science have in the appreciation of the natural world and the formulation of environmental policy? Given that most environmental problems are identified by science one might think that in policy at least it has an essential role. Hence it is surprising to note the widespread criticism of the sciences in recent environmental literature. Sociologists and historians of science, infected by the relativism popular in those studies, have portrayed science as an unreliable ally of environmental policy. Many green writers go further and see in classical science a source of alienation from nature and an ideology of industrial society: they call for or celebrate new scientific paradigms. In this chapter I argue that these positions are mistaken. Science is a reliable ally of environmental policy. Moreover, scientific knowledge and training, properly understood, are components of a proper appreciation of the value of the natural world and show the relation between that appreciation and human well-being.

9.1 SCIENCE: NECESSARY, RELIABLE BUT INSUFFICIENT

9.1.1 Necessary and reliable

Scientific theory and evidence are a necessary condition for a rational ecological policy. Problems of ozone depletion, global warming, acidification of water supplies, knowledge of the decline of bio-diversity, of the state of different habitats, of the effects of agricultural practices on local habitats and so on, could not even be properly *stated* without a scientific vocabulary, let alone be debated.[1] Some sociologists and historians have suggested, however, that while science may be a necessary ally of rational ecological policy, it is an unreliable ally.[2] Thus Yearley writes that science is epistemologically unreliable: its 'observational basis is open to discrepant interpretations . . . the empirical and provisional basis of scientific knowledge – its apparent strength – can be reformulated as an *uncertain* basis'.[3] Shapin similarly refers to 'contingency and reversibility of scientific judgement, and thus the likelihood that what is pronounced true today may, without culpability, be judged wrong tomorrow'.[4] Yearley also points to the more specific problems scientists face when asked to give advice at short notice, on little evidence, on uncertain theoretical foundations, about open systems claims which are difficult to confirm or falsify.

I am happy to accept all the premises of Yearley's argument: that science is fallible, that scientific judgements are revisable, that values and evidence in science underdetermine theory choice – all this standard fare of recent philosophy, sociology and history of science can be admitted.[5] So also can the very particular problems that occur in the sphere of the environmental sciences. Claims about climate change and ozone depletion are, in virtue of being about complex and open systems, difficult to support. Given Yearley's premises does it follow that science is an unreliable friend of the environmentalist?

Augustine in *The City of God* rejects the classical view that a happy life can be realized on earth. One can rely on no earthly goods, not even friends, for even the best of friends may die. Thus in Book XIX, ch. 9 of *The City of God*, Augustine asks: 'What consolation have we in this human society . . . except the unfeigned faith and mutual affections of loyal friends?'[6] He answers that one cannot depend even on friends, since they suffer misfortune and die. Likewise in *The Confessions*, he writes on his misery following the death of a friend: 'every soul is wretched that is bound in affection of mortal things'.[7] We can rely only on that which does not perish.

What response might one make to Augustine? The proper response is this: yes, if a 'reliable' friend is one who could not possibly let one down – then there are no reliable friends to be found on earth. However, that is not what most of us mean by a reliable friend, nor what the classical defenders of friendship meant. A reliable friend is one who displays the virtue of constancy, supports you through bad times, criticizes when the occasion calls and so on. That the person may die and leave one

146

bereft is unfortunate. But this does not show the friend to be unreliable or that we cannot trust any mortal being. A happy life is always a hostage to misfortune

A similar response is owed to Yearley's argument. What would an epistemologically reliable friend *be* for Yearley? One who provided certain, infallible and unrevisable judgements, whose evidence was not open to different interpretations, who could provide such judgements even when faced with complex and open systems. Such a friend, like Augustine's, would not be entirely of this world. He would have a route to knowledge unavailable to the rest of us. *Ex cathedra* utterances moved by divine grace might meet Yearley's criteria, but the non-papal population needs to settle for different standards of reliability. To be epistemologically reliable is to provide the best available knowledge – and science is one, but not the only, source of such knowledge. In the environmental sphere it is as reliable an epistemological friend as one could hope for.[8]

9.1.2 Insufficient

Science, then, is both a necessary and reliable condition for rational environmental policy. It is not, however, *sufficient*. This point is developed in the rest of the book. Ethical and political commitments, and arguments for these, are also required. One cannot 'read' policy from the results of a scientific finding, although both green campaigners and their critics sometimes argue as if they could. I will not rehearse these points again here. One additional point is appropriate, however. The uncertainty, fallibility and revisability of scientific findings itself entails the insufficiency of science. We need principles and judgement to guide us through uncertainty. One principle that is often called upon in these contexts is a 'presumption principle for liberty' defended by some liberals. That principle has been the source of much environmental damage. The presumptive principle asserts that the burden of proof is always on those who want to curtail liberty – to interfere. In environmental matters it has meant that the burden lies on those who claim that some course of action is causing environmental damage: 'more research is needed before curtailment of our action is justified'. No such presumption for liberty should be made: if one has reasonable although not 'conclusive' grounds for believing that a course of action will be severely damaging, then there are grounds for interference. The 'presumption for liberty' in the real world has meant that powerful interests have been able to damage the environment, 'proof' arriving after the event.

Two old-fashioned strategies – 'mini–max' and 'avoid irreversible changes' – provide principles that apply also to conditions of epistemological uncertainty. The mini–max strategy – that one considers the worst outcome of each policy and chooses that which will have the least bad consequences – and the principle of avoiding irreversible decisions have much to recommend them as general guides in the environmental context in conditions of uncertainty. However, these principles themselves require particular judgements in their application. In the case of scientific uncertainty one must make some judgements about the plausibility of different claims in deciding what the worst options are going to be. If one group of scientists tells us that the release of certain gases will lead to global warming and another that they will not, then a mini–max strategy will recommend cutting the release of those gases, thus minimizing the worst result. However, it does so only if one judges the scientists' claims to be plausible. If a crank down the road tells you that a failure to meditate will destroy the energy lines that keep Gaia stable, you need not even consider the option. What goes into a mini–max strategy already relies on some epistemological judgements.

9.2 AGAINST GREENS AGAINST SCIENCE

Given that science is necessary for any rational ecological policy, it is distressing to note the widespread hostility to science amongst some green theorists[9] and activists: no green gathering appears to be complete without its books and workshops on the pseudo-sciences – magic, ley-lines, auras, astrology and every other New Age superstition. At the same time, much green writing seems to place a scientistic faith in 'new sciences' as a source of environmental salvation. The new 'holistic' and 'organic' scientific paradigms taken to be exhibited in 'ecology', 'Gaia' and 'quantum mechanics' provide a break with 'manipulative' classical mechanistic science, and break down the 'separation' of humans and nature. A set of values is read off new sciences, or, worse, a new ontology is taken to provide the basis for a rejection of any value-discussion: once one gets the holistic ontology right the right environmental attitudes follow immediately.

Why this hostility to science and the belief that green politics requires a radically 'new' science? There are two independent sources. The first is a belief that classical science 'separates' or 'alienates' us from nature, and that we need to overcome that separation to have proper concern for the natural world. The second is the belief that science is part of the ideology of industrial society. I will now show that both are misconceived.

9.2.1 Holism, alienation and nature

Holism is popular in recent green thought and for many is taken to be an essential component of green thought.[10] Appeal is made to ecology and quantum mechanics in order to argue that there is no significant distinction between self and the world.[11] The claim that we are part of Gaia is similarly invoked to reject any separation of ourselves and nature. Ecofeminists have also denied the division between culture and nature, mind and body, etc. and in doing so have often defended a holist account of the relation of humans and nature. The division of ourselves and nature represents just part of a web of dualisms which are taken to represent a masculine pattern of thought dominant within the western philosophical tradition.[12]

Why has holism been taken to provide grounds for environmental concern? The answer lies in the assumption that to be connected with an object x in some strong sense is both a necessary and sufficient condition for ethical concern with it. To treat something as an other is to treat it as an object that can be used as we like. If something is connected with us it cannot be so treated. The stronger the connection the stronger the grounds for treating the other well. On this picture of duties to others, an identity of self and others provides the best grounds for obligations to others: they become a species of duties to oneself. As Callicott puts it, if ecology or quantum mechanics entail the 'continuity of self and nature' then:

> if the self is intrinsically valuable, then nature is intrinsically valuable. If it is rational for me to act in my own best interest, and I and nature are one, then it is rational for me to act in the best interest of nature.[13]

Holmes Rolston similarly remarks:

> Ecology does not know an encapsulated ego over and against his or her environment ... The human vascular system includes arteries, veins, rivers, oceans and air currents. Cleaning a dump is not different in kind from filling a tooth. The self metabolically, if metaphorically, interpenetrates the ecosystem. The world is my body.[14]

Hence I have some grounds for filling a dump as I have for filling my teeth.

These arguments from a continuity of self and nature to duties to nature fail. First, nothing in the science of ecology or quantum mechanics entails that there is no significant division between an individual self and its environment. Thus ecology studies the relationships between different populations that are made up of individual organisms. It entails no radically holistic ontology. Hence it does not entail that 'I and nature are one' or that 'the world is my body'. Neither does quantum mechanics force such a position on us. The interpretation of quantum mechanics most commonly cited in defence of this position, the Copenhagen interpretation, in fact rests on a conservative instrumental account of quantum theory which has no such ontological implications. Moreover, there are a number of interpretations which are not even open to a holistic reading.[15] Second, the argument provides the wrong kind of grounds for duties to others. While it appears to give an easy route to duties to the 'non-human' world, the duties it provides are too weak. Duties to oneself are in significant ways *less* stringent than duties to others. Thus, while it may be foolish, and perhaps also a dereliction of one's obligations to oneself, to smoke, take no exercise, let one's teeth rot and generally abuse one's body, abuse of the bodies of others is an altogether more serious affair. What is permissible in the former case is impermissible in the latter. Likewise, to say that filling a dump is like filling our own teeth is to permit ourselves much weaker grounds for so doing than if the dump is considered a part of an independent world inhabited by others. It is in virtue of the fact that non-human beings have separate identities and are not simply extensions of ourselves that we have the duties we have to them. Only such recognition makes sense of environmental concerns. If I am concerned about the fate of a colony of birds it is not because they are an extension of me. It is a concern for individuals for *their* sakes and not my own. The assumption at the basis of the recent popularity of holism, that connections with others are a requirement for obligations to them, is false. A radical separation of humans and nature does not entail that we have no grounds for ethical concern for the natural world. Rather it signifies that we have grounds for a different kind of concern.

The non-human world is distinct from ourselves and in important senses alien to us in ways that are not objectionable and which we could not overcome even if it were desirable to do so. For example, that nature is impersonal and indifferent to human concerns and needs is not something that humans are capable of changing. As Passmore notes:

> the philosopher has to learn to live with the 'strangeness' of nature, with the fact that natural processes are entirely indifferent to our existence and welfare – not *positively* indifferent, of course, but *incapable* of caring about us – and are complex in a way that rules out the possibility of our wholly mastering and transforming them.[16]

Nature's strangeness and indifference to our concerns is not only something that we cannot overcome, but also something that we ought not even to attempt to overcome. The assumption that the discovery of nature's impersonality and indifference is something to be regretted, a cause of a 'disenchantment of the world',[17] needs to be rejected. It is based on an assumption that the only entities which we can value are those that are capable of reciprocating such attitudes to ourselves. The assumption that we can care only for those capable of caring for ourselves reflects an anthropocentric set of values. The depersonalization of nature represents not a disenchantment of the world but the basis for a proper enchantment with it. Appreciation of the strangeness of nature is a component of a proper valuation of it.[18]

It is the otherness of nature to ourselves that provides much of nature's value. Consider John Muir's opposition to the damming of the Hetch Hetchy Valley on the grounds that wild mountain parks should be 'saved from all . . . marks of man's work'.[19] The appeal here is to the value wilderness has in virtue of its not bearing the imprint of human activity. Wilderness, empty mountains, the stars at night, the complex behaviour of non-human living things – all have value as objects of contemplation in part in virtue of their lacking any human significance. Their indifference to our interests, concerns and projects, together with the absence in them of any signs of human presence, is a source of their value. It is for this reason that it is to nature that we often turn to get a sense of perspective and distance from immediate human affairs.

> I am looking out of the window in an anxious and resentful state of mind, oblivious of my surroundings, brooding perhaps on the damage done to my prestige. Then suddenly I observe a hovering kestrel. In a moment everything is altered. The brooding self with its hurt vanity has disappeared. There is nothing now but kestrel. And when I return to thinking of the other matter, it seems less important. And of course this is something which we may also do deliberately: give attention to nature to clear our minds of selfish care.[20]

9.2.2 Science as ideology

A standard complaint in green literature is that science is part of the ideology of 'industrialism' which needs to be rejected with it. Typical is Porritt:

> Modern science and technology are themselves major elements in the ideology of industrialism. There are those who would have us believe that science itself is neutral, yet more and more it is being put to ideological uses to support particular interests, especially by those who already wield the power in our society. Science is simply not geared up to cope with priority problems of humanity.[21]

Porritt's claims display some ambiguity. His claims are compatible with two quite distinct positions. The first is that the aims and goals of scientific research are largely driven by industrial goals. The problems it pursues are often not driven by internal problems of the discipline, but the need for new goods to meet new markets – be these drugs, genetically engineered organisms or new chemicals. That claim is I believe uncontentious – and scientific research is becoming increasingly thus driven through the commercialization of academic institutions. However, to assert on these grounds that 'science' is not neutral is misleading since to say this suggests that the problem lies in the content of the sciences themselves, not just the social environment they inhabit. Talk of the 'non-neutrality' of science suggests a second position that is more radical. It is the view that 'science' is *necessarily* committed to an exploitative view of nature – that it is not simply put to 'ideological uses' but that its very concepts and methods entail a commitment to the domination of nature. Science is in that sense not neutral but necessarily committed to environmentally destructive ways. Hence, to overcome environmental problems requires a radically new science.

Porritt offers no defence of that position. However, it is widespread. Its most sophisticated defenders are to be found in the Frankfurt school.[22] Typical and most explicit is Marcuse. Marcuse claims that science has built into its concepts and methods an interest in instrumental action, in the technical manipulation and control of nature:

> The science of nature develops under the technological a priori which projects nature as potential instrumentality, stuff of control and organization. And the apprehension of nature as (hypothetical) instrumentality *precedes* the development of all particular organization.[23]

The technical manipulation of nature is itself held to be a form of domination, a domination that is linked with the technological domination of humans by others.

The use of science in the destruction of the environment, in the development of technology by the military and other forces of social control, in the rationalization of the political domain and so on, are not 'abuses that arise at the level of their application'. Rather, the interest in domination enters their very construction:

> The point which I am trying to make is that science, *by virtue of its own method* and concepts, has projected and promoted a universe in which the domination of nature has remained linked to the domination of man – a link that tends to be fatal to this universe as a whole.[24]

However, the interest in domination, and the science and technology constituted by this interest, are historically specific and transitory. Marcuse advocates a new science and technology grounded in a difference interest, and with a different view of nature, not as an object to be manipulated but as 'a totality of life to be protected and cultivated'.[25] This change in the aims of science carries with it changes in its content:

Its hypotheses, without losing their rational character, would develop in an essentially different experimental context (that of a pacified world); consequently, science would arrive at essentially different concepts of nature and establish essentially different facts.[26]

Why is science necessarily committed to domination? Following a (mistaken) interpretation of arguments of Husserl,[27] Marcuse's answer is that the mathematical concepts of the sciences themselves reveal an interest in technical control:

the pre-scientific validating ground of mathematical science ... is geometry as the art of measuring, with its specific means and possibilities. This art of measuring in the empirical reality promised and indeed achieved the progressive calculability of nature, subjecting nature to ever more exact 'foresight' in mastering and using nature.[28]

This interest in the mastery of nature is preserved in the mathematical concepts the sciences employ. It is extended to those qualities of nature that cannot be directly manipulated, the secondary qualities, which undergo an indirect quantification by reduction to primary qualities.[29] There is an inherent relation between the concepts of science and their later application in the control and manipulation of nature: 'pure science has an inherently instrumental character prior to all specific application: the Logos of pure science is technology'.[30] Science's interest in the instrumental control and domination of nature and man by man reveals that 'the famous neutrality of pure science ... is an illusion'.[31]

Marcuse's argument is flawed. It assumes that there is a necessary connection between measurement and prediction and technical control, and between technical control and domination. The assumptions are false. One can measure and predict that which one cannot control – witness the history of astronomy. Given that it makes sense to talk of dominating nature, one can control without domination: to reduce greenhouse gases is to try to control nature, but it is not to dominate it. Rather, it is to nurture it by attempting to stop conditions that would decrease, for example, biodiversity. Moreover, even given these assumptions, the claim that mathematical concepts have their origin in the practice of measurement, no more shows that science has an interest in technical control than the origin of some chemical concepts in alchemy shows that modern chemistry has an interest in the transformation of substances into gold. The story of the origin of mathematical concepts tells us nothing of itself about any current commitment to a technical interest. It is also notable that Marcuse identifies science with 'physics' and the methods and concepts of the sciences with those of 'physics'. His thesis would have less plausibility applied, say, to biological theory or evolutionary theory. It gains power only if one assumes a reductionist story in which all the sciences are explanatorily, methodologically and ontologically reducible to physics. Marcuse's argument for a 'technological a priori' to modern science is implausible. Existing science is not necessarily committed to the domination of nature. Correspondingly, no new science with new methods and concepts is required to end the 'domination of nature'.

More recent arguments within the Frankfurt tradition are no more successful. They standardly assume the truth of positivist or instrumentalist portraits of the sciences, and, like Marcuse, they confuse prediction with control and control with domination.[32] The claim that science is an ideology of industrial society has yet to be given a convincing defence.

9.3 AUTONOMY, VALUE AND SCIENCE

Thus far in this chapter my main aim has been to defend science from its green critics. In this section I criticize some of its putative friends. Science is often defended on the grounds that to raise ethical and political questions about the practice of science is to fail to respect 'the autonomy of the sciences'. It is taken to be an attack on the enlightenment values, and to have totalitarian implications. A characteristically robust statement of this view is that of Lakatos:

> *In my view, science, as such, has no social responsibility.* In my view it is society that has a responsibility – that of maintaining the apolitical detached scientific tradition and allowing science to search for truth in the way determined purely by its inner life.[33]

Like many other defenders and critics of 'scientific autonomy', Lakatos's arguments for this position conflates different senses of 'autonomy'. In the following I distinguish three distinct senses of 'autonomy' for the sciences: (1) value-freedom, (2) disciplinary autonomy and (3) ethical autonomy. I argue that while value-freedom and disciplinary autonomy are, in the senses given here, defensible, the ethical autonomy of science is not.

9.3.1 Value-freedom

Critics of the autonomy of science often attempt to go for the jugular by criticizing the 'value-freedom' of the sciences. The concept of value-freedom is itself an ambiguous one and different senses of the term need careful unpicking.[34] The core logical claim of the value-freedom doctrine is that inferences from values to factual claims commit a fallacy.[35] The core normative claim is that the only values that a scientist should employ in deciding the truth or falsity of scientific propositions and theories are the internal cognitive values of science – consistency, explanatory power, simplicity and so on. Ethical and political values ought to play no part in the validation of theories. The thesis can be understood as an injunction against *wish-fulfilment*: that it would be politically or ethically desirable that P does not entail that it is true that P. Thus understood, the thesis appears to be sound and needs to be restated against those who demand 'political correctness' in academic disciplines. This value-freedom doctrine is one central component of the disciplinary autonomy of the sciences. To this I now turn.

9.3.2 Disciplinary autonomy

By the disciplinary autonomy of the sciences I refer to two claims: first that the sciences have internal cognitive values associated with truth-finding which are not reducible to other non-scientific values, and second that they have their own internal problems which are independent of problems that society might impose on them. Lakatos sometimes uses the concept of autonomy in this sense. For example he characterizes the position of the critic of scientific autonomy thus:

> The autonomy of the scientific community must be destroyed. It is the society which should completely determine the scientist's choice of problem, forbid some and lavishly

finance others. The search for truth has no autonomous value.[36]

I have no argument with autonomy in this sense. It should be added, however, that the main real-world threat to disciplinary autonomy is no longer political interference, in particular from Lakatos's opponent, the New Left, but rather the growing commercialization of science.[37] The goals of research and development are set not by the internal goals of scientific disciplines themselves, but by the goals of commerce. It is not outstanding theoretical problems in biology that drive most genetic engineering, but rather commercial problems of companies. One of the problems of the anti-scientific stances of the New Left is that it has undermined a proper defence of the disciplinary autonomy of the sciences – and indeed of other disciplines, not least philosophy.

9.3.3 Ethical autonomy

To assert the ethical autonomy of science is to assert that scientific practices are not answerable *at all* to ethical and political values. This claim is independent of those just made. Value freedom does not entail ethical autonomy. That the truth of the propositions of science is logically independent of value-claims does not entail that the aims and activities of the scientist are not open to ethical appraisal. That the only values relevant to the assessment of the worth of a particular scientific claim are the internal values of science – internal consistency, explanatory power, etc. – does not entail that scientists should thereby be indifferent to the ethical issues raised in the pursuit of their research – e.g. the use of animals and human subjects in experiments. Nor does it entail indifference to the implications that their work has when applied to the political and social contexts in which it occurs. Similarly, disciplinary autonomy does not entail ethical autonomy. That science has internal problems that drive research, and should have the autonomy to pursue internal goals, does not entail that it should be indifferent either to its possible contribution to solving social and environmental problems, or to the way the scientist finds herself driven by external goals which are socially and environmentally damaging. That science should not be determined 'completely' by society[38] does not entail that science should be 'determined *purely* by its inner life'[39] nor that 'science has no social responsibility'. That 'truth' has 'autonomous value' does not entail that it is the only value or that it overrides all others.

The illegitimate move from value-freedom and disciplinary autonomy to ethical autonomy is one that is often made. There is a tendency for professional scientists to regard the only value issues relevant to their work to be those concerned in the validation of scientific theories themselves, and hence to assert that no other value-question can arise. 'I'm a scientist; scientific knowledge is value-free (i.e. assessed by internal standards only); therefore I do not have to consider any value-questions.' This is a non-sequitur, but it is one that often appears to be built into the training of scientists – and it is one that defenders of science like Lakatos also make. The same mistakes are, however, also made by critics of science's ethical autonomy, who appear to think that to show that scientific work does have to answer to ethical and political values requires us to show that one must demonstrate that ethical and political values are relevant to the validation of scientific theories, or that to defend disciplinary autonomy is to defend ethical autonomy. Critics of ethical autonomy insert political and ethical values at the wrong place. Defenders, like Lakatos, respond by giving priority to the values of science above all others.

To defend the ethical autonomy of science is to assume that the value of knowledge about the world has priority over all values, that knowledge is not only a good but one that takes precedence over all others. Hence G. B. Shaw's response to H. G. Wells's defence of vivisection:

> We have it at last from Mr Wells. The vivisector experiments because he wants to know. On the question whether it is right to hurt any living creature for the sake of knowledge, his answer is that knowledge is so supremely important that for its sake there is nothing that it is not right to do.[40]

The ethical autonomy of science is indefensible. Truth and its pursuit are goods, but they do not override all others. Shaw's response continues thus:

> The vivisector-scoundrel has no limits ... No matter how much he knows there is always, as Newton confessed, an infinitude of things still unknown, many of them still discoverable by experiment. When he has discovered what

158

boiled baby tastes like, and what effect it has on the digestion, he has still to ascertain the gustatory and metabolic peculiarities of roast baby and fried baby, with, in each case, the exact age at which the baby should, to produce such and such results, be boiled, roast, fried, or fricasseed.[41]

I examine further the question of the limits of science in the next section. I argue that the individual who thus pursues knowledge in an unrestrained way has failed not only to to understand the place of knowledge amongst other values, but also to understand why knowledge itself has intrinsic value. In defending this position I expand further on the relationship between science, concern for non-human nature and human well-being discussed in chapter 5.

9.4. SCIENCE, WONDER AND THE LUST OF THE EYES

9.4.1. Science, value and human well-being

Why is science of value in itself? The standard answer refers to the intrinsic value of knowledge. But in what does the value of knowledge consist? One answer is that offered by Aristotle:

> In all natural things there is something wonderful. And just as Heraclitus is said to have spoken to his visitors, who were waiting to meet him but stopped as they were approaching when they saw him warming himself at the oven – he kept telling them to come in and not worry, 'for there are gods here too' – so we should approach the inquiry about each animal without aversion, knowing that in all of them there is something natural and beautiful.[42]

The value of knowledge lies in the contemplation of that which is wonderful and beautiful. Such contemplation extends our own well-being since it realizes our characteristic human capacities. There is a relationship between our capacity to appreciate the value of the natural world and human well-being.

This Aristotelian position is developed further by Marx in his remarks on the 'humanization of the senses' in the *Economic and Philosophical Manuscripts*.[43] Both art and science humanize the senses in that they allow humans to respond to the *qualities* that objects possess. We respond in a disinterested fashion – and it is a characteristic feature of humans that they can thus respond to objects. In contrast, our senses are dehumanized when we respond to objects only as items that satisfy narrowly conceived interests:

> *Sense* which is a prisoner of crude practical need has only a *restricted* sense. For a man who is starving the human form of food does not exist, only its abstract form exists; it could just as well be present in its crudest form, and it would be hard to say how this way of eating differs from that of *animals*. The man who is burdened with worries and needs has no *sense* for the finest of plays; the dealer in minerals sees only the commercial value, and not the beauty and peculiar nature of the minerals; he lacks a mineralogical sense; thus the objectification of the human essence, in a theoretical as well as a practical respect, is necessary both in order to make man's *senses human* and to create an appropriate *human sense* for the whole of the wealth of humanity and nature.[44]

Those who can respond to objects only in terms of how far they impinge on narrowly utilitarian or commercial interests fail to develop their specifically human capacities of perception. The farmer who sees the world simply in terms of production yields sees not a rat, a kestrel or a wolf but different kinds of vermin. He sees not a plant with its specific properties and qualities, but a weed. The developer sees not a wood or forest, but an obstacle to a highway. She sees not a landscape or a habitat, but space for buildings. Hence Leopold's contrast: 'The swoop of the hawk . . . is perceived by one as the drama of evolution. To another it is only a threat to a full frying pan.'[45] A person driven by narrowly utilitarian and commercial interests responds not to the 'beauty and peculiar nature' of objects, to 'the whole wealth of . . . nature' but to the world as an object for the satisfaction of a narrow range of interests.

On this interpretation, Marx's remarks on the humanization of the senses parallel his comments on production. Humans, he argues, are distinguished by being able to produce free from needs:

> [Animals] produce only when immediate physical need compels them to do so, while man produces even when he is free of such need . . . Animals produce only according to the standards and needs of the species to which they belong,

while man is capable of producing according to the standards of every species and applying to each object its inherent standard; hence man also produces in accordance with the laws of beauty.[46]

Capitalism dehumanizes in that one produces under compulsion. Our activity is not an end in itself, but a means to another end. Similar remarks might apply to perception. Where other animals can see only in terms of the satisfaction of their own needs, humans are able to perceive in a disinterested fashion. They can respond to the qualities of the objects, freed from the compulsion of need. They exhibit this capacity in science and aesthetic contemplation. Just as capitalism dehumanizes in production, so it also dehumanizes in perception – for it does not allow the individual to develop and exercise this specifically *human* capacity to respond to the world. Communism on this account *humanizes* the senses just as it humanizes productive capacities. That is, it allows us to develop our characteristically human capacities to see.

The Marx that emerges on this interpretation is far more open to the virtues of the contemplative life, far less focused on productive activities as such. He is much more Aristotelian in his account of the good life.[47] Whatever the truth or falsity of this view as an interpretation of Marx – and I think there are difficulties with it – it has considerable merit as a position in its own right. A response to the objects of the non-human world for their own qualities forms part of a life in which human capacities are developed. It is a component of human well-being.

It is in these terms that the specific virtues produced by certain forms of scientific education can be understood. Scientific education involves not simply the apprehension of a set of facts, but also the development of particular intellectual skills and virtues, and capacities of perception. The trained ecologist, be she amateur or professional, is able to see, hear and even smell in a way that a person who lacks such training cannot. The senses are opened to the objects around them. A scientific education can allow the observer to see what is there and to respond to it in a disinterested way. At *this* level, at the level of the development of human capacities, there is a relationship between a scientific training and ethical values. A scientific training *can* issue not only in the traditional intellectual excellences – in the capacity to distinguish good from bad arguments, a willingness to subject work to the critical scrutiny of others and so on – but also in the capacity to perceive and feel wonder at the natural world. For that reason the ecologist may be able to make not merely good judgements about the make-up of different eco-systems, but also good judgements about their *value*. At the level of the development of habits and capacities there *is* a relation between science and value. The practice of science develops not just intellectual virtues but also ethical virtues. It is through the sciences, the arts and kindred practices that an appreciation of the intrinsic value of the natural world is developed. It gives grounds for accepting the authoritative status of *some* evaluative claims made by the practising ecologist.

9.4.2 The lust of the eyes

The virtues developed by the sciences and the arts can be better understood if contrasted with a vice. At the end of section 9.3 I suggested that to take knowledge to be above and independent of other goods involves a failure to recognize what is good about knowledge. The 'humanization of the senses' involves the growth in the capacity for contemplation of objects free from the compulsion of need. One is able to display a disinterested openness to the object – to discover and perceive *its* properties, its 'beauty and peculiar qualities'. It is for this reason that the theoretical practices of science and art have value and a special place in the relation of humans to the natural world.

This relationship of knowledge and object can however be inverted. Knowledge may not issue in a disinterested openness to the object, but rather an object is sought to satisfy the desire to know. Consider the following infamous passage from Claude Bernard:

> The physiologist ... is a man of science, absorbed by the scientific idea which he pursues: he no longer hears the cry of animals, he no longer sees the blood that flows, he sees only his idea and perceives only organisms concealing problems which he intends to solve.[48]

The problem here is not simply Bernard's insensitivity to the *pain* he causes the animal, but his insensitivity *per se*. Consider the following passage from John Fowles:

I came on my first Military orchid, a species I had long wanted to encounter but hitherto had never seen outside a book. I fell on my knees before it in a way that all botanists will know. I identified, to be quite certain, with Professors Clapham, Tutin, and Warburg in hand (the standard British *Flora*), I measured, I photographed, I worked out where I was on the map, for future reference. I was excited, very happy, one always remembers one's 'firsts' of rarer species. Yet five minutes after my wife had finally . . . torn me away, I suffered a strange feeling. I realised I had not actually *seen* the three plants in the little colony we had found.[49]

A significant feature of Bernard's and Fowles's accounts of their scientific encounters with the natural world lies in the way that they are characterized in terms of blindness and deafness. Bernard does not see the blood or hear the screams; Fowles comes away with the realization that he has not seen the orchid. Both have a similar view of the goals of science. What moves the scientist for Bernard is the problems for which the organism provides the solution. The organism has value only as a means to the satisfaction of the scientist's curiosity. Fowles similarly characterizes his early interest in natural history in these terms:

I spent all my younger life as a more or less orthodox amateur naturalist . . . treating nature as some sort of intellectual puzzle, or game, in which to name names and explain behaviours . . . constituted all the pleasures and the prizes.[50]

Organisms become merely means to satisfy the scientist's curiosity – the pleasures of curiosity become the end. For Bernard, this occurs in the course of a celebration of science, for Fowles of a critique. Thus for Fowles, both science and art are just other ways in which nature is reduced to a means to satisfy human interests.

Science, as described by Bernard and Fowles, exhibits and develops not virtues but a vice, a vice to which Augustine refers in the *Confessions* by the memorable phrase 'the lust of the eyes'. Augustine characterizes it thus:

a certain vain desire and curiosity, not of taking delights in the body, but of making experiment with the body's aid, and cloaked under the name of learning and knowledge. Because this is the appetite to know, and the eyes are the chief of the senses we use for attaining knowledge, it is called in Scripture the lust of the eyes.[51]

Where the lust of the flesh goes after the beautiful, the lust of the eyes involves 'curiosity for the sake of experiment [which] can go after quite contrary things ... through a pure itch to experience and find out'.[52] It is exhibited, says Augustine, in the freak show and the desire to see a mangled corpse.[53] In the modern world tourism often provides it with its occasion: an American tourist in Tibet remarked to me after returning from the spectacle of a 'sky burial' – in which the dead are cut up and fed to vultures – that what he really wanted to see now was a public execution. The same phenomenon is revealed in a more polite form in the scientist as described by Bernard and Fowles.

What is wrong with the 'lust of the eyes'? At one level, it displays an absence of the virtues of temperance and practical wisdom in their classical senses. The term 'lust' is appropriate: the person thus affected pursues one good – knowledge – unrestrained by other goods. The consequence can be a quite self-regarding vice – an obsessiveness exhibited for example by Weizenbaum's 'compulsive programmer'[54] whose life is spent in solitude before a computer terminal and who gives up other goods – those of human companionship. It is also, however, often other-regarding – witness vivisection described by Shaw. The lack of limits described by Shaw is at this level a symptom of intemperance. However, it also involves the failure to understand the proper relation of pleasures and their object, and relatedly of the value of knowledge. Augustine's parallel between the lust of the eyes and the lust of the flesh is, in this regard, an illuminating one.

Consider the latter. To see a friend or lover merely as a means to pleasure – sensual or non-sensual – is not to love or befriend at all. It fails to appreciate the goods of friendship and love. We do not befriend and love another merely for the pleasure it brings us. Both friendship and love involve concern for others for their own sake. Pleasure supervenes on a happy relation with the other person. For example, we take pleasure from helping friends, we do not help friends to get pleasure. Correspondingly, the real nature of the object of the relationship matters: a surrogate will not do. The person whose relation to others is driven by 'the lust of the flesh', for whom the psychological state of pleasure in itself was the object of desire, has not understood the value of his relations with others. The value of the relation to others would be purely instrumental, and the specific nature of the object, indeed its reality, would not matter.[55] Similar points apply to knowledge: it involves a 'lust of the eyes' to see an object merely as a means to rid oneself of the itch of curiosity – to gain the 'pleasures' of knowing. Such an instrumental attitude indicates a failure to understand what is valuable about knowledge. We know in order to be able to see and appreciate 'the beauty and peculiar qualities' of the object. One does not seek knowledge of objects to get pleasure, one gets pleasure in knowing about them.

It is in these terms, also, that we are able to understand the limits that the pursuit of knowledge itself imposes on the means to and objects of knowledge, and to grasp the nature of the mistake to which Shaw draws attention. A proper understanding of the goods of scientific knowledge imposes limits on the *means* to discovery. An ecologist who was willing to destroy an environment to know about it, who saw nothing but land that 'conceals from him the problem he is seeking to solve', would not have understood the goods of knowledge.[56] If knowledge is sought because it yields appreciation of the object, then means of discovery which destroy that which is of value or render one blind to its qualities are ruled out. One must sometimes be content with a mystery. There are internal limits to what one will do in order to know.

Likewise, there are limits to what forms an object of knowledge. One does not simply seek objects in order to know. Knowledge is driven by the desire to understand the object. It recognizes a difference between those qualities and objects that form important and significant subjects of knowledge and those that do not. The taste of boiled baby, to use Shaw's macabre example, would not form a a significant object of knowledge. A child's capacity to learn and develop would.

9.4.3 Art, science and decadence

A proper understanding of the value of scientific knowledge involves the acknowledgement of limits in the means to and objects of knowledge. However, it may be the case that scientific institutions and training sometimes encourage the opposite. The world is seen merely as a means to the satisfaction of human curiosity and limits are not recognized. Correspondingly, science can be of a form that while it trains capacities of perception of some properties of objects, it produces also a blindness to others. A scientist trained in the ways of Bernard – and there are scientists thus trained – would be of just such a kind. To the extent that scientific training is of this kind it issues not in virtues but in vices. Some of the criticism of the sciences' role in the relations of humans to the natural world plays on just these points. To the extent that science is thus understood and developed the criticisms have some power. But science need not take this form.

Those who develop such criticism sometimes compare the sciences unfavourably with the arts. Where the sciences always approach nature as a problem to be solved, the arts approach it as an object of contemplation. Where the sciences are always looking for general and abstract features of objects, the arts are concerned with their particular properties. However, while there are differences between scientific and artistic practices, with regard to the criticisms of science just made, the aesthetic attitude to nature is quite as open to inversion as the scientific. It is a virtue of Fowles's position that he is at least consistent here in rejecting both aesthetic and scientific attitudes to nature.[57] Augustine's parallel between the lust of the flesh and the lust of the eyes is again a pertinent one. The lust of the flesh is driven by pleasure that 'goes after objects that are beautiful to see, hear, smell, taste, touch':[58] what is beautiful is sought simply as a means to pleasure just as in the lust of the eyes objects are sought merely as a means to satisfy the itch of curiosity. Pleasure does not supervene on the contemplation of a beautiful object. Contemplation is simply a means to the pleasure. Such an inverted aesthetic attitude to objects is characteristic of a decadent sensibility – an attitude that is captured in Kierkegaard's account of the aesthetic character.[59] The decadent sensibility, like that of the scientist, knows no limits to the means to or object of aesthetic satisfaction. It is constantly restless for *new* objects with new qualities that will satisfy the desire for aesthetic pleasure. Likewise, since the object itself is not what is sought but rather the pleasure, the object can be destroyed or discarded in the pursuit of aesthetic satisfaction. That aesthetic attitude has a real counterpart in the consumer sensibility celebrated by postmodernism – a sensibility for whom last week's objects hold no interest. The endless waste and use of resource it encourages present a much more serious threat to environmental goods than the lust of the eyes.

Both scientific and aesthetic sensibilities can take a 'decadent form' – the role of pleasure and object is open to inversion. However, this chapter is written to praise science and to save it from a premature burial. When they are in order, both science and the arts have a central role to play in the relation of humans to nature. They develop our capacities to respond to the qualities of the non-human world in a disinterested fashion, thus humanizing the senses. Through science and art our distinctive human capacities are developed and our relation to nature goes beyond a narrowly utilitarian one. The sciences and arts form central allies in the appreciation of the value of the non-human world and in the realization of human well-being.

10

MARKET, HOUSEHOLD AND POLITICS

In the last six chapters I have been concerned to reject market-based approaches to environmental policy, and to defend a central place for the sciences, arts and kindred practices in arriving at decisions about the environment. In this final chapter I place the arguments for these positions within the wider context of debates in political theory, particularly those between proponents of socialism and capitalism concerning the defensibility of markets. I do so by way of three distinctions that have been central to discussion of the market – between: (1) market and household, (2) market and politics, and (3) market and non-market associations. I examine two positions critical of the market that have been informed by these distinctions: the first is found in Marx and aims to construct a non-market order; the second which goes back to Hegel and has been popular in recent political philosophy seeks to place boundaries around the market. I highlight major problems with the second position, and argue that the first ought not yet to be buried.

10.1 HOUSEHOLD AND MARKET

[Aristotle's] famous distinction of householding proper and money-making, in the introductory chapter of his *Politics* . . . was probably the most prophetic pointer ever made in the realm of the social sciences; it is certainly still the best analysis we possess.[1]

Whether or not Aristotle's analysis is prophetic in the sense Polanyi intends, it has major relevance for modern ecological problems. His distinction between householding and money-making has had a deserved influence in the history of ecological and Marxian economics.[2]

Wherein lies the difference between householding and money-making? 'All articles of property can have two possible uses':[3] as items to be used – say a sandal to be worn – or as an item to be exchanged with others. Associated with these two uses are two modes of acquisition. That of the household, the 'economic', considers acquisition only with respect to the object's primary use, as an object that satisfies a need:

> It follows that one form of acquisition . . . is naturally a part of the art of household management. It is a form of acquisition which the manager of a household must either find ready to hand, or himself provide and arrange, because it ensures a supply of objects, necessary for life and useful to the association of the polis or the household which are capable of being stored.[4]

These objects constitute true wealth. In opposition to Solon Aristotle asserts that this wealth has bounds: 'the amount of household property which suffices for a good life is not unlimited'.[5]

The second form of acquisition, the chrematistic,[6] is concerned with the accumulation of the means of exchange, of currency: 'It is the characteristics of this second form which lead to the opinion that there is no limit to wealth and property'.[7] This form of wealth-making is often confused with the first, but the two are distinct. While there is a limit to the accumulation of natural goods, namely the needs they satisfy, there is no limit to the acquisition of the means of exchange: 'There is no limit to the end it seeks; and the end it seeks is wealth of the sort we have mentioned [i.e., wealth in the form of currency] and the mere acquisition of money'.[8] Whereas exchange in the household is entered into only to acquire what is useful, the second form of acquisition becomes its own end.[9]

Modern society is one in which the art of acquiring wealth without limit has become the driving force of economic life. The accumulation of means of exchange is its principle motive. It is in this regard that Marx cites Aristotle: the end of increasing capital becomes the aim of the economy, and such an end knows no limits.[10] The institutional mechanisms behind that movement I do not discuss here – on this question Marx's economic analysis is still of considerable value. I focus rather on the issue central to Aristotle's own discussion (which after all predated the modern economic institutions discussed by Marx), that is, the market's implications for individuals' conceptions of their interests and what it is to live well.

Individuals' conceptions of their interests do not exist in a social vacuum: they presuppose particular institutional contexts. Different institutions carry with them different understandings of a person's interests. Consider, for example, traditional societies. Within traditional society, status and honour are institutionally defined to be in one's interests. Thus to lose status for the sake of another would be to act altruistically, to sacrifice one's interests for those of another. To give up status for wealth would be 'vulgar'. Within the modern market setting, an individual's interests are defined in terms of the accumulation of rights over material goods. To give up such goods – to contemplate a fall in one's 'standard of living' – is to act in a self-sacrificial way; and politicians and economists who speak on environmental matters assure us that individuals cannot be expected to be thus self-sacrificial. Status is largely defined in terms of material goods: to lack the means of exchange necessary to acquire them is to be socially invisible.

Within the modern market economy Solon's view of wealth holds sway: 'there is no bound to wealth stands fixed for men'.[11] The modern economic textbook begins with that assumption. Human wants are infinite and can never be satisfied: hence, scarcity of resources and the economic problem of access to scarce resources are necessary features of all societies. There are in this view no boundaries to the growth of wealth. Efficiency is defined in terms of the ever-increasing satisfaction of wants. Thus Pareto-optimality – a new state of affairs S_1 is efficient if there is no alternative state S_2 such that a person prefers S_2 to S_1, and no one prefers S_1 to S_2. To be efficient is to meet wants effectively: new wants and their satisfaction represents a spiral of increasingly efficient states. The institution of the market defines individuals' interests in terms of the never-ending acquisition of goods to satisfy their wants.[12]

Aristotle, in setting up the distinction between household and market, is not simply drawing a contrast between two sets of institutions and the views of well-being they presuppose. He is also drawing a contrast between an objective and proper conception of well-being and a misconception. Solon's view, that there are no limits to wealth, is founded on a mistaken view of what it is to live well. It is to confuse mere living with living well. In their 'anxiety about livelihood' individuals forget their 'well-being'.[13] The contrast is taken up in the *Nicomachean Ethics* in the course of a discussion of friendship:

> Those who make self love a matter of reproach ascribe it to those who award the biggest share of money, honours and bodily pleasures to themselves. For these are the goods desired and eagerly pursued by the many on the assumption that they are the best; and hence they are also contested.[14]

The individual 'greedy for these goods' has made an error. The error lies not in 'self-love', in wanting for oneself what is best in life, but in a failure to identify the goods that make up a good life. The egoist is one who has a narrow view of such goods, who asks of friendship, for example, 'what do I get out of it?'. The answer is not to enumerate possible material benefits, but to point out the egoist's misconceptions concerning the goods of life. Friendship is not merely an external means to a good life, but one of its central components. The egoist's vice, 'pleonexia' – wanting more than is proper – is not simply an other-regarding vice, but a self-regarding one. The egoist confuses 'mere living' with 'living well'. To treat the environment simply as a resource for the ever increasing satisfaction of newly dreamt-up wants is an other-regarding vice: it is to treat the inarticulate – future generations and non-humans – as if they did not matter. However, it is also a self-regarding vice. To treat a forest merely as a resource is to assume a narrow conception of the goods of life. It is to fail to see for example what is wonderful and beautiful in a forest. The central social and political question that has to be addressed concerns the institutional context in which such a wider and more satisfactory conception of the goods of life is made possible and encouraged.

10.2 HOUSEHOLD, POLITICS AND NON-MARKET ASSOCIATIONS

Aristotle's critique of the pursuit of wealth without limit relies on a contrast between the market and a different institutional setting – the household – in which individuals might be expected to have a different understanding of their interests, one in which wealth has boundaries (although this understanding might itself be distorted by the market).[15] For this reason it is the household rather than the market which is to provide the model for political economy, since the polis is concerned with the acquisition of wealth for the good life, not for mere living.[16] Aristotle's contrast between the household and the market, while it retained considerable power in the eighteenth-century debates on commerce – it was central to the civic humanist critique of commercial society[17] – no longer has the immediate force it had. The household in classical antiquity was a productive unity – indeed, the principle productive unit of the ancient economy.[18] It remained a central productive unit up to the eighteenth century. In the modern economy it serves primarily as a place of consumption of goods and services.[19] If it is invoked by politicians and economists, as it was in the UK in the Thatcher years, it serves merely as a model of financial budget management.

However, the contrast between the market and other institutional contexts remains a live one – and one that has been employed either to criticize the market or to demarcate its boundaries. Two contrasts are particularly significant here. The first is that between the *market* and *politics* – and between the related roles of private individual and public citizen: it is to be found in embryo in Rousseau, and in more developed form in Hegel's distinction between civil society and state in the *Philosophy of Right* and in Marx's 'On the Jewish question' in the distinction between the citizen of the democratic polity and the private member of civil society. The second contrast is that between market and non-market associations such as professions, trade unions, guilds, academic institutions and so on:[20] on the one hand, early defenders of commercial society took such associations as their primary targets; on the other syndicalist, anarchist and guild versions of socialism appealed to such associations as the units of co-operative social order.[21]

That individuals in different contexts display different conceptions of their interests is not foreign to mainstream economics. The distinction between politics and economics has been particularly well worked. Thus, when Sagoff in *The Economy of the Earth* draws on the distinction between the preferences an individual has in the role of consumer and those that she has as a citizen,[22] he draws on a distinction that has a long history within economics.[23] Sagoff draws the contrast between the social roles thus:

> As a citizen I am concerned with the public interest: with the good of the community, rather than simply the well-being of my family. . . . In my role as a *consumer* . . . I concern myself with personal or self-regarding wants and interests; I pursue the goals I have as an individual.[24]

These different preference orders map on to differences between what 'I want' against what 'we want' and these in turn map on to the distinction between a person's wants and her values. While as a consumer an individual expresses her wants, as a citizen she expresses her judgements 'about what is right or good or appropriate in the circumstances'.[25] For Sagoff it is in the role of citizen that the individual deliberates about environmental goods.

What is significant about Sagoff's use of the distinction when placed in contrast with that of earlier social and political theory, is the degree to which Sagoff and others within mainstream economic literature take for granted the institutional contexts of different preference orders. What in the work of, say, Rousseau, Hegel and Marx appears as an account of the relationship between different institutional frameworks, in Sagoff becomes simply a matter of two different preference orders. Members of American society have 'conflicting preference maps'[26] that simply exist side by side. 'I take different points of view when I vote and when I shop. I have an "Ecology Now" sticker on a car that drips oil everywhere it is parked.'[27] I vote for laws that express my values and constrain my actions as a consumer.

The main message of Sagoff's work is that the use of cost-benefit analysis in politics is founded on a misconception. It treats politics as if it were a process of aggregating consumer preferences and not as one whereby citizens arrive at public judgements about what is of value. That criticism of cost-benefit analysis has recognizable affinities with that developed in this book. However, as it stands, it is one that suffers, like neo-classical economic theory, from a failure to consider the institutional context in which preferences are formed, and hence the consequent social and political questions about the relationship between different institutions, or the defensibility of the institutions themselves. The split of 'private want' and 'public value' is treated as a matter of divergent preference orders that are given and unavoidable: the institutional foundations – the 'American nation'[28] and 'the market' – are nowhere questioned. In 10.3 I sketch the social and political issues raised by Sagoff's position, outline the kind of social and political theory it requires, and express some scepticism about its plausibility. In 10.4 I defend an unpopular alternative which is more radical in its criticism of the market.

10.3 THE MARKET IN ITS PLACE?

Sagoff assumes that it is both possible and desirable that individuals have distinct and competing preferences that exist side by side in different settings. The individual plays one role, that of citizen, within the nation, and another, that of consumer, within the market. His main critical concern is that the forms of rationality appropriate to the market have begun to impinge on the political, where they are inappropriate. In arguing thus Sagoff implicitly assumes that the institutional problem is one of boundary maintenance – of keeping apart the kinds of good and rationality appropriate to different institutional spheres. The position he assumes has been articulated by Walzer[29] and has been popular within recent political theory. It has been particularly influential on that part of socialist theory which accepts a role for markets, but one that is bounded and does not encroach on other spheres.[30]

For Walzer, liberal politics involves an 'art of separation'[31] which creates freedoms by building walls between different institutions – churches, schools, universities, families and markets. The walls serve two purposes. First, they ensure that goods in one setting are not convertible into goods in another. Economic success should not bring political power, political power should not determine religious authority and so on. The aim is 'complex equality' – in which different goods are distributed according to the distinct understanding of different institutions and practices, and not by some other dominant external institution.[32] Second, and this is implicit in the last sentence, the walls protect the *integrity* of each institution and practice – each institutional setting has its 'particular patterns of rules, customs and cooperative arrangements',[33] and politics should keep each separate – including itself as a practice. In particular, in the USA the problem is that of 'the confinement of the market to its proper space'. This and not the Marxist goal of 'the abolition of the market' should be the aim.

Sagoff's work can be best understood within this theoretical setting. The problem is of creating a wall that maintains the integrity of political practices – that ensures that it answers to debate and does not become a surrogate market place.

Walzer's position has obvious attractions, and indeed many of the arguments of this book could be incorporated into its theoretical framework. However, in the end I do not believe it is adequate for two sets of reasons. First, within the economic sphere itself to leave the allocation of most resources to the market is incompatible with the realization of environmental goods. The market responds only to those preferences that can be articulated through acts of buying and selling. Hence the interests of the inarticulate, both those who are contingently so – the poor – and those who are necessarily so – future generations and non-humans – cannot be adequately represented.[34] Moreover, a competitive market economy is necessarily orientated towards the growth of capital, and such an orientation is incompatible with a sustainable economy. While talk of planning is not popular for reasons discussed below, I find it difficult to see how environmental goods could be realized without planning within the economic sphere itself. The question is not one of market or plan, but rather what forms of planning are compatible with other goods, in particular that of autonomy.[35] It might be objected that this argument misses the point – that the purpose of Walzer's and Sagoff's position is to lift environmental decisions out of the market and place them within the political. However, given this move it is very unclear just where and what the boundary of the political and the market is supposed to be: there are very few economic decisions that do not have environmental consequences.[36]

The problems with the nature of the boundary between the political and economic point to the second set of problems which are of more relevance to the arguments of this chapter. Neither Walzer nor Sagoff and others who defend similar views appear to give a compelling account of the relation between economic and political spheres, in particular of the different concepts of interests associated with the different institutions. The 'preference schizophrenia' celebrated by Sagoff provides the clue to the problems. The 'consumer' is conceived as bound by two constraints – the moral values she has as a citizen and the laws that express those values. Each self-interested consumer is seen as being involved in an inner contest with his own values and an external struggle with legal decree. The former struggle is expressed in the kind of advice addressed to the 'green consumer', the latter in laws enacted to control environmentally damaging behaviour. My scepticism about Sagoff's position lies in doubts about the efficacy of either mechanism. The problem on the 'value' side lies in part in free-rider problems. An individual might hold that it is not the case that everyone ought to drive a car, but also believe, quite rightly, that her driving a car will make no significant difference. 'Consumers' in the market relate to each other as isolated actors who are unable to co-ordinate their actions.

On the legal side, it often pays to act illegally and often does not pay to enforce. The treatment of the economic actor primarily as a *consumer* is, here, misleading. It is within the productive process that ecological damage primarily occurs, and it is the productive enterprise that law primarily needs to control. The efficacy of the law often relies on the co-operation of productive enterprises – the discovery of sources of environmental damage is difficult to ascertain and the enforcement of laws uncertain and costly. In *this* respect the market-orientated critics of positions which, like Sagoff's, rely on law have some power. To control polluting activities one must address the *interests* of the economic actor.[37] However, it is a question not of putting an interest in the ever-increasing accumulation of wealth to environmental ends – that view is implausible – but rather of changing the institutional context in which interests are thus conceived.

The problems of Sagoff's position are those of Walzer's also. It is not enough to talk of the 'art of separation' and of drawing and maintaining boundaries. One requires some account of how an individual's view of herself as 'a citizen' is not merely to be an abstract and ineffective moralizing figure, who talks in the voice of conscience occasionally to the 'rational economic actor'. Any such account involves some picture of the institutions which act as a bridge between an individual as 'self-maximizing agent' and an individual as 'a citizen' whose behaviour is founded in public discourse about value. It is a virtue of Hegel's position that he addresses this question, that he not only defends the co-existence of private member of civil society and public individual, but also attempts to outline institutions that bridge that gap – in the language of Hegel, that 'mediate' between particular and universal interests: the 'corporations' provide that link.[38] While his own solution may appear implausible it raises the right issues. The problem with the picture defended by Walzer, Sagoff and others is that this institutional question is not addressed. Citizenship is simply set up as an ideal – as a public community that exists alongside the market, which is to be kept uninfected by it, and in which the individual expresses her 'better side'. While such views often begin from a criticism of Marx, one is left in the end with a picture of the relation of political and economic realms of which Marx is properly critical:

> Where the political state has attained its full degree of development man leads a double life, a life in heaven and a life on earth, not only in the mind, in his consciousness, but in *reality*. He lives in the *political community*, where he regards himself as a *communal being*, and in *civil society*, where he is active as a *private individual*.[39]

Hence the problem that Marx addresses in *On the Jewish Question*, that of bringing heaven down to earth – of creating an institutional context in which individuals are able to have a conception of themselves as 'citizens' not in abstract but in their actual lives. His solution is well known – that of 'abolishing . . . the market and the conditions which give rise to it'.[40] How adequate is Marx's solution?

10.4 THE MARKET, CIVIL SOCIETY AND TOTALITARIANISM

Marx's solution is often taken to have totalitarian implications.[41] The rejection of the totalitarian regimes of Eastern Europe is often conceived of in terms of the 're-invention of civil society' – and Marx's call for the abolition of civil society has recently been viewed in this context.[42] The disappearance of the 'private individual' for the 'communal being' is taken to contain the seeds of totalitarian developments.

That retrospective verdict on Marx is unfair. Part of the problem lies in the way the term 'civil society' is employed. The term is used in a number of different senses but two stand out:

(1) civil society refers to the market and

(2) civil society refers to associations that are independent of the state.

These two senses are often used interchangeably, in particular in critiques of Marx.[43] However, they are by no means the same nor necessarily partners – indeed, the opposite is true. The proponents of the free market have fought on two fronts: against 'state socialist' incursions into the market on the one hand, and against associations and combinations – unions, professional associations and other combinations – on the other. It is often forgotten, for example, that Adam Smith wrote before any significant socialist movement – and his defence of commercial society is aimed as much against independent associations of producers as it is against state interference.[44]

Where totalitarianism is concerned, it is civil society in the second sense that is of significance, not the first. Through most of history markets have played a marginal role in economic life. An economy in which the unfettered market becomes *the* institutional framework for economic life is a recent phenomenon. However, for all that persons have suffered from tyrannical and oligarchical forms of government in the past, totalitarianism itself is a recent phenomenon. It is born of the disappearance not of the market, but of independent associations. The distinguishing feature of totalitarian movements is that they recognize no association or activity that is not subordinate to their own political ends – in Himmler's words 'There is no task that exists for its own sake'.[45] The possibility of such movements is itself founded on the loosening of other loyalties and associations in modern society, of the creation of the isolated individual. The market economy itself has been a major source of the loosening of such ties.

When Marx calls for the disappearance of the opposition of the 'citizen' and the 'private individual of civil society', it is the opposition of 'citizen' to the individual *within the market* with which he is concerned. Civil society, thus conceived, is understood already to lack independent associations. It is the 'old civil society' of feudalism that contained 'separate societies within society'.[46] The political revolution that overthrew feudalism

> destroyed all the estates, corporations, guilds and privileges which expressed the separation of people from its community. The political revolution thereby *abolished* the *political character of civil society*. It shattered civil society into its simple components – on the one hand *individuals* and on the other the *material* and *spiritual elements* which constitute the vital content and civil situation of these individuals.[47]

If Marx's analysis has any totalitarian seeds, they lie not in his critique of the market, but in his critique of feudalism. It may be that he rather too quickly accepts the story of the development of modern society as one in which the market succeeds in dis-associating individuals into isolated individuals – and that in his own picture of the future world community he tends to speak in universalistic terms of individuals thus disassociated.[48]

10.5 NON-MARKET ASSOCIATIONS AND ENVIRONMENTAL GOODS

Non-market institutions have not disappeared, and those who continue to look beyond market society – an unfashionable pursuit these days – need to recognize their importance. In *this* sense, that socialist tradition which appeals to the contrast between the market and non-market institutions provides the more promising source of a non-market order. It is within such institutional settings that individuals often develop conceptions of their interests at odds with those in the market. The concept of 'non-market' institutions includes a variety of different kinds of association: voluntary associations like natural-history societies, climbing clubs, and the like, public institutions resourced by the state, but not *of* the state – universities, schools, hospitals, conserv-ation councils and so on – through to associations that exist within the economic sphere but in which participants engage with each other in non-market ways – trade unions, professional associa-tions and so on. Such associations form a mixed bag: some exist merely to promote particular interests, others only to promote some good, while many do both. Where such associations are concerned with the development of a practice with its own internal goods, individuals often display a resistance to market mechanisms – although the market has undermined some and is increasingly encroaching on many others.[49] It is in these contexts that the practices in which our characteristic human capacities are developed – sciences, arts, crafts and so on – live a precarious existence, and the Aristotelian distinction between living and living well is maintained – in which individuals see their good as not simply in terms of wealth, power and status, but also in terms of the realization of excellences that define such practices.

A good society is one in which the well-being of its members is best realized. I have argued at various places in this book that human well-being is not to be identified with either the realization of psychological states or the satisfaction of preferences – but with the possession and realization of objective goods which include the achievement of certain human excellences. Politics, I argued in chapter 6, should be about the pursuit of the good life – and thus conceived it will be such that it allows a plurality of human practices to flourish: it also needs to adjudicate between these practices when, in conditions of social choice, they offer different judgements about the value of objects around us. That view of politics and public life is also necessary if human society is to be ecologically rational – for at least three reasons. First, it is within the context of such practices that an appreciation of and a concern for the goods of the natural world occurs. In particular, the development of human capacities within the sciences and arts, properly conducted, opens humans to the goods around them for reasons noted in chapter 9. Second, as I note in Chapter 3, they also place individuals within an historical tradition in which the well-being of those in the present is tied to that of those in the future. Third, it is in the context of such practices that living well is distinguished from living – that the boundaries in the human acquisition of material goods are recognized. Politics and political economy informed by such practices are recognizably not about 'chrematistics' – or 'economics' in the sense it is now used in economics departments[50] – but 'economics' in the Aristotelian sense. It is the art of household management that recognizes that there are limits to the material goods required for the good life.

To conceive thus of the good society and good life requires that politics should not be treated as a market pursued by other means. It is in this context that I have criticized cost-benefit analysis. However, in this chapter I have sketched some reasons for holding that what is required is not simply the construction and maintenance of boundaries around the market, but a rejection of the market as the principal institutional framework of economic life. Within such a framework productive units are driven by competition to continuous expansion, and consumers find their interests institutionally defined in terms of the unlimited acquisition of goods. An ecologically rational society requires a different institutional context in which interests are not thus defined.[51]

Much has been written in the sociology of green politics about the development of new social movements and the revitalization of civil society.[52] Half of that story I welcome. Civil society, in the sense of a society of public associations independent of the state in which the goods of human life are discussed and pursued, provides one of the hopes of an ecological politics. However, civil society in *that* sense needs protection not just from the state but from the market. However, the idea that 'new social movements' provide the agents for a new society I find less convincing. Not only do they lack social power, they also often reveal a deplorable irrationality which is quite at odds with the associations and goods required for an ecologically rational society. My pre-dilections are for 'older' social movements.[53] However, I do not pretend to offer here an account of possible agents of social change. That would require a very different book. This book is written rather in the spirit that Anthony Kenny prays:

> Some find something comic in the idea of an agnostic praying to a God whose existence he doubts. It is surely no more unreasonable than the act of a man adrift in the ocean, trapped in a cave, or stranded on a mountainside, when he cries for help though he may never be heard or fires a signal which may never be seen.[54]

In the absence of knowledge of an agent of social change it is still rational to speak.

NOTES

1 HUMAN WELL-BEING AND THE NATURAL WORLD

1 The use of 'us' invites such responses: Who is 'we'? To which class, gender, race, nationality, time, species do 'we' belong? The use of the ambiguous 'we' in the first paragraph is deliberate. In a book written in the 'first world', it also invites the response – what of the deteriorating environment of the third world? A criticism that might be made of this book, as it is made of 'deep' positions, is that the focus on non-human nature and future generations betrays a blindness to the plight of existing humans. I reply thus: that I do not discuss in detail third-world poverty – including the degradation of the lived environment of both urban and rural communities – does not entail that I believe it to be unimportant. There is no necessary incompatibility between concern for existing humans and concern for non-humans and future generations. However, the major weaknesses of both mainstream economic and political theory and the institutions they support are, for reasons developed in later chapters, more clearly evident in their failure to incorporate non-humans and future generations.

2 The approach of Austrian economics is different. I discuss it elsewhere in the book, but not here.

2 NATURE, INTRINSIC VALUE AND HUMAN WELL-BEING

1 Naess (1984) p. 266. However, Naess's use of the term is unstable and he sometimes uses 'intrinsic value' to refer to objective value. See n. 4

2 Moore (1922) p. 260.

3 Worster (1985) p. xi.

4 Thus, for example, Naess and Rothenberg (1989) initially define 'intrinsic value' as value which is 'independent of our valuation' (p. 11) but then later characterize it in terms of a contrast with instrumental

182

value (pp. 74–5). In his own account of deep ecology Naess employs the term in the sense of non-instrumental value (see n. 1 and Naess (1973)). Others are more careful. Thus, while Attfield (1987) is committed to both an objectivist meta-ethics and the view that the states of some non-humans have intrinsic value, he *defines* intrinsic value as non-instrumental value and distinguishes this from his 'objectivist understanding of it'. Callicott (1985) distinguishes non-instrumental value from objective value, using the term 'inherent value' for the former and 'intrinsic value' for the latter. However, the use of these terms raises its own problems since there is little agreement in the literature as to how they are to be employed. For example, Taylor (1986) pp. 68–77 makes the same distinction but uses 'inherent value' to describe Callicott's 'intrinsic value' and 'intrinsic value' to describe his 'inherent value', while Attfield (1983) ch. 8, uses the term 'inherent value' to refer to something quite different. Another exceptionally clear discussion of the meta-ethical issues surrounding environmental ethics is Routley (1980).

5 This kind of argument is to be found in particular in the work of McCloskey (1980) and (1983).

6 Cf. Gauthier (1986) pp. 46–9 and Callicott (1985).

7 Stevenson (1944) p. 174.

8 Ibid. p. 178.

9 I take the operators from Blackburn (1984) pp. 193ff.

10 Cf. Routley (1980).

11 Ibid. pp. 121–3.

12 Ross (1930) p. 140. Ross held four things to have intrinsic value – 'virtue, pleasure, the allocation of pleasure to the virtuous, and knowledge' (p. 140).

13 Moore (1903) pp. 28, 83ff. and 188ff.

14 Moore (1922) p. 260.

15 I do not follow Moore's own discussion here. Moore's own use of the term is closer to the weaker than the stronger interpretation. Thus, for example, the method of isolation as a test of intrinsic value proceeds by considering whether objects keep their value 'if they existed *by themselves*, in absolute isolation' (Moore (1903) p. 187).

16 A similar argument is to be found in Gunn (1980) pp. 29–34. It should be noted, however, that, while the argument in the text fails, there is an independent reason for supposing that rarity cannot be a source of value: since everything is rare under some description, rarity as such cannot confer value on an object. As I argue in 7.1, it is best understood as an amplifier of value: if an object has value under some description, it has greater value if it is rare under that description.

17 Thompson partially defines intrinsic value and hence an environmental ethic in terms of a contrast with such values: 'those who find intrinsic value in nature are claiming . . . that things and states which are of value are valuable for what they are in themselves and not because of their relation to us' (Thompson (1990) p. 148). This characterization is inadequate, in that it rules out of an environmental ethic positions such as that of Muir who values certain parts of nature

because of the absence of the marks of humans. I take it that Thompson intends a contrast to the third set of values – values objects can have in virtue of being instrumental for human satisfaction.

18 Cited in Dubos (1980) p. 135.
19 A relatively sophisticated version of the argument is to be found in Rolston (1989a) pp. 92–5; cf. Callicott (1985). I discuss their views further in chapter 9.
20 Although now a little old, Jammer (1974) remains a good survey of the basic different interpretations of quantum theory.
21 It should also be noted that the view, popular among some green thinkers (see, for example, Capra 1975), that the Copenhagen interpretation entails a radically new world view that undermines the old classical Newtonian picture of the world, is false. The Copenhagen interpretation is conceptually conservative and denies the possibility that we could replace the concepts of classical physics by any others (see Bohr (1934) p. 94 and Heisenberg (1959) p. 46: I discuss this conservatism in O'Neill (1991a) ch. 6). I return to the appeal to quantum mechanics in chapter 9.
22 Hume (1972) Book III, §1, p. 203.
23 Mackie (1977) p. 42.
24 Cf. McDowell (1985) p. 111.
25 Cf. McDowell (1985) p. 113 and Dancy (1986).
26 See McDowell (1985) and McDowell (1983). Cf. Wiggins (1987a) Essays III and IV. For critical discussion of this approach, see Blackburn (1985), Dancy (1986), Hookway (1986), Wright (1988).
27 For such a Humean response, see Blackburn (1985).
28 Cf. Hookway (1986) p. 202.
29 Hence I also reject Feinberg's claim that the goods of plants are reducible to those of humans with an interest in their thriving (Feinberg (1980)).
30 Wright (1963) ch. 3.
31 Ibid. p. 50. Cf. Taylor (1986) pp. 60–71.
32 See Cooper (1975) pp. 19ff.
33 Wright (1963) pp. 50–1.
34 I discuss this example in more detail in O'Neill (1991b).
35 Hence, there is no need to invoke scientific hypotheses such as the Gaia hypothesis to defend the existence of such goods, as does for example, Goodpaster (1978) p. 323.
36 Attfield (1987), p. 21. Cf. Rolston (1988), Goodpaster (1978) and Taylor (1986).
37 See Attfield (1987) for this kind of position. For a different attempt to bridge the gap between objective goods and moral oughts see Taylor (1986) chs 2–4.
38 Aristotle (1985) Books viii–ix.
39 Ibid. 1168b.
40 This would clearly involve a rejection of Aristotle's own view that animals are made for the sake of humans (Aristotle (1948) 1256b 17 p. 25). However, as I note in chapter 9, other remarks of Aristotle in his biological work suggest a more adequate position.

41 To take this approach would be to adopt a classical virtues-based account of concern for non-humans (for discussion see Dombrowski (1984) and for a modern reworking Clark (1977)) as against modern utilitarian and Kantian perspectives (Singer, 1976, 1979 chs 3, 5; Regan 1988). It is illuminating in this regard to compare Porphyry with Singer on why one should abstain from killing animals. Where Singer argues from the purely impersonal perspective of the utilitarian, that one should maximize pleasure/preference satisfaction, Porphyry begins with an account of what it is to live the good life – that of 'the contemplation of real being' (Porphyry (1965) Book I, §29) – and seeks to convince his interlocutor, the fallen Firmius Castricius, that to live such a life requires abstinence from meat (ibid. especially Book I, §§28ff.). While Porphyry's neo-platonist account of the good life is I believe radically mistaken, his virtues-based strategy for defending concern for animals is not.

42 This line of argument has the virtue of fitting well with Aristotle's own account of happiness, given an inclusive interpretation of his views. For further discussion of this see chapter 6.

3 FUTURE GENERATIONS AND THE HARMS WE DO OURSELVES

1 For a discussion of this point, see Barry (1977).

2 Golding (1972). Cf. Passmore (1980).

3 See, for example, Sikora (1978) and Attfield (1983) chs 6 and 7.

4 Rawls (1972) section 44.

5 See Barry (1977), Richards (1971) and Routley (1978).

6 See especially the debates that emerged from Parfit (1982) and (1984), Part 4.

7 Utilitarianism in particular comes in a large number of varieties ranging from person-affecting versions (Narveson 1967), through average utilitarianism to the total view outlined in the text. These different versions have very different implications for our obligations to future generations.

8 Goodin (1985) p. 177. For another clear statement of this assumption, see Barry (1977). The classic account of the opposing view – that we can be harmed by events after our deaths – is found in Aristotle's discussion of Solon (Aristotle (1985) Book I, chs 10–13).

9 See, for example, Barry (1977).

10 See O'Neill (1988b) for discussion of these narratives.

11 Bell (1953) p. 396.

12 See Crowe (1968).

13 Ibid. ch. 6.

14 Eliot (1919) p. 15.

15 A notable exception is Sagoff (1988) pp. 60–5.

16 Golding (1972).

17 See, for example, Sikora (1978) and Attfield (1983) chs 6 and 7.

18 Revised versions of Rawlsian principles are particularly popular: see,

for example, Richards (1971) and Barry (1977).

19 Routley (1978).
20 Kuhn (1977a).
21 See Gay (1967).
22 Eliot (1932).
23 See Oakeshott (1962) for a modern presentation of that view. I discuss his views further in chapter 8.
24 By 'a subjectivist theory of well-being' I mean here this view that well-being consists in having certain psychological states. There are other senses of the phrase which need to be distinguished from this one and which are not my concern in this chapter. For a recent unpicking of different senses, see Wood (1990). See also Crisp (1990), Griffin (1986) Part one, Kraut (1979) and Parfit (1984) Appendix I. I criticize desire-fulfilment accounts of well-being that fall between subjective state and objective conceptions in chapter 5. It should be noted also that subjectivism as an account of well-being is logically independent of subjectivism as a meta-ethical position. It is possible to be an objectivist in meta-ethics and hold that as a matter of normative fact, the well-being of humans consists in their having certain subjective states, and to be a subjectivist in meta-ethics who holds an objectivist account of well-being.
25 See Epicurus, 'Letter to Menoeceus' in Bailey (1926) and Lucretius (1965) Book III, 830–1094 for the classical statement of this view.
26 Cf. Nagel (1979).
27 See Aristotle (1985) 1095b 26–30 and 1159a 14–25.
28 Herodotus (1954) p. 13.
29 Augustine (1976) Book V, ch. xiv, p. 204.
30 See the scholium on Epicurus *Principle Doctrines* xxix, in Bailey (1926) pp. 367–8.
31 Hardin (1977).
32 Within the third world a more direct force causes peasants to be unable to express any intergenerational identity, i.e. poverty. If one does *not* graze one's land to the limits there will be no future for one's kin. Hence, even when one recognizes the effects of environmentally insensitive practices, one has no alternative. The continuing existence of those whom one wants to benefit requires such practices.
33 See Pocock (1975) chs 13 and 14, and 'The mobility of property and the rise of eighteenth-century sociology', in Pocock (1985).
34 Pocock (1975) p. 458.
35 Mises (1951) p. 62 and (1949) pp. 595–8 and 620–4. My arguments here owe much to Polanyi (1957a) chs 14–15.
36 For Smith's view, see Smith (1976), especially Book I, ch. 10, part 2. See Poole (1991) ch. 1 for a discussion relevant to the present arguments.
37 See Dubos (1980) ch. 7.
38 Weil (1952) p. 96.
39 While Marx criticizes the market, he recognizes the way it has thus liberated individuals. See, for example, Marx (1973) pp. 156–65.
40 Marx (1972) p. 776.

4 THE CONSTITUENCY OF ENVIRONMENTAL POLICY

1 These two measures can often diverge, for in general individuals want more for compensation for loss than they will pay for the gain of the same item (see Pearce and Turner (1990) p. 128–9).
2 Kaldor (1939) and Hicks (1939). I do not discuss here the well-known problem with this test, that both a proposal, P_1, and a proposal to reverse P_1, P_2, can pass the test.
3 Little (1951).
4 Bergson (1938).
5 Pearce et al. (1989) pp. 60–2.
6 See ibid., ch. 3.
7 Popper (1961) preface.
8 The view has become standard within neo-classical tradition. For a defence in the Austrian tradition, see Mises (1949) ch. 18
9 Pigou (1952) p. 25; cf. Ramsey (1928) p. 543.
10 Cf. MacIntyre (1985) ch. 15.
11 Pigou (1952) p. 107.
12 It should be noted that the other standard view of well-being assumed in economic theory, the desire-fulfilment account (Ramsey (1931); Griffin (1986) chs 1 and 2), is not open to this objection. Individuals usually desire that certain objective states of affair obtain. Hence, a desire-satisfaction account allows that individuals may suffer from illusions of the kind found in holiday B. Moreover, persons might simply desire that their lives have a particular narrative order with a particular end. However, I believe desire-fulfilment accounts of well-being are unsatisfactory for independent reasons which are developed in chapter 5.
13 Pearce et al. (1989) p. 150.
14 See Aristotle (1948) chs vii-xi and Smith (1976) Book IV, ch. 1 and Book II ch. 2, esp. pp. 306–8.
15 Smith op. cit. pp.307–8.
16 See Stone (1987) pp. 66–77.
17 Attfield and Dell (1989) p. 36.
18 Ibid. p. 29.
19 Bellamy (1984).
20 Attfield and Dell (1989) pp. 36–7.

5 JUSTIFYING COST-BENEFIT ANALYSIS: ARGUMENTS FROM WELFARE

1 A proof of that theorem will be found in any basic micro-economic textbook. See, for example, Feldman (1980).
2 One of the virtues of Hayek's version of Austrian economics is that it starts from the claim that this assumption is false. Marx's account of the business cycle can also be stated in terms of information lack and the spread of disinformation (O'Neill 1989).

3 I raise problems for this assumption in chapter 7.

4 For 'pure' public goods an additional assumption is required – that the consumption of the good by A does not reduce B's consumption.

5 There are other reasons not mentioned in the text that real market economies depart from 'optimality', most notably those concerned with increasing returns to scale.

6 The other standard solution appeals to property rights. This work stems from Coase (1960). I have already suggested in chapter 3 that this fails to deal with problems of future generations. It has more general problems that stem from its neo-classical foundations e.g. that it assumes that the costs of enforcing property rights are zero. For a discussion within the mainstream, see Pearce and Turner (1990) ch. 5 and Rose-Ackerman (1977). More significantly in the context of this and the following chapter, it inherits from its neo-classical foundations purely want-regarding criteria for optimal outcomes. The criticism of that position developed within the text can be straightfowardly re-run against property rights responses to market failure.

7 Pearce *et al.* (1989) pp. 5ff.

8 Those who start from Austrian assumptions often reject cost-benefit analysis as an intrusion of bureaucrats into the market sphere. The arguments in this book start from the opposite direction – that it involves the intrusion of market rationality into the political and ethical sphere, that it treats politics as a surrogate market rather than a forum – see Elster (1986).

9 Barry (1990) p. 38.

10 Cited in Veach (1962) p. 41.

11 Pigou (1952) ch. 1 §5 and ch. 2.

12 Aristotle *Metaphysics* 1072a 29. For an account of the objective account and a contrast with subjective-state and desire-fulfilment accounts, see Parfit (1984) Appendix I and Griffin (1986) part one.

13 Pigou (1952) ch. 2 §3.

14 Griffin (1986) p. 14. See also Goodin (1986).

15 Griffin (1986) p. 17.

16 Kuhn (1970b) p. 234.

17 Kuhn (1970a) p. 170.

18 Any arguments for such a sociological position are all ultimately self-defeating, since the thesis in question applies to those arguments themselves.

19 This is not to deny that there is something right about Kuhn's claims. The complexity of the norms and skills that are embodied in science, the fact that not all norms are articulated, the requirement for non-rule-governed judgement in applying general norms to new particular cases, all mean that often the best *practical* criterion one can have for choosing between different theories is often the decision of trained scientists. Kuhn in *that* sense is right. But even here there are limits. There are general norms of rationality to which scientists and non-scientists alike can appeal. Scientists are not 'the highest court of appeal'. For further discussion see my chapter 8.

20 I owe this example to Crisp (1989) p. 132.

21 Nagel (1986) pp. 195ff.
22 Cf. Raz (1986) ch. 12.
23 I develop this point in more detail in O'Neill (1991–2).
24 Sen (1986) p. 37; see also Sen (1985).
25 Sen (1986) p. 37.
26 Ibid. p. 38.
27 Compare Aristotle on friendship (Aristotle (1985) Books viii and ix).
28 Sen himself recognizes that plurality: see Sen (1980–1).
29 Cited in Dillon (1991) pp. xxiv–xxv. It should be noted that my arguments in this paragraph do not entail that all commitments to ideals are similarly constitutive of a person's well-being nor that there cannot be a conflict between, to use Nagel's terminology, 'living well and living right' (Nagel (1986) ch. X). Some commitments might have ethical importance but only a peripheral significance to a person's life. I may believe strongly that I ought to assist others in need but, given that this is not a central commitment of *my life*, that I am not for example a dedicated nurse, while to assist may matter, it may be peripheral to how well my own life is said to go *for me*. To assist others in need may conflict with my well-being in the sense that it may involve giving up time on projects that are more central to my own life. Such conflicts, however, are contingent, and standardly a consequence of the institutions in which we must pursue our lives. It is a mark of good social, economic and political institutions that these conflicts are minimized – that 'to live well' and 'to live right' are rendered as congruent as they can be.
30 Pigou (1952) p. 11.
31 As noted above and in the next section this extension of the range of 'measuring rod of money' lies at the heart of the Pearce report. Pearce *et al.* (1989) ch. 3.
32 I return to this point in the last chapter of the book. See also O'Neill (1992a).
33 Pearce *et al.* (1989).
34 Pearce and Turner (1990) p. 41.
35 I suspect much of the work in this area of cooking the books – of shadow-pricing preferences for environmental goods and not others.
36 I draw here on Burgess *et al.* (1991) although their theoretical perspective is one with which I disagree.
37 The dispute raises a complex set of issues about authority, inequality, and rational scepticism which I discuss in chapter 8 and pluralism raised in chapter 7. Here I ignore such complications.
38 As in the science case I believe the appeal to the competent agent is more satisfactory than that to the informed agent. What distinguishes the trained ecologist from her untrained counterpart is not that she has collected a mass of extra facts about the marshes and its inhabitants but rather that she has gained new powers, and not just the cognitive powers of good theoretical judgement, but also observational powers to see and hear what is in the marshes: she no longer sees a mush of mud, grass and insects, but a variety of flora and fauna. The appeal to the competent agent also has a good pedigree. Compare, for example,

Hume's attempt to distinguish different standards of taste by reference to the capacities of the agent (Hume 1970). A discussion of Hume that has been influential on the arguments developed here is Wiggins (1987b). See also Crisp (1993).

39 Compare Leopold's claim in his essay, 'Conservation esthetic', that 'ecological science has wrought a change in the mental eye' (Leopold (1989) p. 173). That essay is much more valuable than the better known, but less satisfactory, essay 'The land ethic' (ibid. pp. 201–20).

40 Mill (1861a) ch. 2.

41 See Green (1907) §162ff.

42 It should be noted that to say this is not to say that human practices, attributes and responses are irrelevant to what we value. It is to deny the view that values are mere expressions of preference.

43 This is not of course to say that each and everyone should become a trained ecologist: there are other ways of realizing our human powers, including our powers to see from a disinterested perspective, e.g. the arts, rock-climbing when it is a branch of mountaineering (and not merely of gymnastics), walking for its own sake, bird-watching and so on. This point applies also to my discussion in chapter 9. Neither does the text entail that every educated ecologist displays the characteristic virtues outlined in the text; some may not, a point to which I return in chapter 9. It does I believe entail that the good society will be one in which such practices flourish. Moreover, as I show in the next chapter, in a properly constituted community the pursuits of others extend ourselves.

6 PLURALISM, LIBERALISM AND THE GOOD LIFE

1 Barry (1990) p. 66.

2 As Raz notes, the concept of 'political neutrality' (Raz (1986) ch. 5) is open to several interpretations. It can refer to neutrality of justification – that political action and procedures should not be justified or undertaken on the grounds that they promote some conception of the good – or to neutrality of effect – that political action or procedures should not have the effect of promoting one conception of the good over another. Liberals standardly defend neutrality of justification. There are also ambiguities about the site of neutrality – specific decisions, political institutions, economic and social institutions and so on. Behind many defences of political neutrality is a concern that the state should not impose a particular conception of the good life by decree or law. That misses the central point of defenders of the classical conception of politics who from Aristotle through to Marx and Mill have been concerned mainly with the nature of political and social institutions rather than specific laws: Aristotle's *Politics* is concerned with the forms of vice and virtue associated with different constitutional arrangements. Mill likewise frames the issue in terms of

institutions – 'the first question on respect to any *political institutions* is, how far they tend to foster in members of the community the various desirable qualities moral and intellectual' (Mill (1861b) pp. 28–9, my emphasis). Marx is concerned with the social and economic arrangements that allow the realization of our characteristically human capacities. To reject political neutrality is not thereby to embrace a paternalistic state.

3 Dworkin (1978) p. 127.

4 It should be noted, however, that there would remain some major problems with cost-benefit analysis for the liberal. In particular, in using aggregative principles of optimality, like its classical utilitarian parent, it does not recognize the separateness of persons; hence, the concept of 'rights' cannot be generated from within it. A liberal cost-benefit analysis would require additional moral side-constraints.

5 Rawls (1972) §50 pp. 325–32.

6 Aristotle (1948) 1280b 38f. p. 139.

7 Ibid. 1324a 22.

8 Larmore (1987) p. 43.

9 Standard examples range from Republican virtues of the French revolution through the totalitarian socialism of the Bolsheviks to Devlin's conservatism.

10 Aristotle (1948) Book II, ch. II.

11 In broad terms I think Aristotle's defence of the family, understood as a defence of special relations, is sound, while his defence of private property is not. For a discussion of the latter see Irwin (1987).

12 Aristotle (1948) 1261b 10ff. Cf. Aristotle (1946) I.7.

13 Aristotle (1948) 1252b 27ff. pp. 5–6. I should note here that while I find Aristotle's identification of the good of an entity in terms of its maturity plausible with respect to biological individuals, I believe it is less convincing when applied to social institutions. However, nothing in the rest of the chapter turns on this point.

14 In the following I assume an inclusivist reading of Aristotle's account of *eudaimonia*. (For a classic account of that interpretation, see Ackrill (1980). For a recent useful account of the debate between inclusivist and dominant interpretations which takes a different position to that assumed here, see Kenny (1991).) The central substantive claim in the text – that given a pluralist account of the good life one can combine a rejection of neutrality and a defence of social plurality – does not, however, stand or fall with inclusivist interpretations of particular Aristotelian texts.

15 Aristotle (1985) 1097b 14ff. Cf. 1172b 31–4.

16 Ibid. 1096b 23ff.

17 Aristotle (1948) 1253a 26–9. See also 1253a 2–4.

18 Aristotle (1985) 1097b 8–11.

19 For a useful discussion, see Irwin (1988) §219.

20 Aristotle (1985) 1166a 8.

21 Ibid. 1160a 8–30

22 See Berlin (1969) and Williams (1979).

23 See Rawls (1972) ch. VII.

24 Larmore (1987) p. 43
25 Aristotle (1948) Book VII, ch. vii.
26 For criticism of standard defences of neutrality see n. 34.
27 Thus far I believe Habermas is right about the felicity conditions on the speech acts involved in argument, but not about all speech acts (Habermas 1984). His further claims concerning the ideal speech situation I find much less plausible.
28 For Hobbes's views, see his diatribe against the scholastics (Hobbes (1968) chs 5 and 46).
29 This position is rejected by those who, like Larmore and Habermas, argue that the norms of rational discourse themselves provide the justification for political neutrality (Larmore (1987) ch. 3; Habermas (1986) p. 170). Thus Larmore suggests that the following 'universal norm of rational dialogue' provides a justification for political neutrality. 'When two people disagree about some specific point, but wish to continue talking about the general problem they wish to solve, each should prescind from the belief that the other rejects, (1) in order to construct an argument on the basis of his other beliefs that will convince the other of the disputed belief, or (2) in order to shift to another aspect of the problem, where the possibilities of agreement seem greater. In the face of disagreement, those who wish to continue the conversation should retreat to *neutral ground*, with the hope of either resolving the dispute or by passing it' (Larmore (1987) p. 53). The argument fails, for to accept the constraints of rational dialogue already presupposes a particular conception of the good which has long been itself contested. Thus a central issue between defenders of the enlightenment and their conservative critics resides in the question of how far traditions and ways of life should be open to rational reflection according to the 'universal' norms of rational discourse. For the conservative to require such reflection and discourse is already to betray a rationalist outlook that fails to appreciate the place of unreflective judgements and commitments in a well-ordered society. In a similar fashion, some defenders of Islam in the UK have been rightly suspicious of placing their beliefs in the domain of public debate on the grounds that it induces reflection that has already undermined other faiths in post-Enlightenment Europe: faith requires a central place for unquestioned authority and dogma. The appeal to the need for public rational discourse already presupposes a particular account of the good for individuals. This is not to criticize that account or the Enlightenment values of autonomy that provide its foundation. It is to deny that politics understood in terms of a rational dialogue is neutral. It is not, and, as I have shown in 5.5, the most able liberal defender of that view, J. S. Mill, recognizes that it is not.

In defending his account Larmore also appeals like Dworkin to 'equality of respect' between persons (Dworkin (1978); Larmore (1987) pp. 59ff.). Both assume that 'equality of respect' between persons entails equality of respect of their beliefs. This is false. If all individuals do deserve equality of respect and concern it is in virtue of the *capacities* they all share, not what they actually realize through their use. Thus it might be the case that individuals deserve equal respect in virtue for example of their capacity to reason. It does not follow that the actual beliefs at which they arrive are also owed equal respect: some are owed contempt, although we may still tolerate them. Equal consideration of individuals in virtue of their capacities does entail that they should have equal opportunities to realize those capacities. This however involves not neutrality between conceptions of the good, but a commitment to some particular conception and a rejection of those that thwart the development of an individual's human powers. The view that Dworkin rejects – 'that the content of equal treatment cannot be independent of some theory of the good for man or the good life' (Dworkin (1978) p. 127) – is a sound one.

30 On the contrast between politics as a surrogate market and politics as a forum see Elster (1986). Free-market defenders of neutrality like Hayek reject such surrogate market mechanisms on the grounds that they fail to do the job of the market: liberal neutrality requires the greatest extension of the market. Hayek quite consistently also rejects a conception of politics as a conversation about the ends of life. Neutrality requires non-rational mechanisms, like those of the market, which involve no inspection of the ends individuals choose to pursue. The role of politics is that of setting the framework for the working of such neutral, non-rational mechanisms (Hayek 1973, 1976, 1979). That position is I believe more internally coherent than that defended by Larmore.

31 See Raz (1986) ch. 15.

32 See Thucydides (1954) Book II, § 37, p. 145. This part of Pericles' funeral oration strongly influenced Mill (Mill (1853) pp. 524ff.).

33 See Mill (1866) p. 371.

34 Mill (1861b) pp. 28–9.

35 Ibid. pp. 64–6 and *passim*. Cf. Mill (1853) pp. 324ff. and 334ff.

36 Mill (1861a) ch. 2, pp. 257–62.

37 Mill (1859) p. 187.

38 Likewise, if a religious tradition, to maintain itself, demands that its children undergo a schooling that is closed from outside influence, then the Millian liberal, unlike his modern neutral counterpart, will reject that demand (cf. Raz (1986), ch. 15).

39 There are of course a number of other differences between the theorists which I do not discuss: Mill has, for all the charges of elitism, a much more favourable assessment of the capacities of the ordinary citizen than either Plato or Aristotle. On the other hand, his hedonism sits uneasily with his account of the human good, a difficulty Aristotle does not face.

40 Mill (1859) p. 197.

41 Ibid. p. 202.

42 Mill (1866) pp. 357–8.

43 This is an instance of a more general point about the arguments of *On Liberty*. The harm principle is concerned with demarcating the kinds of intervention that are legitimate in different parts of a person's life, and not, as is often supposed, with where one may intervene and

where one may not. Intervention in the form of social sanctions and legal penalties is illegitimate where a person's actions concern only herself. Persuasion, instruction, advice, remonstration, entreaty and avoidance are legitimate (Mill 1859, pp. 135 and 226).

44 Mill (1866) p. 331.
45 For a discussion of truth and convergence in Mill, see Skorupski (1989) ch. 10, sections 9 and 10 and *passim*.
46 Raz (1986) provides an excellent restatement of perfectionist liberalism which is self-conscious about its roots in the liberalism of Mill.
47 Naess (1973) p. 96.
48 Aristotle (1948) 1263b 35.
49 Mill (1859) p. 188
50 Compare Gellner: 'the anthropologists were roughly liberals in their own society and Tories on behalf of the societies they were investigating' (Gellner (1974) p. 31).

7 PLURALISM, INCOMMENSURABILITY, JUDGEMENT

1 The following owes a great deal to Griffin (1977) and (1986) ch. 5. There are some terminological differences between his account and that defended here – 'incommensurability' and 'incomparability' are not distinguished in the way they are here. There are also substantive differences – he holds that all objects are strongly comparable where I hold only that they are weakly comparable.
2 Bentham's utilitarianism provides the clearest example of such a position. There is a single intrinsic value, pleasure, and, a corresponding felicific unit of measurement which not only ranks objects, but indicates the amount of pleasure each will produce. (Bentham (1970) ch. 4).
3 Attfield and Dell (1989) p. 29. Compare the definition of commensurability in Raz (1986) p. 322.
4 Attfield and Dell (1989) p. 30.
5 Ibid. p. 30.
6 Geach (1967).
7 There are examples of the uses of 'red' which do appear to be attributive, e.g. 'That's a red Granny Smith' said of a slightly less than green Granny Smith apple. It would be false to infer 'That's a red apple'. (I owe this point to conversations with Frank Sibley. Compare Owen (1986) p. 277.) It might be that one needs to distinguish not types of adjectives but different *uses* of adjectives. Given this, it *might* be that 'good' has both attributive and predicative uses – a point developed in Hampshire (1971). However, I remain sceptical of the claim that there are predicative uses of 'good' and 'better' that range over all objects and states of affair.
8 See Austin's claim that 'good' like 'real' is 'substantive hungry' (Austin (1962) pp. 68–70).
9 See Kierkegaard (1992).

194

10 A consequence is that, even given strong commensurability, there might still be a role for judgement in choices between objects of the kind outlined in later sections of this chapter.

11 This does not, of course, entail that the valuations made from different perspectives are merely 'projections'. Different 'evaluative utterances' made in different practices of the same object could all be true just as different non-evaluative utterances could be. The point is neutral between a realist and a non-realist meta-ethics.

12 See Ratcliffe (1977) pp. 6–10 for a discussion that is both interesting and influential. The criteria I note here are taken from that text.

13 The distinctions above clarify the dispute between different accounts of the relationships between incommensurability and plurality. As both Brennan (1992) and Stocker (1990) note, incommensurability need not be founded on the existence of a distinct set of perspectives, practices, traditions or roles. *Within* these incommensurability is possible. However, it does not follow that a distinct source of incommensurability is not what Nagel calls the fragmentation of value which raises more acute problems of comparability (see Nagel (1979) and (1986); cf Taylor (1982)). A rather different debate is that between Stone (1987) and Callicott (1990) which focuses on Stone's claim that adequate moral appraisal requires a plurality of moral *theories*: one should be utilitarian in one setting, Kantian in another and so on. Thus stated, pluralism is indefensible. At best Stone can be understood as drawing attention to the plurality of goods that no moral theory of the kind modern utilitarianism or Kantianism offer is able to deal with adequately.

14 See Pigou (1952) ch. 2.

15 See Stocker (1990). It should be noted that some hedonists allow that, while only pleasure is intrinsically good, pleasures are irreducibly diverse. (See Neurath (1912) whose views I discuss later.)

16 See Lemmon (1987), Nagel (1987), Taylor (1982), Williams (1979). For a useful selection of papers on the theme, see Gowans (1987).

17 The other two axioms that define the rational agent in neo-classical economics are those of completeness and reflexivity.

18 That intransitivity is a mark of commensurability is a claim defended by Raz (1986) pp. 324ff. The arguments of this section owe a great deal to a paper given by Guttenplan (1991). For a good recent discussion see Kavka (1991).

19 See Arrow (1963).

20 Rawls (1972) pp. 42ff. and 61ff. Compare the trumping rule of Dworkin (1977) p. xi.

21 Rawls's initial formulation of his priority rule would for example *never* allow us to give up just a little freedom for quite massive gains in physical well-being: he qualifies it later (p. 542).

22 Rawls (1972) p. 34. As Rawls appears to realize, his characterization of his position as 'intuitionist' is odd: it has no necessary connection with 'intuitionism' as it has been traditionally understood in ethics, and in particular with the epistemological assumptions of Moore, Ross, Prichard and others. Rawls's attitude to 'intuition' or 'judgement' is

ambivalent: while he seeks to replace it as far as possible with rules he allows that in the end it cannot be entirely eliminated.

23 That is, two principles may be consistent, but form part of an inconsistent set that includes a true description of a particular situation. See Williams (1987) for a careful statement of this point.

24 Aristotle (1985) 1141b 15ff. See also Aristotle (1985) Book X, ch.10.

25 See Kant (1948) [389 vii] p. 55. For a discussion, see O'Neill (1987).

26 It is this place for practical judgement in adjudicating conflicts of value that I take it lies at the basis of the case for weak comparability of values. We can make rational choices between different objects or states of affairs *without* calling on general principles of comparison.

27 Plato (1956) §329ff. and 349ff., Aristotle (1985) Book VI, ch. 13; Aquinas (1963) 1a 2ae Question 65. My own discussion owes much to Geach (1977) pp. 162ff.

28 See Hayek (1935) and Lange and Taylor (1956). For different appraisals of the outcome of the debate, see Buchanan (1985) ch. 4 and Shapiro (1989).

29 Mises's argument is quite distinct from the more powerful epistemological arguments that Hayek later introduced and which have become the focus of discussion. Unfortunately the lack of discussion of Mises's original argument has meant that the commensurability assumption he defends has become a dogma of much economic analysis.

30 Mises (1949) p. 209; compare Mises (1951) part II and (1920). See also the critique of Neurath in Weber (1978) ch. II, §12, pp. 100–7. Weber's argument is more careful than that of Mises. He argues that some 'value indicators' (plural) must take the place of prices for rational planning, and he expresses some doubt as to what they might be. No simple commensurability assumption is made.

31 Neurath (1919) p. 146.

32 Neurath (1928) p. 263. In developing this point Neurath is also criticizing earlier ecological economists such as Popper-Lynkeus and Ballod-Atlanticus who attempted to work exclusively with energy units. For a history of this forgotten tradition of ecological economies, and the place of Neurath in it, see Martinez-Alier (1987).

33 Thus, contrary to the received mythology about positivism, some of the positivist accounts of social and economic planning allowed for a role for non-technical judgements which their Austrian opponents in the socialist calculation debate denied. However, Neurath's own account of ethical judgement differs substantially from that defended in this book. Neurath was a utilitarian and Epicurean who saw the good of social policy as the maximization of happiness understood as pleasure. However, he rightly rejected the existence of units of pleasure on which calculations could be made (Neurath 1912).

34 Pearce *et al.* (1989) p. 115.

35 Compare Nagel (1987) esp. p. 184.

36 'some people who lack knowledge but have experience are better in action than others who have knowledge' (Aristotle (1985), 1141b 16ff.). The connection between good judgement and perception is central to

Aristotle's account of practical reason. See, for example, Aristotle (1985) 1109b 23.

37 That opposition is to be found within much of the work of both generations of the Frankfurt school. However, science, engineering and other technical subjects require the application of good judgement just as much as do ethics and aesthetics (see Kuhn 1977a).

38 I discuss these options further in chapter 10.

39 This point is central to institutional economics (see Hodgson 1988).

40 Sagoff (1988) ch. 4.

41 For typical uses of the phrase, see Pigou (1952) p. 11 and *passim* and Pearce *et al.* (1989) ch. 3.

42 See, for example, Griffin (1977) p. 52 and Pearce and Turner (1990) p. 121.

43 See Borges (1970).

44 Raz (1986) pp. 345ff.

45 Raz (1986) pp. 348–9.

46 Marx (1974) p. 109.

47 Aristotle (1985) 1133b 19 This remark is cited by Marx in Marx (1970) ch. 1 §3, pp. 64–5. Marx goes on to present an account of Aristotle's failure to develop an account of exchange value, but this further discussion is not relevant to the claim made here. For a discussion, see Meikle (1979) and Collier (1991–2).

48 That point runs through his work, from the section on money in the *Economic and Philosophical Manuscripts* through to the distinction between use-value and exchange-value in the first chapter of *Capital*.

8 AUTHORITY, DEMOCRACY AND THE ENVIRONMENT

1 I owe this point to Ravetz who raised it in a discussion at Lancaster University in the mid-1980s. For good examples of such generalized scepticism see Burgess *et al.* (1991).

2 Oakeshott (1962) pp. 1–2. For Hayek against rationalism, see Hayek (1960) chs. 2–4 and (1988) ch. 4. For a discussion of the place of 'authority' in early conservative thought, see Nisbet (1970) ch.4.

3 For the place of the social division of knowledge in Hayek's case for the market and against planning, see Hayek (1949a and 1949b). Like Oakeshott, Hayek's case depends on the claim that not all knowledge can be articulated in propositional form.

4 Oakeshott (1962) p. 7.

5 Ibid. p. 8. Oakeshott's characterization of practical knowledge clearly parallels Aristotle's concept of practical wisdom, *phronēsis*. However, there are differences. Aristotle, rightly, does not believe that practical knowledge is necessarily 'unreflective'. In making non-reflectivity a necessary feature of practical knowledge, Oakeshott's conservatism shows itself to be much stronger than that of Hegel or even Burke.

6 I adapt the term from one employed by Collier (1990).

7 MacIntyre (1985) p. 187. The concept of practice is clearly closely

related to Aristotle's concept of 'praxis' – of action which is done for its own sake and not just for ends beyond it (Aristotle, (1985) 1139a 35–b4).

8 MacIntyre (1985) p. 189. I argue below that this claim is false.

9 Compare Winch's Wittgensteinian analysis of authority, which gives an excellent account of what I have termed 'internal authority': 'The acceptance of authority is not just something which, as a matter of fact, you can get along without if you want to participate in rule-governed activities; rather to participate in rule-governed activities, *is*, in a certain way, to accept authority. For to participate in such an activity is to accept that there is *a right and a wrong way of doing things*, and the decision as to what is right and wrong can never depend *completely* on one's own caprice' (Winch (1967) p. 99).

That this is the case is not accidental. MacIntyre in an earlier discussion of 'authority' makes an explicit reference to Winch's analysis (MacIntyre (1967) pp. 52–4). His concept of 'practice' has Wittgensteinian as well as Aristotelian roots.

10 I am aware that my usage is far from standard here. In particular, it differs markedly from that of Weber (Weber (1978) ch. III). 'Legal-rational authority' is authority that for Weber is impersonal and in my terms depends on a person's institutional position. 'Traditional' and 'charismatic' authority are both for Weber 'personal'. The differences with Weber here are partly terminological, but also partly substantial – Weber's concept of 'traditional' authority, in particular, appears to me to conflate a number of distinct sources of authority.

11 See Aristotle (1985) 1095b 26–30 and 1159a 14–25 and my earlier discussion in 4.2.

12 Cf. Winch (1967) pp. 102ff. and Keat (1993).

13 The problem is set out clearly in Austin (1954) lecture III and it is his account I follow here. The problem was also one that concerned J. S. Mill (1831; 1859 ch. 3; 1861b chs 1–7). However, on the question of authority as on others, Mill's views were necessarily not those of the orthodox utilitarian, nor is it clear that he had a consistent approach over his life. In allowing differences in judgements about the quality of pleasure (Mill (1861a) ch. 2) in his later work his approach becomes more Aristotelian in character, as is his solution. For discussions of Mill's views, see Freidman (1968), Pateman (1982), Skorupski (1989) ch. 10.

14 Austin (1954) p. 58.

15 Ibid. p. 73 [390].

16 Ibid. p. 63 [392].

17 Ibid. p. 79 [394].

18 Ibid. p. 62ff.

19 Williams (1985) pp. 108–10. Unlike Sidgwick, whom Williams discusses, Austin is not committed to expediency that 'the vulgar' should not know utilitarian principles that ground their moral rules and sentiments (Sidgwick (1877) pp. 448–9). Austin is committed to the diffusion of 'the leading principles of ethics' albeit with the primary end of justifying wage labour and private property to a disaffected working class (Austin (1954) pp. 65–73).

20 See Mill (1937).

21 Aristotle (1948) 1281b 39ff, p. 145.

22 The distinction between *phronēsis* and *techne*, between practical wisdom and craft, is sometimes drawn in terms of the latter being concerned only with universals and the former with particulars (see, for example, Beiner (1983) p. 92). This is mistaken. The contrast is drawn thus between *techne* and *sophia*, science, but not between practical wisdom and craft. The distinction here is in terms of their respective objects, action and production (Aristotle (1985) 1140a 1ff.). For the parallels between practical wisdom and craft-knowledge, see ibid. 1141b 15ff.

23 Cf. Aristotle (1985) 1141b 28ff.

24 There are real problems, however. There are goods in life other than the pursuit of politics. One conservative criticism of participatory democracy – that it would lead to the rule of the politically active – has some power and need not entail either a non-public or a 'consumerist' view of the goods of life as is sometimes claimed. Other shared activities take time and energy. The politically active are just those least suited to be rulers, for it is they who are likely to view power as a good. The ancient remedy of selection by lot appears to me a better solution than the modern remedy of elective oligarchy, since it selects precisely those who do not want to serve (cf. Burnheim (1985). See also Aristotle's definition of the citizen: 'citizens . . . are all who share in the civic life of ruling and being ruled in turn' (1948, 1283b)). A democratic politics does require a 'democratic culture' in which individuals participate in a variety of associations that develop political judgement and skills. It does not require that all participate in politics narrowly conceived all of the time. Moreover, for reasons I discuss in chapter 10, it is only given participation in certain non-political associations that one can expect individuals to make democratic decisions that reflect concerns for future generations and non-humans, rather than for narrowly conceived interests.

25 Cf. Walzer (1983).

26 Burgess *et al.* (1991) p. 517.

27 Tawney (1964) p. 87. Compare the end of the section on money in Marx (1844).

28 Nelkin (1984) p. 29. I discuss this problem in detail in O'Neill (1990) and (1992a). A similar point can be made with respect to the other main source of public knowledge – journalism: on the way that the market undermines the goods of journalism, see O'Neill (1992b).

29 These are often found in books on 'Informal Logic' or 'good reasoning'. The best of these do have good exercises or hints for the development of such skills. However, at the same time, they often fall into the error of holding that the analysis of informal argument is *simply* a question of discovering *new rules* or principles that 'standard' logic fails to appreciate. Often it is not a question of new rules but of judgement as to when and how to apply existing rules to particular cases. That judgement itself cannot be caught in rules. It requires practical knowledge acquired in the practice of argument.

30 For an example, see Yearley (1991) p. 142. Unfortunately, as recent examples of bad forensic evidence reveal, not all bad science fails the lawyer's art.

31 See Keat (1981) ch. 1 for a discussion.

32 Consider, for example, the work of Sale (1985) and others on bio-regions. They write as if history and culture did not exist, that one could read off the units of politics from the science of ecology.

33 The project of a unified science took four distinct forms: (1) a reductionist project in which all the sciences would be logically derivable via bridge-laws from physics; (2) a project for a unified language of science; (3) a programme for a unified method for all sciences; and (4) a project that would orchestrate the different sciences, such that, for any specific problem, all relevant sciences could be called upon. All four doctrines were defended by positivists in different stages of positivism's history. However, the last, which has been largely ignored, was that central to the encyclopaedic project of the *International Encyclopedia of Unified Science*: 'The purpose of this work is to explore the foundations of the various sciences and to aid the integration of scientific knowledge. The universe does not follow the division of departments of a university.'

34 See Neurath (1944) *passim* and (1946).

35 Aristotle (1985) 1141b 15ff.

36 Aristotle (1948) 1281a 40ff., p. 143. See also Aristotle's reference back to this passage in 1282a 15ff.

37 Cf. Luxemburg (1971) p. 306.

38 Aristotle (1948) 1282a 17ff., p. 147.

39 MacIntyre (1967) pp. 188–9.

40 These form the core of the Austrian case for the market (Hayek 1949a and 1949b).

41 I take the distinction from Hirschman (1970).

42 Hayek (1949b) pp. 85ff.

43 O'Neill (1989) and (1990).

44 Aristotle (1948) 1282a 3ff., pp. 145–6.

9 SCIENCE, POLICY AND ENVIRONMENTAL VALUE

1 Environmental problems reveal the weakness of the forms of relativism fashionable in the sociology and history of science. They have their source not in our words but in the world. If ozone depletion is a fact, then changing our culture or discourse so that we talk in different terms will not change rising cancer rates. Similarly, if scientific argument is merely rhetoric then there is no reason to take its conclusions seriously.

2 Yearley (1991) ch. 4 is the main proponent of this view. See also Shapin (1992).

3 Yearley (1991) p. 137.

4 Shapin (1992) p. 28.

5 Although see Stove (1982) ch. 1 for a useful corrective.
6 Augustine (1972) p. 862.
7 Augustine (1944) Book iv, ch. 4, p. 50.
8 A point to note here is that all Yearley's arguments about the relation of science and environmentalism can be made in terms of the relation of science and engineering. It might be that the criticisms of Yearley are unfair – that what he intends to criticise is the way that science is sometimes treated as a source of infallible, certain and unrevisable knowledge by green activists and the public and is sometimes presented by scientists in this way. This is certainly the intention of Shapin. If this is the point, then, in so far as some activists and members of the public do have these views, and it is not clear to me how far they do, they need to be disabused and to the extent that scientific experts make a call on these views they deserve epistemological censure. However, to make those points in terms of 'the unreliability of science' is quite mistaken and suggests a quite different possibility – that some other more 'reliable' source is available. That this is the case, is false.
9 See, for example, Atkinson (1991), who attempts to employ the entire weight of recent social constructionist views of science.
10 See, for example, Capra (1982), Spretnak and Capra (1985) ch. 2 and Naess (1973). For a powerful statement of the opposite view according to which nature's separation from us is the source of an environmental ethic, see Reed (1989). While Reed's position is closer to that defended here, his anti-humanist elaboration of this view is not one I share. For an excellent discussion of these issues, see Brennan (1988).
11 See Rolston (1989b) and Callicott (1985).
12 For a good account of eco-feminism, see Plumwood (1986).
13 Callicott (1985).
14 Rolston (1989b) p. 23.
15 For a development of criticisms of recent 'ecological holism', see the discussions in Sylvan (1985) esp. Part II, pp. 10–12, Sylvan (1990) and Brennan (1988) chs 5–8.
16 Passmore (1980) Appendix, p. 8.
17 The term is Weber's, for whom the process of rationalization of modern society which includes the development of modern science represents a disenchantment of the world: see, for example, Gerth and Mills (1948) pp. 139ff. and 357.
18 There is also a necessary relation between ethical concern for an object and true beliefs about it: proper concern for an object x presupposes the possession of a core set of true beliefs about x. This is not just because if one has false beliefs about x concerned actions for x are likely to be misplaced, true as this is. It is that if one has systematically false beliefs about x, there is a sense in which x is not the object of one's concern at all. Hence the justifiable complaint lovers sometimes make on parting: 'you never really loved me; you loved someone else you mistook me for'. A similar complaint can be made of those in green movements who insist on an anti-scientific, mythologized and personalized picture of the natural world: the natural world simply isn't the object of their concern.

19 Cited in Dubos (1980) p. 135. Cf. Routley (1981).
20 Murdoch (1970) p. 84.
21 Porritt (1984) p. 50.
22 In addition to the work of Marcuse discussed below, see also Horkheimer (1973) and Adorno and Horkheimer (1972). For a survey, see Leiss (1972). Habermas shares the view that science is constituted by an interest in technical control, but rejects the possibility of a science which is not thus constituted (Habermas 1970).
23 Marcuse (1968) p. 126.
24 Ibid. p. 135. Cf. Marcuse (1972a) pp. 223–4.
25 Marcuse (1972b) p. 61.
26 Marcuse (1968) p. 136.
27 Husserl (1970) is the main source of Marcuse's arguments. I show this to be a misinterpretation in O'Neill (1988a). Another source of his views, as it is of many recent deep greens, is Heidegger.
28 Marcuse (1965) pp. 284–5.
29 Ibid. p. 284.
30 Ibid. p. 286.
31 Ibid. p. 286.
32 Thus, for example, Fay (1978) assumes a positivist account of the physical sciences and Habermas (1978) assumes a pragmatic account of the meaning of scientific terms. For an excellent critical discussion, see Keat (1981) esp. ch. 3.
33 Lakatos (1970) p. 258.
34 See Keat (1981) esp ch. 2 and (1989) for a careful unpicking of different senses.
35 This claim is often defended by appeal to a non-realist account of values thus: 'value-utterances have no truth-value and hence cannot entail or be entailed by scientific statements that do'. This is a valid argument. One needn't, however, invoke that argument to hold the invalidity of standard inferences from values to facts. The fallacy of relevance is all one needs to deny moves from evaluative to factual claims when these are illegitimate. Even given that value-utterances do have a truth-value, their truth-value is normally irrelevant to the truth of any scientific claim. This said, to allow value realism does allow that not all claims about values are logically independent of all factual claims. If, for example, one allows that statements of the form 'X is good for A' made of biological entities are factual and evaluative, then some biological 'need-claims' about those entities will logically entail value claims.
36 See Nelkin (1984) and O'Neill (1990).
37 Lakatos (1970) p. 257
38 Lakatos (1970) p. 257.
39 Ibid. p. 258 (my emphasis).
40 Shaw (1927) p. 478.
41 Ibid. pp. 478–9.
42 Aristotle (1972) Book I, ch. 5, 645a 16ff.
43 Marx's early work can be given an ecologically benign reading in these terms but I am not sure how far such a benign reading can be sustained. For a more sceptical view, see O'Neill (1991–2).

44 Marx (1844) pp. 353–4.
45 Leopold (1989) p. 173. Hence his claim that 'recreational development is a job not of building roads into lovely country, but of building receptivity into the still unlovely human mind' (ibid. p. 177): one could then see what is wonderful in 'the weed in the city lot' as well as in the large redwood.
46 Ibid. p. 329. For criticism of Marx's claims about animals, see Benton (1988) pp. 4–18. It is not clear to me that this affects the substance of Marx's claims here. The human good can be defined in terms of the *characteristic* capacities of humans, not their *distinctive* capacities.
47 Marx's position has other Aristotelian features, in particular with respect to leisure, *scholē*. Generally, persons can live a fully human life only if they have some part of their life free of necessity (see Aristotle (1985) 1177b 4ff.; (1948) 1333a 30ff., 1334a 11ff.), a point that Marx famously makes in *Capital* Vol III (Marx (1972) p. 820). It is only then that one has the luxury of being able to contemplate in a disinterested fashion.
48 Bernard (1957) p. 103.
49 Fowles (1979) p. 61.
50 Ibid. p. 51.
51 Augustine (1944) p. 197. For a recent discussion of Augustine's theme, see Clark (1990) pp. 96–102.
52 Augustine (1944) p. 198.
53 Compare Plato (1974), Book IV, 439–40, in which Plato employs the example of the desire to look upon corpses to illustrate desires in a state of disorder and the role of *thumos*, spirit, in taking the side of reason to bring order to them.
54 Weizenbaum (1976) ch. 4.
55 See Lodge (1984) pp. 324–6.
56 Consider, for example, the Spartina archipelago experiments in which, to test the MacArthur–Wilson equilibrium theory of insular bio-geography six islands were 'defaunated . . . with methyl bromide gas' (Rey 1984, p. 102).
57 Fowles (1979) p. 68 and *passim*.
58 Augustine (1944) p. 198.
59 Kierkegaard (1992).

10 MARKET, HOUSEHOLD AND POLITICS

1 Polanyi (1957a) pp. 53–4; cf. Polanyi (1957b). For criticism of Polanyi's interpretation of Aristotle see Meikle (1979).
2 For its place in modern ecological thought, see Martinez-Alier (1987). For its role in Marx's thought, see Collier (1991–2) (to which my own discussion owes much), Meikle (1979) and the text below.
3 Aristotle (1948) Book I, ch. 9 (1257a 6), p. 28.
4 Aristotle (1948) Book I, ch. 8 (1256b 27ff.) p. 26. Compare Marx's distinction between use-value and exchange-value.
5 Aristotle (1948) 1236b 31.

6 The use of the term 'chrematistic' which I outline here is that which Aristotle employs most widely in *The Politics* and it is in this sense that Marx and later ecological writers employ it. Aristotle does however, sometimes use it in a more neutral sense: for an account of the different uses, see Barker in Aristotle (1948) pp. 226–7.

7 Aristotle (1948) 1256b 40ff., p. 27.

8 Aristotle (1948) Book I, ch. 9 (1257b 28ff.), p. 31.

9 In Marxian terms, Aristotle distinguishes here the circuit commodity–money–commodity from that of money–commodity–money: 'The circuit C–M–C starts with one commodity, and finishes with another which falls out of circulation and into consumption. Consumption, the satisfaction of wants, in one word use-value, is its end and aim. The circuit M–C–M, on the contrary, commences with money and ends with money. Its leading motive, and the goal that attracts it, is therefore mere exchange-value' (Marx (1970) ch. 4, p. 148).

It is the circuit M–C–M that forms the object of criticism in Aristotle.

10 Marx (1970) ch. 4, pp. 150–1.

11 Quoted in Aristotle (1948) Book I, ch. 8 (1256b 34), p. 26.

12 This is not to say that *some* of the wants thus created are not ones that it is good that one should have. Smith, Hume and other early proponents of commercial society were not without some justification in referring to its civilizing tendencies. This point is taken up by Marx in his later works, where he talks of capitalist society creating individuals with 'universal relations, all-round wants and universal capacities' (Marx (1973) p. 158). There is a tension here, however, between on the one hand praising the market for creating an individual who has wider cultural and social needs and on the other criticizing the market for manufacturing endless wants such that '*lack of moderation* and *intemperance* become its true standard' (Marx (1844) p. 358). Some general account of human well-being of the kind sketched in the early works is required to distinguish these.

13 Aristotle (1948) 1257b 40f., p. 32.

14 Aristotle (1985) 1168b 16ff.

15 Aristotle (1948) Book I, ch. 9 (1257b 35ff.) pp. 31–2.

16 See, for example, Aristotle (1948) Book I, ch. 8 (1256b 26–39), p. 26.

17 See Pocock (1975) ch. 13, 14 and *passim*, and (1985) ch.6.

18 On the marginal place of commerce in the classical economy, see St Croix (1981) esp. ch. III iv.

19 See Polanyi (1957a) pp. 53–5 and Weber (1978) ch. IV §.2, pp. 375ff.

20 See Smith (1976) Book I, ch. X, part II and Book V, ch. I, part III art. II.

21 For a survey, see Black (1984) chs 14 and 15. An excellent case for this version of socialism is to be found in Neurath (1942). For an interesting recent discussion which employs the contrast as a basis of a critique of classical liberal political economy, see Gamwell (1984).

22 Sagoff (1988) esp. pp. 8ff., 50ff., 65ff. and *passim*.

23 See, for example, Tulloch (1967) and Sen (1977). For a useful brief discussion with further references, see Goodin (1986) §III. The existence of more than one preference-ranking is a problem for neo-classical theory which assumes a single preference-ordering, a point

I noted in chapter 7. The standard move *within* neo-classical theory is that 'public' preferences do not depart from 'private' preferences – rather they represent the outcomes of such preferences in the context of prisoner dilemma or assurance games in which the individual has the same preferences, but, from enlightened self-interest, follows a different strategy for their realisation. While it may be the case that some public preferences can be thus explained in terms of such strategic rationality, as a general explanation it is implausible. It fails to address the effect of institutional context on preference formation.

24 Sagoff (1988) p. 8.
25 Ibid. p. 9.
26 Ibid. p. 52.
27 Ibid. p. 53.
28 On the problems with the appeal to nationhood in Sagoff, see O'Neill (1992c).
29 Walzer (1983) and (1984).
30 See, for example, Miller (1989).
31 Walzer (1984).
32 Walzer (1983) defends this at length.
33 Walzer (1984) p. 325.
34 See chapter 4. Cf. Martinez-Alier (1987).
35 See Neurath (1942) and Bottomore ((1990).
36 Reading Sagoff it is very unclear just where the market is supposed to be an appropriate institution for decision-making. Decisions that are 'too trivial, too personal, or too knotty to be argued *in foro publico* . . . should be left to some non-political solution, usually a market' (Sagoff (1988) p. 44). The colour of neckties and the number of frisbees as against yo-yos are offered as examples. At the level of consumer preference these are trivial and personal, and a society that made public pronouncements on such matters would exhibit the madness of the Little-Endian decrees of Lilliput (Swift (1953), part one, ch. 4). However, at the point of production they may not be at all trivial: choices in dye-making processes, for example, can have major environmental implications. It is only by treating economic actors primarily as consumers that Sagoff appears to leave a lot of room for markets. If one focuses on productive process the role of markets in Sagoff's account shrinks rapidly.
37 See, for example, Dales (1968). For criticism, see Chapter 5 note 6.
38 Hegel (1967) paragraphs 250–6, 295, 308, 311 and *passim*.
39 Marx (1843) p. 220.
40 Ibid. p. 241. This is the most forthright rejection of the market by Marx. It is little quoted, principally, I suspect, because it occurs in a passage in which Marx – himself of Jewish origin – expresses a grotesque and indefensible caricature of 'Judaism'. For some pertinent remarks see Arendt (1986) pp. 34–5.
41 See Kolakowski (1974) and Nisbet (1970). Such views are also implicit in the rejection of Marx by Walzer (1984).
42 See, for example, Keane (1988a) and (1988b). More generally, the move

towards the idea of 'complex equality' and the 'art of separation' has been made within socialist theory as a response to the failure of the 'actually existing socialism' of Eastern Europe and China. The very idea of a 'planned economy' and non-market order has few defenders. The verdict of 'failure' on Eastern European and Chinese economies is one with which I have no quarrel. Their failure, moreover, was particularly marked in the environmental sphere – a point defenders of the constrained market often rightly highlight (see, for example, Pearce and Turner (1990) ch. 12). The lack of democracy and independent associations were important factors in such failures, and to understand this and the economic and political peculiarities of these regimes one needs to look at the particular history of the Russian and Chinese empires. I am unconvinced that ideas of planning or a predominantly non-market order should thereby be placed off the agenda. I will not attempt in this chapter to rebut all the charges made against these ideas. The strongest economic argument against this view remains, I believe, Hayek's epistemological arguments (Hayek 1949a and 1949b); I comment critically on these in O'Neill (1989) and (1990). Here I restrict discussion to the major political criticism made of the idea of a planned economy, that it is totalitarian.

43 Typical in this regard is Walzer who writes that 'for Marx separation, in so far as it was real, was something to be overcome. Separated institutions – churches, universities, even families – have no part of his program . . .' (Walzer (1984) p. 318) and gives as evidence Marx's comments about how civil society creates 'an individual separated from the community, withdrawn into himself, wholly preoccupied with his private interest and acting in accordance with his private caprice'. As I show below, Marx takes the issue of separate institutions and that of the separated individual to be quite distinct. The market is founded on the abolition of separate institutions and the creation of the separated individual. Now, I believe he is wrong about this, but it does not follow that in aiming to abolish the market he aims to abolish separated institutions. Because he believes (falsely) that this has already occurred he is mainly silent on such institutions. This is not to say that the anarchist tradition and later writers like Neurath who envisage a more pluralistic non-market economy are not much clearer here than is Marx.

44 See, in particular, Smith (1976) Book I, ch. X part III – which contains the famous passage 'people of the same trade seldom meet together, even for merriment and diversion, but the conversation ends in a conspiracy against the public' (p. 144). That passage, even in market society, falsifies the story of associations. They are, even when conspiracies, not always *merely* conspiracies. They may protect also the internal standards of a craft or profession. The opposition to associations remains a strong one in defences of the free market. See, for example, Hayek (1979) ch. 15.

45 Cited in Arendt (1986) p. 322.

46 Marx (1843) p. 232.

47 Ibid. pp. 232–3.
48 However, it is possible to interpret Marx here in terms of a criticism of the particular *form* which independent associations took in pre-capitalist society, rather than of their existence *per se*. Thus, in *The Civil War in France* the confederal structure of the Paris Commune is praised. In doing so Marx notes its likeness to medieval communes, but he then distinguishes it from them. See Marx (1871) pp. 288ff. Cf. Keat (1982).
49 See O'Neill (1990) and (1992a).
50 As Collier notes, 'it would be in the interests of accuracy if the economics departments in most universities were re-styled "Departments of Chrematistic"' (Collier, 1991–2).
51 This last point is not a new one. The distinction between 'economic' and 'chrematistic' forms of the acquisition of material goods has been central to a body of literature in ecological economics developed over the last century, that has been largely forgotten. Martinez-Alier's excellent book *Ecological Economics* does much to reassert it. Within this tradition Neurath develops his picture of a socialist society as a 'societas societum' – a view in which economic life is not governed by market principles, but in which 'civil society' in the sense of thriving public association exists. Thus he rejects the centralization of powers and functions in the state in favour of dispersed overlapping authorities: 'We know from the Middle Ages how "overlapping" authorities can work. There could be international organizations which would be responsible for the administration of the main natural resources, e.g. an organization dealing with iron, others with coffee, rubber, foodstuffs which could act as members of an international planning board – such organizations could be in action before a world commonwealth would be organized' (Neurath (1942) p. 433).
    Similarly 'big rivers with their banks could be "internationalized"' (ibid. p. 434). More local units of self-government with powers of regional planning might exist alongside such larger functional units (ibid. p. 435; cf. Sylvan 1993). The forms of functional international units Neurath describes are of the kind required if global resources are to be used in an ecologically rational way, in particular to overcome international 'tragedy of the commons' problems. His solution also avoids the narrow localism of some green thinkers (Sale 1985) and the authoritarian statism of others (see Ophuls (1977) and Heilbroner (1975), esp. ch. 4), and rejects the assumption, which has dogged much twentieth-century political thought and action, that we must choose between the 'internationalism of the "money-order"' (ibid. p. 434) or state-planning. His position has not had the discussion it deserves.
52 The work of Melucci has been influential in this regard. See Melucci (1988) and (1989).
53 I remain unconvinced that the classical Marxist concept of class has lost its power (see Graham (1992) chs 4 and 5). It strikes me that its main problem is not that the working class has disappeared – in the sense Marx uses the term it has not – but that the majority of the world's

population remain peasants who live an increasingly precarious existence. It is only from European and North American centred perspectives that 'post-industrialism' would seem the major issue, rather than industrialization and the demise of agriculturally fertile soils.

54 Kenny (1986) p. 210.

BIBLIOGRAPHY

Ackrill, J. L. (1980) 'Aristotle on *Eudaimonia*', in A. Rorty, ed., *Essays on Aristotle's Ethics*, Berkeley: University of California Press.
Adorno, T. and Horkheimer, M. (1972) *The Dialectic of the Enlightenment*, trans. J. Cumming, New York: Herder & Herder.
Aquinas, T. (1963) *Summa Theologiae*, London, Eyre & Spottiswoode.
Arendt, H. (1986) *The Origins of Totalitarianism* (1st edn 1951), London: André Deutsch.
Aristotle (1946) *Rhetorica*, trans. R. Roberts, Oxford: Clarendon Press.
—— (1948) *Politics*, trans. E. Barker, Oxford: Oxford University Press.
—— (1972) *De Partibus Animalium I*, trans D. Balme, Oxford: Clarendon Press.
—— (1985) *Nicomachean Ethics*, trans. T. Irwin, Indianapolis: Hackett.
Arrow, K. (1963) *Social Choice and Individual Values* (2nd edn), New Haven: Yale University Press.
Atkinson, A. (1991) *Principles of Political Ecology*, London: Belhaven Press.
Attfield, R. (1983) *The Ethics of Environmental Concern*, Oxford: Blackwell.
—— (1987) *A Theory of Value and Obligation*, London: Croom Helm.
—— and Dell, K., eds (1989) *Values, Conflict and the Environment: Report of the Environmental Ethics Working Party*, Oxford: Ian Ramsey Centre.
Augustine (1944) *Confessions*, trans. F. Sheed, London: Sheed & Ward.
—— (1972) *City of God*, trans. H. Bettenson: Harmondsworth, Penguin.
Austin, J. (1954) *The Province of Jurisprudence Determined*, London: Weidenfeld & Nicolson.
Austin, J. L. (1962) *Sense and Sensibilia*, Oxford: Clarendon Press.
Bailey, C., ed. (1926) *Epicurus, the Extant Remains*, Oxford: Clarendon Press.
Barry, B. (1977) 'Justice between generations', in P. Hacker and J. Raz, eds, *Law, Morality, and Society*, Oxford: Clarendon Press.
—— (1990) *Political Argument*, (2nd edn) New York: Harvester Wheatsheaf.
Beiner, R. (1983) *Political Judgement*, London: Methuen.
Bell, E. T. (1953) *Men of Mathematics*, vol II, Harmondsworth: Penguin.
Bellamy, D. (1984) *I-Spy Book of Nature*, London: IPC Magazines.
Bentham, J. (1970) *An Introduction to the Principles of Morals and Legislation*, London: Methuen.

Benton, T. (1988) 'Humanism = speciesism: Marx on humans and animals', *Radical Philosophy* 50: 4–18.

Bergson, A. (1938) 'A reformulation of certain aspects of welfare economics', *Quarterly Journal of Economics* 52: 310–34.

Berlin, I. (1969) *Four Essays on Liberty*, Oxford: Oxford University Press.

Bernard, C. (1957) *Introduction to the Study of Experimental Medicine*, trans. H. Green, New York: Dover.

Black, A. (1984) *Guilds and Civil Society*, London: Methuen.

Blackburn, S. (1984) *Spreading the Word*, Oxford: Clarendon Press.

—— (1985) 'Errors and the phenomenology of value', in T. Honderich, ed., *Morality and Objectivity*, London: Routledge.

Bohr, N. (1934) *Atomic Theory and the Description of Nature*, Cambridge: Cambridge University Press.

Borges, J. (1970) 'Three versions of Judas', in *Labyrinths*, Harmondsworth: Penguin.

Bottomore, T. (1990) *The Socialist Economy*, New York: Harvester Wheatsheaf.

Brennan, A. (1988) *Thinking about Nature*, London: Routledge.

—— (1992) 'Moral pluralism and the environment', *Environmental Values* 1: 15–33.

Buchanan, A. (1985) *Ethics, Efficiency and the Market*, Oxford: Clarendon Press.

Burgess, J., Harrison C. and Maiteny P. (1991) 'Contested meanings: the consumption of news about nature conservation', *Media, Culture and Society* 13: 499–519.

Burnheim, J. (1985) *Is Democracy Possible?*, Cambridge: Polity Press.

Callicott, J. B. (1985) 'Intrinsic value, quantum theory, and environmental ethics', *Environmental Ethics* 7: 257–75.

—— (1990) 'The case against moral pluralism', *Environmental Ethics* 12: 99–124.

Capra, F. (1975) *The Tao of Physics*, London: Wildwood House.

—— (1982) *The Turning Point*, London: Wildwood House.

Clark, S. (1977) *The Moral Status of Animals*, Oxford: Clarendon Press.

—— (1990) *A Parliament of Souls*, Oxford: Clarendon Press.

Coase, R. (1960) 'The problem of social cost', *The Journal of Law and Economics* 3: 1–22.

Collier, A. (1990) *Socialist Reasoning*, London: Pluto.

—— (1991–2) 'Value, rationality and the environment', Seminar series on *Socialism and the Environment*, Kent University.

Cooper, J. (1975) *Reason and Human Good in Aristotle*, Cambridge, Mass.: Harvard University Press.

Crisp, R. (1989) 'The road to objectivity', *Philosophical Books* 30: 129–36.

—— (1990) 'Sidgwick and self-interest', *Utilitas* 2: 267–80.

—— (1992) 'Aristotle's inclusivism', St Anne's College, Oxford.

—— (1993) 'Naturalism and non-naturalism in ethics', in S. Louibond and S. Williams, eds, *Substance, Values, Truth: a Festschrift for David Wiggins*, Oxford: Blackwell.

Crowe, M. (1968) *A History of Vector Analysis*, Notre Dame: Notre Dame University Press.

Dales, J. (1968) *Pollution, Property and Prices*, Toronto: University of Toronto Press.

Dancy, J. (1986) 'Two conceptions of moral realism', *Proceedings of the Aristotelian Society*, Supp. vol. 60: 167–87.

Dillon, J. (1991) 'Steve MacKenna: a biographical sketch', in Plotinus, *The Enneads*, trans. S. MacKenna, Harmondsworth: Penguin.

Dombrowski, D. (1984) *Vegetarianism*, Amherst: University of Massachusetts Press.

Dubos, R. (1980) *The Wooing of Earth*, London: The Athlone Press.

Dworkin, R. (1977) *Taking Rights Seriously*, London: Duckworth.

—— (1978) 'Liberalism', in S. Hampshire, ed., *Public and Private Morality*, Cambridge: Cambridge University Press.

Eliot, T. S. (1919) 'Tradition and the individual talent' (1919), in *Selected Essays*, London: Faber & Faber (1951).

—— (1932) 'The metaphysical poets', in *Selected Essays, 1917–1932* New York, Harcourt Brace

Elster, J. (1986) 'The market and the forum: three varieties of political theory', in J. Elster and A. Hylland, eds, *Foundations of Social Choice Theory*, Cambridge: Cambridge University Press.

Fay, B. (1978) *Social Theory and Political Practice*, London: Allen & Unwin.

Feinberg, J. (1980) 'The rights of animals and unborn generations', in *Rights, Justice and the Bounds of Liberty*, Princeton: Princeton University Press.

Feldman, A. (1980) *Welfare Economic and Social Choice Theory*, Dordrecht: Martinus Nihoff.

Fowles, J. (1979) 'Seeing nature whole', *Harper's Magazine* 259: 49–68.

Freidman, R. (1968) 'An introduction to Mill's theory of authority', in J. B. Schneewind, ed., *Mill*, London: Macmillan.

Gamwell, F. (1984) *Beyond Preference*, Chicago: University of Chicago Press.

Gauthier, D. (1986) *Morals by Agreement*, Oxford: Oxford University Press.

Gay, P. (1967) *The Enlightenment*, London: Weidenfeld & Nicholson.

Geach, P. (1967) 'Good and evil', in P. Foot, ed., *Theories of Ethics*, Oxford: Oxford University Press.

—— (1977) *The Virtues*, Cambridge: Cambridge University Press.

Gellner, E, (1974) 'Concepts and society', in B. Wilson, ed., *Rationality*, Oxford: Blackwell.

Gerth, H. H. and Mills, C. W., eds (1948) *From Max Weber*, London: Routledge & Kegan Paul.

Golding, M. (1972) 'Obligations to future generations', *The Monist* 56: 85–99.

Goodin, R. E. (1985) *Protecting the Vulnerable*, Chicago: University of Chicago Press.

—— (1986) 'Laundering preferences', in J. Elster and A. Hylland, eds, *Foundations of Social Choice Theory*, Cambridge: Cambridge University Press.

Goodpaster, K. (1978) 'On being morally considerable', *Journal of Philosophy* 75: 308–25 (323).

Gowans, C., ed. (1987) *Moral Dilemmas*, Oxford: Oxford University Press.

Graham, K. (1992) *Karl Marx: Our Contemporary*, New York: Harvester Wheatsheaf.

Green, T. H. (1907) *Prologomena to Ethics* (5th edn), Oxford: Clarendon Press.

Griffin, J. (1977) 'Are there incommensurable values?', *Philosophy and Public Affairs*: 739–59.

—— (1986) *Well-Being*, Oxford: Clarendon Press.

Gunn, A. (1980) 'Why should we care about rare species?', *Environmental Ethics* 2: 17–37.

Guttenplan, S. (1991) 'Preference and rationality', paper given at Sussex University.

Habermas, J. (1970) 'Technology and science as "ideology"', in *Towards a Rational Society*, Boston: Beacon Press.

—— (1978) *Knowledge and Human Interests* (2nd edn), London: Heinemann.

—— (1984) *The Theory of Communicative Action*, vol. 1, trans. T. McCarthy, Boston: Beacon Press.

—— (1986) *Autonomy and Solidarity*, London: Verso.

Hampshire, S. (1971) 'Ethics: a defence of Aristotle', in *Freedom of Mind and other Essays*, Princeton: Princeton University Press.

Hardin, G. (1977) 'The tragedy of the commons', in G. Hardin and J. Baden, eds, *Managing the Commons*, San Francisco: Wm Freeman.

Hayek, F., ed. (1935) *Collectivist Economic Planning*, London: Routledge.

—— (1949a) 'Economics and knowledge', in *Individualism and Economic Order*, London: Routledge & Kegan Paul.

—— (1949b) 'The uses of knowledge in society' in *Individualism and Economic Order*, London: Routledge & Kegan Paul.

—— (1960) *The Constitution of Liberty*, London: Routledge & Kegan Paul.

—— (1973) *Law, Legislation and Liberty*, vol I, London: Routledge & Kegan Paul.

—— (1976) *Law, Legislation and Liberty*, vol II, London: Routledge & Kegan Paul.

—— (1979) *Law, Legislation and Liberty*, vol III, London: Routledge & Kegan Paul.

—— (1988) *The Fatal Conceit*, London: Routledge.

Hegel, F. (1967) *Philosophy of Right*, trans. T. Knox, Oxford: Clarendon Press.

Heilbroner, R. (1975) *An Inquiry into the Human Prospect*, London: Calder & Boyars.

Heisenberg, W. (1959) *Physics and Philosophy*, London: Allen & Unwin.

Herodotus (1954) *The Histories*, trans. A. de Selincourt, Harmondsworth: Penguin.

Hicks, J. (1939) 'The foundations of welfare economics', *Economic Journal*, 49: 696–712.

Hirschman, A. O. (1970) *Exit, Voice and Loyalty*, Cambridge, Mass.: Harvard University Press.

Hobbes, T. (1968) *Leviathan*, Harmondsworth: Penguin.

Hodgson, G. (1988) *Economics and Institutions*, Cambridge: Polity Press.

Hookway, C. (1986) 'Two conceptions of moral realism', *Proceedings of the Aristotelian Society*, supp. vol. 60: 189–205.

Horkheimer, M. (1973) *The Eclipse of Reason*, New York: Continuum Books.

Hume, D. (1970) 'Of the standards of taste', in *Four Dissertations*, New York: Garland.

—— (1972) *A Treatise of Human Nature*, London: Fontana.

212

Husserl, E. (1970) *The Crisis of European Sciences*, trans. D. Carr, Evanston: Northwestern University Press.

Irwin, T. H. (1987) 'Generosity and property in Aristotle's *Politics*', *Social Philosophy and Policy* 4: 37–54.

—— (1988) *Aristotle's First Principles*, Oxford: Clarendon Press.

Jammer, M. (1974) *The Philosophy of Quantum Mechanics*, New York: John Wiley.

Kaldor, N. (1939) 'Welfare propositions of economics and interpersonal comparisons of utility', *Economic Journal* 49: 549–52.

Kant, I. (1948) *Groundwork of the Metaphysic of Morals*, in H. Paton, ed., *The Moral Law*, London: Hutchinson.

Kavka, G. (1991) 'Is individual choice less problematic than collective choice?', *Economics and Philosophy* 7: 143–65.

Keane, J. (1988a) *Democracy and Civil Society*, London: Verso.

—— ed. (1988b) *Civil Society and the State*, London: Verso.

Keat, R. (1981) *The Politics of Social Theory*, Oxford: Blackwell.

—— (1982) 'Liberal rights and socialism', in K. Graham, ed., *Contemporary Political Philosophy*, Cambridge: Cambridge University Press.

—— (1989) 'Relativism, value-freedom and the sociology of science', in M. Krausz, *Relativism: Interpretation and Confrontation*, Notre Dame: University of Notre Dame Press.

—— (1993) 'Scepticism, authority and the market', in N. Abercrombie, R. Keat and N. Whiteley, ed., *The Authority of the Consumer*, London: Routledge.

Kenny, A. (1986) *A Path from Rome*, Oxford: Oxford University Press.

—— (1991) 'The Nicomachean conception of happiness', *Oxford Studies in Ancient Philosophy*, supp. vol.: 67–80.

Kierkegaard, S. (1992) *Either/Or: a Fragment of Life*, Harmondsworth: Penguin.

Kolakowski, L. (1974) 'The myth of human self-identity', in L. Kolakowski and S. Hampshire, eds, *The Socialist Idea*, London: Weidenfeld & Nicolson.

Kraut, R. (1979) 'Two conceptions of happiness', *The Philosophical Review* 88: 167–97.

Kuhn, T. (1970a) *The Structure of Scientific Revolutions* (2nd edn), Chicago: University of Chicago Press.

—— (1970b) 'Reflections on my critics', in I. Lakatos and A. Musgrave, eds, *Criticism and the Growth of Knowledge*, Cambridge: Cambridge University Press.

—— (1977a) 'Objectivity, value judgement and theory choice', in *The Essential Tension*, Chicago: Chicago University Press.

—— (1977b) *The Essential Tension*, Chicago: Chicago University Press.

Lakatos, I. (1970) 'The social responsibility of the scientist', in *Mathematics, Science and Epistemology: Philosophical Papers* vol. 2, ed. J. Worral and G. Currie, Cambridge: Cambridge University Press (1978).

Lange, O. and Taylor, F. (1956) *On the Economics of Socialism*, ed. B. Lippincott, New York: McGraw-Hill.

Larmore, C. (1987) *Patterns of Moral Complexity*, Cambridge: Cambridge University Press.

Leiss, W. (1972) *The Domination of Nature*, New York: Braziller.

Lemmon, E. J. (1987) 'Moral dilemmas', in C. Gowans, ed., *Moral Dilemmas*, Oxford: Oxford University Press.

Leopold, A. (1989) *A Sand County Almanac*, Oxford: Oxford University Press.

Little, I. (1951) *A Critique of Welfare Economics*, Oxford: Clarendon Press.

Lodge, D. (1984) *Small World*, Harmondsworth: Penguin.

Lucretius (1965) *On Nature*, trans. R. Geer, Indianapolis: Bobbs-Merill.

Luxemburg, R. (1971) *Selected Political Writings*, ed. R. Howard, New York: Monthly Review Press.

McCloskey, H. J. (1980) 'Ecological ethics and its justification', in D. Mannison, M. McRobbie and R. Routley, eds, *Environmental Philosophy*, Canberra: Australian National University.

—— (1983) *Ecological Ethics and Politics*, Totowa, NJ: Rowman & Littlefield.

McDowell, J. (1983) 'Aesthetic value, objectivity and the fabric of the world', in E. Schaper, ed., *Pleasure, Preference and Value*, Cambridge: Cambridge University Press.

—— (1985) 'Values and secondary qualities', in T. Honderich, ed., *Morality and Objectivity*, London: Routledge.

MacIntyre, A. (1967) *Secularisation and Moral Change*, London: Oxford University Press.

—— (1985) *After Virtue* (2nd edn), London: Duckworth.

Mackie, J. (1977) *Ethics*, Harmondsworth: Penguin.

Mannison, D., McRobbie, M. and Routley, R., eds (1980) *Environmental Philosophy*, Canberra: Australian National University.

Marcuse, H. (1965) 'On science and phenomenology', in R. S. Cohen and M. Wartofsky, eds, *Boston Studies in the Philosophy of Science*, vol. II, New York: Humanities Press.

—— (1968) *One-Dimensional Man*, New York: Abacus.

—— (1972a) *Negations*, Harmondsworth: Penguin.

—— (1972b) *Counter-Revolution and Revolt*, London: Allen Lane.

Martinez-Alier, J. (1987) *Ecological Economics*, Oxford: Blackwell.

Marx, K. (1843) 'On the Jewish question' in *Early Writings*, ed. L. Colletti, Harmondsworth: Penguin, (1974).

—— (1844) *Economic and Philosophical Manuscripts*, in *Early Writings*, ed. L. Colletti, Harmondsworth: Penguin (1974).

—— (1871) 'The civil war in France', in K. Marx and F. Engels, *Selected Works*, London: Lawrence & Wishart (1968).

—— (1970) *Capital*, vol. I, London: Lawrence & Wishart.

—— (1972) *Capital*, vol. III, London: Lawrence & Wishart.

—— (1973) *Grundrisse*, Harmondsworth: Penguin.

—— (1974) *The German Ideology*, ed. C. Arthur, London: Lawrence & Wishart.

Meikle, S. (1979) 'Aristotle and the political economy of the *Polis*,' *Journal of Hellenic Studies* 79: 57–73.

Melucci, A. (1988) 'Social movements and the democratization of everyday life', in J. Keane, ed., *Civil Society and the State*, London: Verso.

—— (1989) *Nomads of the Present*, London: Hutchinson Radius.

Mill, J. (1937) *An Essay on Government*, Cambridge: Cambridge University Press.

Mill, J. S. (1831) *The Spirit of the Age* in *Essays in Politics and Culture*, ed. G. Himmelfarb, New York: Anchor (1963).

—— (1853) 'Grote's History of Greece', in J. S. Mill *Dissertations and Discussions*, vol. II (2nd ed), London: Longman (1867).

—— (1859) *On Liberty*, in M. Warnock, ed., *Utilitarianism*, London: Collins (1962).

—— (1861a) *Utilitarianism*, in M. Warnock ed., *Utilitarianism*, London: Collins (1962).

—— (1861b) *Representative Government* (new edn), London: Routledge (n.d.).

—— (1866) 'Grote's Plato', in *Dissertations and Discussions*, vol. III, London: Longman (1867).

Miller, D. (1989) *Market, State and Community*, Oxford: Clarendon Press.

Mises, L. von (1920) 'Economic calculation in the socialist commonwealth', in F. Hayek, ed., *Collectivist Economic Planning*, London: Routledge (1935).

—— (1949) *Human Action*, London: William Hodge.

—— (1951) *Socialism*, London: Jonathan Cape.

Moore, G. E. (1903) *Principia Ethica*, Cambridge: Cambridge University Press.

—— (1922) 'The conception of intrinsic value', in *Philosophical Studies*, London: Routledge & Kegan Paul.

Murdoch, I. (1970) *The Sovereignty of the Good*, London: Routledge & Kegan Paul.

Naess, A. (1973) 'The shallow and the deep, long range ecology movement', *Inquiry* 16: 95–100.

—— (1984) 'A defence of the deep ecology movement', *Environmental Ethics* 6: 265–70.

—— and Rothenberg, D. (1989) *Ecology, Community and Lifestyle*, Cambridge: Cambridge University Press.

Nagel, T. (1979) 'Death', in *Mortal Questions*, Cambridge: Cambridge University Press.

—— (1986) *The View from Nowhere*, Oxford: Oxford University Press.

—— (1987) 'The fragmentation of value', in C. Gowans, ed., *Moral Dilemmas*, Oxford: Oxford University Press.

Narveson, J. (1967) 'Utilitarianism and new generations', *Mind* 76: 62–72.

Nelkin, D. (1984) *Science as Intellectual Property*, New York: Macmillan.

Neurath, O. (1912) 'The problem of the pleasure maximum', in *Empiricism and Sociology*, Dordrecht: Reidel (1973).

—— (1919) 'Through war economy to economy in kind', in *Empiricism and Sociology*, Dordrecht: Reidel (1973).

—— (1928) 'Personal life and class struggle', in *Empiricism and Sociology*, Dordrecht: Reidel (1973).

—— (1942) 'International planning for freedom', in *Empiricism and Sociology*, Dordrecht: Reidel (1973).

—— (1944) *Foundations of the Social Sciences*, Chicago: University of Chicago Press.

—— (1946) 'The orchestration of the sciences by the Encyclopedism of logical empiricism', in R. S. Cohen and M. Neurath, eds (1983) *Philosophical Papers 1913–1946*, Dordrecht: Reidel.

—— (1973) *Empiricism and Sociology*, Dordrecht: Reidel.
Nisbet, R. (1970) *The Sociological Tradition*, London: Heinemann.
Oakeshott, M. (1962) *Rationalism in Politics*, London: Methuen.
O'Neill, J. (1988a) 'Marcuse, Husserl and the crisis of the sciences', *Philosophy of the Social Sciences* 18: 327–42.
—— (1988b) *Six Presentations of a Mathematical Discovery*, Lancaster: Lancaster University.
—— (1989) 'Markets, socialism and information', *Social Policy and Philosophy* 6: 200–10. Reprinted in E. Frankel Paul, F. Miller and J. Paul, eds, *Socialism*, Oxford: Blackwell (1989).
—— (1990) 'Property in science and the market', *The Monist* 73: 601–20.
—— (1991a) *Worlds Without Content*, London: Routledge.
—— (1991b) 'Exploitation and workers' councils', *Journal of Applied Philosophy* 8: 263–7.
—— (1991–2) 'Humanism and nature', paper given to the Seminar Series *Socialism and the Environment*, University of Kent.
—— (1992a) 'Egoism, altruism and the market', *Philosophical Forum* 23: pp.278–88.
—— (1992b) 'Journalism in the market place', in A. Belsey and R. Chadwick, eds, *Ethical Issues in Journalism and the Media*, London: Routledge.
—— (1992c) 'Should environmentalists be nationalists?', paper given to the conference on environmental ethics, Lancaster University.
O'Neill, O. (1987) 'Abstraction, idealization and ideology in ethics', in J. D. Evans, ed., *Moral Philosophy and Contemporary Problems*, Cambridge: Cambridge University Press.
Ophuls, W. (1977) 'The politics of a sustainable society', in D. Pirages, ed., *The Sustainable Society*, New York: Praeger.
Owen, G. E. (1986) 'Aristotle on the snares of ontology', in *Logic, Science and Dialectic*, London: Duckworth.
Parfit, D. (1982) 'Future generations: further problems', *Philosophy and Public Affairs* 11: 113–72.
—— (1984) *Reasons and Persons*, Oxford: Clarendon Press.
Passmore, J. (1980) *Man's Responsibility for Nature* (2nd edn), London: Duckworth.
Pateman, T. (1982) 'Liberty, authority and the negative dialectics of J. S. Mill', *Radical Philosophy* 32: 16–22.
Pearce, D., Markandya, A. and Barbier, E. (1989) *Blueprint for a Green Economy*, London: Earthscan.
Pearce, D. and Turner, K. (1990) *Economics of Natural Resources and the Environment*, New York: Harvester Wheatsheaf.
Pigou, A. (1952) *The Economics of Welfare*, (4th edn) London: Macmillan.
Plato (1956) *Protagoras*, trans. W. K. Guthrie, Harmondsworth: Penguin.
—— (1974) *The Republic*, trans. D. Lee, Harmondsworth: Penguin.
Plumwood, V. (1986) 'Ecofeminism: an overview and discussion of positions and arguments', *Australian Journal of Philosophy, Supplementary Volume: Women and Philosophy*: 120–38.
Pocock, J. (1975) *The Machiavellian Moment*, Princeton: Princeton University Press.

—— (1985) *Virtue, Commerce, and History,* Cambridge: Cambridge University Press.

Polanyi, K. (1957a) *The Great Transformation,* Boston: Beacon Press.

—— (1957b) 'Aristotle discovers the economy', in *Primitive, Archaic, and Modern Economies,* Boston: Beacon Press.

Poole, R. (1991) *Morality and Modernity,* London: Routledge.

Popper, K. (1961) *The Poverty of Historicism,* London: Routledge & Kegan Paul.

Porphyry (1965) *On Abstinence From Animal Food,* trans. T. Taylor, London: Centaur Press.

Porritt, J. (1984) *Seeing Green,* Oxford: Blackwell.

Ramsey, F. (1928) 'A mathematical theory of saving', *Economic Journal,* 38: 543–59.

—— (1931) 'Truth and probability', in *The Foundations of Mathematics,* London: Routledge & Kegan Paul.

Ratcliffe, D., ed., (1977) *A Nature Conservation Review,* Cambridge: Cambridge University Press.

Rawls, J. (1972) *A Theory of Justice,* Oxford: Oxford University Press.

Raz, J. (1986) *The Morality of Freedom,* Oxford: Clarendon Press.

Reed, P. (1989) 'Man apart: an alternative to the self-realization approach', *Environmental Ethics* 11: 53–69.

Regan, T. (1988) *The Case for Animal Rights,* London: Routledge.

Rey, J. (1984) 'Experimental tests of island biogeographic theory', in D. Strong, D. Simberloff, L. Abele and A. Thistle, eds, *Ecological Communities: Conceptual Issues and the Evidence,* Princeton: Princeton University Press.

Richards, D. (1971) *A Theory of Reasons for Action,* Oxford: Clarendon Press.

Rolston III, H. (1988) *Environmental Ethics,* Philadelphia: Temple University Press.

—— (1989a) 'Are values in nature subjective or objective?' in *Philosophy Gone Wild,* Buffalo: Prometheus Books.

—— (1989b) 'Is there an ecological ethic?', in *Philosophy Gone Wild,* Buffalo: Prometheus Books.

Rose-Ackerman, S. (1977) 'Market models for pollution control', *Public Policy* 25: 383–406.

Ross, W. D. (1930) *The Right and the Good,* Oxford: Clarendon Press.

Routley, R. and V. (1978) 'Nuclear energy and obligations to future', *Inquiry* 21: 133–79.

—— (1980) 'Human chauvinism and environmental ethics', in D. Mannison, M. McRobbie and R. Routley, eds, *Environmental Philosophy,* Canberra: Australian National University.

Routley, V. (1981) 'On Marx as an environmental hero', *Environmental Ethics,* 3: 237–44.

Sagoff, M. (1988) *The Economy of the Earth,* Cambridge: Cambridge University Press.

St Croix, G. (1981) *The Class Struggle in the Ancient World,* London: Duckworth.

Sale, K. (1985) *Dwellers in the Land: the Bioregional Vision,* San Fransisco: Sierra Club.

Sen, A. (1977) 'Rational fools: a critique of the behavioural foundations of economic theory', *Philosophy and Public Affairs* 6: 317–44.

—— (1980–1) 'Plural utility', *Proceedings of the Aristotelian Society* 80: 193–215.

—— (1985) 'Well-being, agency and freedom', *Journal of Philosophy* 82: 169–221.

—— (1986) 'The standard of living', in *The Tanner Lectures on Human Values VII*, Cambridge: Cambridge University Press.

Shapin, S. (1992) 'Why the public ought to understand science-in-the-making', *Public Understanding of Science*, I: 27–30, reprinted as 'A magicians cloak cast off for clarity', *The Times Higher Education Suppliement* 1006: 15.

Shapiro, D. (1989) 'Reviving the socialist calculation debate: a defense of Hayek against Lange', *Social Philosophy and Policy* 6: 139–59.

Shaw, G. B. (1927), reply to H. G. Wells, *The Sunday Express*, August. Reprinted in J. Wynne-Tyson, ed., *The Extended Circle*, London: Sphere (1990).

Sidgwick, H. (1877) *The Methods of Ethics* (2nd edn), London: Macmillan.

Sikora, R. (1978) 'Is it wrong to prevent the existence of future generations?', in R. Sikora and B. Barry, eds, *Obligations to Future Generations*, Philadelphia: Temple University Press.

Singer, P. (1976) *Animal Liberation*, London: Jonathan Cape.

—— (1979) *Practical Ethics*, Cambridge: Cambridge University Press.

Skorupski, J. (1989) *John Stuart Mill*, London: Routledge.

Smith, A. (1976) *Wealth of Nations*, Chicago: University of Chicago Press.

Spretnak, C. and Capra, F. (1985) *Green Politics*, London: Paladin.

Stevenson, C. L. (1944) *Ethics and Language*, New Haven: Yale University Press.

Stocker, M. (1990) *Plural and Conflicting Values*, Oxford: Clarendon Press.

Stone, C. (1987) *Earth and Other Ethics*, New York: Harper & Row.

Stove, D. (1982) *Popper and After*, Oxford: Pergamon.

Swift, J. (1953) *Gulliver's Travels*, London: Collins.

Sylvan, R. (1985) 'A critique of deep ecology', *Radical Philosophy* 40: 2–12 and 41: 10–22.

—— (1990) *In Defence of Deep Environmental Ethics*, Canberra: Australian National University, Preprint Series in Environmental Philosophy.

—— (1993) 'Anarchism', in R. Goodin and P. Pettit, eds, *A Companion to Contemporary Political Philosophy*, Oxford: Blackwell.

Tawney, R. (1964) *Equality*, London: Unwin.

Taylor, C. (1982) 'The diversity of goods', in A. Sen and B. Williams, eds, *Utilitarianism and Beyond*, Cambridge: Cambridge University Press.

Taylor, P. (1986) *Respect for Nature*, Princeton: Princeton University Press.

Thompson, J. (1990) 'A refutation of environmental ethics', *Environmental Ethics*, 12: 147–60 (148).

Thucydides (1954) *The Peloponnesian War*, trans. R. Warner, Harmondsworth: Penguin.

Tulloch, G. (1967) *Towards a Mathematics of Politics*, Ann Arbor: University of Michigan Press.

Veach, H. B. (1962) *Rational Man*, Bloomington: Indiana University Press.

Walzer, M. (1983) *Spheres of Justice*, Oxford: Blackwell.
—— (1984) 'Liberalism and the art of separation', *Political Theory* 12: 315–30.
Weber, M. (1978) *Economy and Society*, Berkeley: University of California Press.
Weil, S. (1952) *The Need for Roots*, London: Routledge & Kegan Paul.
Weizenbaum, J. (1976) *Computer Power and Human Reason*, San Francisco: Freeman.
Wiggins, D. (1987a) *Needs, Values, Truth: Essays in the Philosophy of Value*, Oxford: Blackwell.
—— (1987b) 'A sensible subjectivism', in *Needs, Values, Truth: Essays in the Philosophy of Value*, Oxford: Blackwell.
Williams, B. (1979) 'Conflicts of values' in A. Ryan, ed., *The Idea of Freedom*, Oxford: Oxford University Press.
—— (1985) *Ethics and the Limits of Philosophy*, London: Collins.
—— (1987) 'Ethical consistency' in C. Gowans ed., *Moral Dilemmas*, Oxford: Oxford University Press.
Winch, P. (1967) 'Authority', in A. Quinton, ed., *Political Philosophy*, Oxford: Oxford University Press.
Wood, A. (1990) *Hegel's Ethical Thought*, Cambridge: Cambridge University Press.
Worster, D. (1985) *Nature's Economy*, Cambridge: Cambridge University Press.
Wright, C. (1988) 'Moral values, projections and secondary qualities', *Proceedings of the Aristotelian Society*, supp. vol. 62: 1–26.
Wright, G. H. von (1963) *The Varieties of Goodness*, London: Routledge & Kegan Paul.
Yearley, S. (1991) *The Green Case*, London: Harper Collins.

INDEX

Ackrill, J. L. 191n
acquisition, modes of 169
Adorno, T. 202n
aesthetics: and diversity 100–1; and environmental evaluation 100–1, 107–9, 159–61, 165–7
alienation, holism and nature 149–52
anthropocentrism 2–3, 24–5
Aquinas, St Thomas 32, 114, 196n
Arendt, H. 205n, 206n
argument: and cost-benefit analysis 67–71; and pluralism 92–5
Aristotle 3, 7, 32, 66, 96, 100, 114, 159, 184–9n, 196–200n, 202n–4n; on authority and democracy 133–5, 140–4; and the classical conception of politics 84–92, 190n; on human flourishing 20, 23–4, 86–7, 159, 170–1, 191n; on household and money-making 3, 168–71, 203–4n; and pluralism 85–92; and practical judgement 114, 140–4, 196n, 197n, 199n; *see also* self-sufficiency
Arrow, K. 112, 195n
art, science and decadence 165–7
Atkinson, A. 201n
Attfield, R. 183n, 184n, 185n, 187n, 194n
Augustine 37, 146–7, 163–4, 166, 186n, 201n, 203n
Austin, J. 132, 194n, 198n
Austrian economics 1, 2, 4, 53, 111, 115–16, 118–20, 142–3, 182n, 187–8n, 193n, 200n
authority: Aristotle on 133–5;

democracy and the environment 123–44; external 129–30, 135–8; forms of 126–31; impersonal, in practices 127–9; internal 129–30, 138; limits of 135–44; problems of 131–5; producers and users 141–4; rationalism and irrationality 124–6; scepticism about 123–4, 136; separation of internal and external 136–7; and utilitarianism 131–3
autonomy of science: disciplinary 156–7; ethical 157–9; and value and science 155–9
autonomy of persons 5–6, 82, 130, 192n

Bailey, C. 186n
Barry, B. 63, 83, 185n, 186n, 188n, 190n
Beiner, R. 199n
beliefs: pluralism, and goods 90–2; and rational argument 92–5
Bell, E.T. 29–30, 36, 185n
Bellamy, D. 187n
Bentham, J. 194n
Benton, T. 203n
Bergson, A. 187n
Berlin, I. 89, 191n
Bernard, C. 162–4, 166, 203n
Black, A. 204n
Blackburn, S. 183n, 184n
Bohr, N. 184n
Borges, J. 197n
Bottomore, T. 205n
Brennan, A. 195n, 201n
Buchanan, A. 196n
Burgess, J. 189n, 197n, 199n